The Road
To Independence

The Road
To Independence

A Documentary History of the Causes
of the American Revolution: 1763-1776

By JOHN BRAEMAN

G. P. Putnam's Sons
New York

Contents

Preface

THIS book is intended primarily for the interested general reader and student. I have written a brief narrative history of the background of the American Revolution based upon the latest scholarship, with the key documents inserted directly in the text as illustrative material.

At the end of the book, I have included a select bibliography of the leading works on the background of the American Revolution. But I would like to take this opportunity to acknowledge my indebtedness to three distinguished scholars whose work has greatly influenced my thinking on the period: Edmund S. Morgan, Lawrence H. Gipson, and the late Sir Lewis Namier.

I would also like to thank the staffs of the following libraries for their kind assistance in gathering the material for this volume: Ohio State University Library, Ohio State Museum, the New York Public Library, Columbia University Library, and Brooklyn College Library.

I wish also to thank my friends Ronald W. Linker, of Pennsylvania State University, Paul Goodman, of Brooklyn College, and John C. Rule, of Ohio State University, for their assistance and encouragement. I am, of course, solely responsible for all errors of fact and interpretation.

For reasons of space, I have had to edit many of the documents. In editing, I have capitalized the beginning of each sentence; otherwise I have followed the text in the source indicated without modernizing the spelling, capitalization, or punctuation, except where noted. I wish to thank the following individuals and institutions for permission to reprint copyright material or documents in their possession: Her Majesty's Stationery Office, for W. L. Grant and James Munro, eds., *Acts of the Privy Council, Colonial Series* (6 vols., London, 1908–1912); Clifford K. Shipton and the American Antiquarian Society, for Clarence S. Brigham, ed., *British Royal Proclamations Relating to America, 1603–1783* (Worcester, Mass., 1911); the American Historical Association, for "A French Traveller in the Colonies," I, *American Historical Review*, XXVI, No. 4 (July, 1921); the Carnegie Institution of Washington, for Edmund C. Burnett, ed., *Letters of Members of the Continental Congress* (8 vols., Washington, D.C., 1921–1938); the University of Chicago Press, for Thomas W. Copeland, *et al.*, eds., *The Correspondence of Edmund Burke* (3 vols. to date, Chicago, 1958–   ); Walter Muir Whitehill and the Colonial Society of Massachusetts, for the Colonial Society of Massachusetts *Publications;* Thompson R. Harlow and the Connecticut Historical Society, for the Connecticut Historical Society *Collections;* the *English Historical Review* and Lady Namier, for Lewis Namier, "Charles Garth, Agent for South Carolina," *English Historical Review*, No. CCXVI (October, 1939); the Henry E. Huntington Library and Art Gallery, for Francis Bernard to the Board of Trade, August 15, 1765 and August 31, 1765, Huntington Library MSS., H.M. 1947, and for Douglass Adair and John A. Schutz, eds., *Peter Oliver's Origin and Progress of the American Rebellion: A Tory View* (San Marino, Calif., 1961); Richard Walsh and the Maryland Historical Society, for the *Maryland Historical Magazine;* Howard C. Meyers, Jr., for Albert H. Smyth, ed., *The Life and Writings of Benjamin Franklin* (10 vols., New York, 1905–1907); Stephen T. Riley and the Massachusetts Historical Society, for the Massachusetts Historical Society *Proceedings* and *Collections;* the Institute of Early American History and Culture and the University of North Carolina Press, for Edmund S. Morgan, ed., *Prologue to Revolution: Sources and Documents on the Stamp Act Crisis, 1764–1766* (Chapel Hill, N.C., 1959); Oxford University Press, for Merrill Jensen, ed., *American Colonial Documents to 1776* [*English Historical Documents,* IX] (New York, 1955); Princeton University Press, for Julian Boyd, ed., *The Papers of Thomas Jefferson* (16 vols. to date, Princeton, N.J., 1950–   ); G. P. Putnam's Sons, for Harry A. Cushing, ed., *The Writings of Samuel Adams* (4 vols., New York and London, 1904–1908); Macmillan & Company Ltd. and St. Martin's Press, for Sir John Fortesque, ed., *The Correspondence of George III from 1760 to December 1783* (6 vols., London, 1927–1928); Mrs. Granville T. Prior and the South Carolina Historical Society, for the *South Carolina Historical and Genealogical Magazine;* Randolph W. Church and the Virginia State Library, for John P. Kennedy, ed., *Journals of the House of Burgesses of Virginia, 1761–1765* (Richmond, 1907); and Yale University Press, for Clarence E. Carter, ed., *The Correspondence of General Thomas Gage* (2 vols., New Haven, 1931–1933).

I. Introduction

ALTHOUGH not enjoying the public interest lavished upon the Civil War, the American Revolution was probably the single most decisive event in this nation's history. And not surprisingly, given its central importance, historians continue to argue over its causes and significance. Much of the disagreement arises from the fact that there were thirteen separate colonies involved, and that the impact of events differed from one to another. But an even more important reason is that the revolution came almost accidentally. Most colonists wished at first no more than the redress of grievances; it was only gradually that events nurtured the nascent national self-consciousness of the colonists into a demand for independence from the mother country. To explain this change of mind is fundamental to any study of the background of the American Revolution.*

Page Smith has recently pointed out that the first generation of writers on the Revolution—men who lived through and them-

* In writing this survey of trends in the historiography of the American Revolution, I have drawn heavily upon the following excellent studies: Edmund S. Morgan, "The American Revolution: Revisions in Need of Revising," *William and Mary Quarterly,* Third Series, XIV (January, 1957), pp. 3-15; Morgan, *The American Revolution: A Review of Changing Interpretations* (Service Center for Teachers of History: Washington, D.C., 1958); Page Smith, "David Ramsay and the Causes of the American Revolution," *William and Mary Quarterly,* Third Series, XVII (January, 1960), pp. 51-77; Richard B. Morris, "Class Struggle and the American Revolution," *ibid.,* XIX (January, 1962), pp. 3-29; Cecelia M. Kenyon, "Republicanism and Radicalism in the American Revolution: An Old-Fashioned Interpretation," *ibid.,* XIX (April, 1962), pp. 153-182; Wesley Frank Craven, "The Revolutionary Era," in John Higham, ed., *The Reconstruction of American History* (New York, 1962), pp. 46-63; and Jack P. Greene, "The Flight from Determinism: A Review of Recent Literature on the Coming of the American Revolution," *South Atlantic Quarterly,* LXI (Spring, 1962), pp. 235-259.

selves participated in the conflict—stressed the importance of the question of constitutional principle. David Ramsay, the ablest of this generation, showed how religious differences, constitutional usuage, increasing economic maturity, libertarian ideas, and social equality had predisposed the colonists to the "belief, that their local assemblies stood in the same relation to them, as the Parliament of Great Britain to the inhabitants of that island." The difficulty came when the British ministry undertook after 1763 to reaffirm and reenforce the subordination to the mother country that had previously rested so lightly upon the colonies. Ramsay laid no tyrannical designs to George III; rather he blamed a failure of statesmanship. The British attempts at taxation set the stage for the Revolution, and the colonists, Ramsay concluded, fought that contest for a principle—the principle of no taxation without representation.

The next generation of historians of the American Revolution lost much of the balance and perspective their fathers had maintained. Imbued with the superheated patriotism of Jacksonian democracy, writing for a public yearning for a glorious national past, George Bancroft pictured the Revolution as part of God's plan for mankind—the decisive event in the long travail of human liberty. Behind the British actions lay not poor statesmanship, but a conscious plot to subvert freedom. "The ruling passion of George III, early developed and indelibly branded in, was," Brancroft wrote, "the restoration of the prerogative." By contrast, the revolutionary leaders emerged as heroes larger than life; they fought "for freedom itself. They were inspired by the thought that the Providence which rules the world demanded of them heroic self-denial as the champions of humanity." The American Revolution, Bancroft held, was a struggle "for the advancement of the principles of everlasting peace and universal brotherhood."

Bancroft's conclusions were echoed by the distinguished English Whig historian, Sir George Otto Trevelyan. In his *Early History of Charles James Fox* (1880), Trevelyan pictured George III as a king "so formidable, so pertinacious, so insatiable of

power and so very particular as to the means which he employed
in the pursuit of it" that he threatened English liberties. Arrayed
against George III's bid to establish "a system of personal government" stood the Rockingham Whigs. This small band of
dedicated men fought a losing battle against the king's horde of
corrupt placemen until the American Revolution. Trevelyan's
massive four volumes on *The American Revolution* (1898–1907)
pictured colonial resistance to the ministry's exactions as part
and parcel of this larger struggle against royal tyranny. The
Revolution, he wrote, was a "defensive movement" in behalf of
essential English institutions, "genuine national self-government
and real ministerial responsibility against the purpose and effort
of a monarch to defeat the political progress of a race."

Such an account appealed to the filiopietistic inclinations of
most Americans, historians or not, in the nineteenth century.
But with the turn of the century the current shifted against this
"heroic" interpretation of the Revolution. What Morton G. White
has called "the revolt against formalism" was in full swing, and
more and more historians were heeding Frederick Jackson
Turner's injunction to look beneath the surface of events to find
the vital forces at work. In the intellectual climate of the progres-
sive era, these vital forces were, first and foremost, economic ones.
This new brand of interpretation was not long in being applied
to the American Revolution. Turner's ablest student, Carl
Becker, laid down, in his *History of Political Parties in the Province of New York, 1760–1776* (1909), his celebrated aphorism
that New York politics before the Revolution revolved around
two questions of equal importance—the question of home rule
and that of who should rule at home. Publication of Charles
Beard's *An Economic Interpretation of the Constitution* (1913)
gave further impetus to the idea that social and economic divisions within the colonies were basic in shaping the history of
the period.

The most important application of the economic interpretation to the American Revolution was by a young Columbia-
trained historian, Arthur M. Schlesinger, Sr., first in his book

The Colonial Merchants and the American Revolution (1918)
and then in his highly influential essay "The American Revolution Reconsidered" (1919). Schlesinger did not question the
prevailing appraisal of British policy: George III was aiming at
"personal autocracy." Where Schlesinger differed from his fellow historians was in reducing the stature of the leaders of colonial resistance to less than heroic proportions. His thesis was
simple: hurt financially by the new policy of strict imperial
control, the seaboard merchants sparked the resistance to the
British measures and "aroused the populace to a sense of British
injustice." The constitutional argument—the cry of No Taxation Without Representation—was, Schlesinger contended, mere
sound and fury. "The popular view of the revolution as a great
forensic controversy over abstract government rights will not
bear close scrutiny," he declared. "The major emphasis is thus
placed upon the clashing of economic interests."

Why then did so many of these same merchants end as loyalists
or at best lukewarm supporters of the Revolution? The merchants, Schlesinger explained, aware of the material benefits
membership in the empire brought, shied at independence;
frightened by "the growth of republican feeling and leveling sentiment which the controversy occasioned," they looked "askance
at a doctrine of home rule which left it uncertain who was to
rule at home." But they had released forces which, "like Franken-
stein," they found impossible to handle, and lost control to "the
democratic mechanic class." The heroes of Schlesinger's account
were "the mechanics and petty shopkeepers of the towns"—a
"proletarian element . . . for the most part unenfranchised"—
and "the democratic farmers of the interior"—men who "brought
to the controversy a moral conviction and bold philosophy which
gave great impetus to the agitation for independence."

The main features of the Schlesinger thesis—the clash of economic interests between the colonies and mother country, on
the one hand, and internal social and economic divisions within
the colonies themselves, on the other—were incorporated in
Charles and Mary Beard's *The Rise of American Civilization*

and Vernon Parrington's *Main Currents of American Thought,*
both published in 1927. A whole generation took its ideas of
the American Revolution—indeed, of the entire American past
—from those two books. But even in the heyday of the popularity
of the economic interpretation, dissenting voices were heard. The
so-called imperial school stood for a different approach. In
Britain, Lewis Namier and his followers demolished the traditional picture of George III. And the United States in the years
since the Second World War has witnessed the rise of an aggres-
sive revisionist school among younger historians of the revolutionary period. However much these schools differed in their
approaches, the net effect has been similar—to restore the question of constitutional principle to primacy.

The keynote of the imperial school was that the American
Revolution could be understood only within the context of the
empire as a whole. Taking this approach, these historians emerged
with a much more favorable appraisal of British policy than their
predecessors had. George L. Beer set the tone in his studies of
British colonial policy. As early as 1893, in his master's thesis,
*The Commercial Policy of England toward the American Colo-
nies,* Beer defended the British policy as remarkably liberal. In
this and subsequent volumes, he made two crucial points: that
before 1763, the colonists had, on the whole, acquiesced in the
application of the laws of trade; and second, that "it would be
difficult to estimate whether colony or metropolis was called
upon to bear a greater proportion of the sacrifice demanded by
the prevailing ideal of a self-sufficient commercial Empire."
Then why the Revolution? Beer denied that economic issues
were primary. The colonists had so prospered under the existing
system that by the 1760's they felt strong enough to go it alone.
"The fundamental question at issue," Beer concluded in his
British Colonial Policy, 1754–1765 (1907), "was the political
independence of the American colonies."

A similar conclusion was reached by the distinguished Yale
historian Charles M. Andrews. The Revolution was "primarily,"
he believed, "a political and constitutional movement." By 1763,

the colonial assemblies had become "powerful legislative bodies.
. . . There was taking shape a new idea of a colony, a self-
governing dominion, the members of which were competent to
develop along their own lines, while working together with the
mother country as part of a common state." But the English ruling classes remained wedded to the traditional notions of colonial dependence—political and commercial—to the mother
country, and "they interpreted the attitude of the colonists as
something radical and revolutionary." There was no alternative
to independence. "On one side," Andrews declared in his 1925
presidential address before the American Historical Association,
"was the immutable, stereotyped system of the mother country,
based upon precedent and tradition and designed to keep things
comfortably as they were; on the other, a vital dynamic organism,
containing the seeds of a great nation, its forces untried, still
to be proved. It is inconceivable that a connection should have
continued long between two such yoke fellows, one static, the
other dynamic, separated by an ocean and bound only by the
ties of a legal relationship."

A pupil of Andrews, Leonard W. Labaree, illuminated the
constitutional crisis brought on by the growing self-consciousness
and power of the colonial assemblies in his brilliant monograph
Royal Government in America (1930). The eighteenth century,
Labaree showed, saw the balance of power in the colonies shift
from the crown and its instruments, the royal governors, to the
assemblies. "The constitutional history of the provinces in the
eighteenth century is fundamentally the history of a series of
controversies between the assemblies and the prerogative in which
the former won victory after victory." These successive victories
by the assemblies set the stage for the final showdown. "After
1763," Labaree concluded "the British officials felt that parliament must be called upon to intervene on behalf of the royal
authority. But by that time the assemblies had come to consider themselves so entirely as local parliaments, coordinate in
status with the parliament of Great Britain, that interference in

their affairs by a so-called supreme legislature was intolerable to them. Thereafter, the final crisis could not be long postponed."

The most productive of the imperial school has been Lawrence H. Gipson, author of a monumental study of "The British Empire before the American Revolution" that has now reached ten volumes. Gipson treats the Revolution as an outgrowth of "the Great War for the Empire" that raged between Britain and France in the eighteenth century. That conflict left Britain heavily in debt and facing the extra burden of providing adequate security measures for North America. The tax burden borne by the colonies was far less than that of their compatriots across the Atlantic. The British measures taken after 1763 to tighten up the laws of trade and draw a revenue from America were designed to right the balance. But these measures ran counter to the increasing political, cultural, and economic maturity of the colonies, whose separatist impulses were given free play by the removal of the hostile French and Indians from their flank. The break-up of the Empire, Gipson believes, "may be attributed largely to a fundamental constitutional defect—that the machinery for governmental control and maintenance of the Empire could not be easily adjusted to meet the changing needs demanded by the growing maturity of the older colonies."

Further support for the primacy of constitutional and political issues has been supplied by the research of Sir Lewis Namier and his followers in eighteenth-century British politics. The Namier school rehabilitated George III; he was no longer a would-be tyrant, but a hard-working and able monarch exercising the authority granted him under the existing British constitution. The fundamental principle of this British constitution was the sovereignty of the king in parliament—and it was, according to Eric Robson, a leading Namier disciple, the incompatability of this principle with the colonial demand for greater autonomy that brought on the American Revolution. "This junction between King and Parliament in Great Britain itself," Robson explained in his book *The American Revolution* (1955), "was bound to carry the supremacy of the British Parliament in the colonies; the fact that George III so thoroughly and completely stood by the constitutional principles of his time rendered a conflict between Great Britain and the colonies wellnigh inevitable. The conflict with the American colonies was engaged in and conducted by George III and his ministers to uphold the supremacy of Parliament at Westminster. It was this, rather than the rights of the Crown, which was at stake."

There has appeared since World War II a new school of interpretation which Jack Greene has aptly styled the "neo-Whig" school. Whereas the imperial school looked at the Revolution from the outside—from the vantage point of the home country— the neo-Whigs have focused "upon American grievances against Britain, the central question in their studies being why Americans were angry in the fateful years after 1763." But this difference in approach masks a deeper split. Although not as uncritically pro-British as many historians have claimed, the imperial school, looking at British policy in the context of the larger problem of imperial administration, treated British policies and difficulties sympathetically. The neo-Whigs are more prone to sympathize with colonial grievances; the colonists, they believe, were in fact defending American liberties from novel and oppressive British measures after 1763.

Oliver Dickerson's *The Navigation Acts and the American Revolution* (1951) was the pioneering work in this neo-Whig reinterpretation. Dickerson held that the laws of trade did not bear injuriously upon the colonists in the eighteenth century. Nor was there, he argued, serious grievances against, or evasion of, the system. After 1763, however, the British government substituted a policy of taxation to raise revenue for the older system of trade regulation. The discontent aroused by this departure was aggravated by the establishment of the American Board of Customs Commissioners in 1767—an action which Dickerson termed "England's most fateful decision." The "customs racketeering" of the new board not only alienated such important future revolutionary leaders as John Hancock of Massachusetts and Henry

Laurens of South Carolina, but sparked violent colonial resistance. The riot over the seizure of Hancock's sloop *Liberty*, the Boston Massacre, and the Gaspee Affair—milestones in the road to revolution—were all provoked by the activities of the rapacious customs officials. The American complaints were not mere masks for conflicting economic interests; the colonists had legitimate grievances.

A similar conclusion was reached by Edmund S. and Helen M. Morgan in their *The Stamp Act Crisis: Prologue to Revolution* (1953). The book's thesis was that devotion to principle animated the colonial resistance against the Stamp Act. Denying the oft-repeated charges of inconsistency levied against the colonists, the Morgans showed that from the start the colonists denied Parliament's authority to levy any taxes, internal or external, for revenue purposes—and that they adhered to this principle for the ten years from the Stamp Act Crisis to the Revolution. In hailing the repeal of the Stamp Act, the colonists interpreted the Declaratory Act to mean that Parliament had supreme legislative authority, but that taxation was another matter. Most Britons, on the contrary, thought the right of taxation was an inseparable part of Parliament's supreme legislative authority. When the colonists resisted the Townshend Act, more and more Englishmen began to fear that the colonists aspired to independence, while more and more Americans feared a British plot to enslave them. Although "the situation was not irretrievable" at the time of the repeal of the Stamp Act, the Morgans concluded, "there was nevertheless a genuine and irreconcilable conflict between Parliament's insistence on its authority to tax the colonies and the American's denial of that authority."

Two years after the Morgans' book appeared, Robert E. Brown published a blistering attack upon the internal class-conflict interpretation of the Revolution. His *Middle-Class Democracy and the Revolution in Massachusetts, 1691–1780* challenged the widely accepted view that the colonies had an undemocratic and restricted franchise and showed for Massachusetts at least that most adult males qualified for the vote. Thus the Revolution was not a struggle to achieve democracy; it was fought to preserve an already existing democratic social order. "When the common people talked of dying for their liberties or pledging their lives and property for the defense of their liberties, they were not dealing in abstractions." There is no doubt, Brown argued, "that the British intended to curtail colonial democracy as a necessary step toward recovery of British authority and the prevention of colonial independence. The result was the very thing the British had tried to prevent—American independence."

Bernhard Knollenberg's *Origin of the American Revolution* (1960) pushed the beginnings of the contest back to 1759 when the British military victories emboldened the government to inaugurate a stricter policy of colonial regulation. The disallowance of the Virginia Two Penny Act in 1759, followed by the Massachusetts writs of assistance controversy, raised grave constitutional issues. More provocations followed the treaty of Paris: stricter enforcement of the trade laws, the Proclamation of 1763, the Sugar Act of 1764, and, most importantly, the Stamp Act of 1765. Until the adoption of these provocative measures, Knollenberg holds, the colonists were, on the whole, satisfied with the existing imperial system. But these new measures, "concentrated in the span of a few years, all contributed to the colonial fear that the British grovernment would go further and further in depriving the colonies of the large measure of self-government in internal affairs they had so long enjoyed and justly valued." Thus the stage was set for the coming of the Revolution.

A recent article by Thad W. Tate in the *William and Mary Quarterly* (1962), "The Coming of the Revolution in Virginia: Britain's Challenge to Virginia's Ruling Class, 1763–1776," makes the same point about that pivotal colony. Tate discounts the importance in arousing revolutionary sentiment of such factors as the indebtedness of the planters to British merchants, or the resentment of speculators against British western policy, or internal conflict between radicals and conservatives. The Virginians, Tate finds, moved to revolution when the British measures after 1763 challenged their long-established local autonomy.

"All the major public resolutions, addresses, and petitions of the colony," he finds, "spoke against a threat to 'ancient, legal, and constitutional rights.' . . . The Revolution did not open in force until the announcement of the Stamp Act. From there until the beginning of armed conflict with Dunmore in the fall of 1775 political or constitutional issues were the occasion for every outbreak of protest within the colony."

The neo-Whig interpretation has been buttressed by such recent monographs as Carl Ubbelohde's *The Vice-Admiralty Courts and the American Revolution* (1960); David S. Lovejoy's *Rhode Island Politics and the American Revolution, 1760–1776* (1958); and W. W. Abbot's *The Royal Governors of Georgia, 1754–1775* (1959). Despite the differing emphases of each individual work, there is a broad consensus of opinion among the members of the neo-Whig school. All agree, in Jack Greene's words, "that the Revolution was essentially a conservative movement, a defense of American rights and liberties against provocations by the mother country."

II. Britain Tries a New Departure

THE first act in the drama that would culminate in the Declaration of Independence began during the Seven Years War, when the "Great Commoner," William Pitt, moved to halt the illegal wartime trade between the mainland colonies and the French West Indies—a trade that was materially aiding French resistance. The most effective weapons of the customs officers in suppressing this traffic were the writs of assistance: these general writs gave customs officers a free hand to call upon local officials for assistance and to enter, by force if necessary, warehouses, stores, or homes to search for smuggled goods, without presenting any evidence for suspecting the presence of such goods. Such writs had been granted to customs officers by the Supreme Court of Judicature of Massachusetts during the war; but these would expire six months after the death of George II in October, 1760, and sixty-three Boston merchants retained lawyer James Otis, Jr., to oppose the petition by the customs officers for their renewal.

Whether Otis was moved by principle, or by resentment because the new governor, Francis Bernard, had refused to appoint his father to the chief justiceship, will never be known. But in his address before the court on February 24, 1761, Otis presented the first major colonial challenge on constitutional grounds to British authority. Attacking such general writs as an "instrument of arbitrary power . . . destructive of English liberty and the fundamental principles of law," Otis denied the authority of Parliament "to establish such a writ. . . . An act against the constitution is void." The following version of Otis's speech was prepared by John Adams at a later date from rough notes taken at the trial:

Printed: Charles Francis Adams, ed., *The Works of John Adams* (10 vols., Boston, 1850–1856), II, pp. 523-525.

"MAY IT PLEASE YOUR HONORS,

I was desired by one of the Court to look into the books, and consider the question now before them concerning writs of assistance. I have accordingly considered it, and now appear, not only in obedience to your order, but likewise in behalf of the inhabitants of this town, who have presented another petition, and out of regard to the liberties of the subject. And I take this opportunity to declare, that whether under a fee or not (for in such a cause as this I despise a fee) I will to my dying day oppose with all the powers and faculties God has given me, all such instruments of slavery on the one hand, and villany on the other, as this writ of assistance is.

It appears to me the worst instrument of arbitrary power, the most destructive of English liberty and the fundamental principles of law, that ever was found in an English law-book. . . .

In the first place, may it please your Honors, I will admit that writs of one kind may be legal; that is, special writs, directed to special officers, and to search certain houses, &c. specially set forth in the writ, may be granted by the Court of Exchequer at home, upon oath made before the Lord Treasurer by the person who asks it, that he suspects such goods to be concealed in those very places he desires to search. The act of 14 Charles II. which Mr. Gridley mentions, proves this. And in this light the writ appears like a warrant from a Justice of the Peace to search for stolen goods. Your Honors will find in the old books concerning the office of a Justice of the Peace, precedents of general warrants to search suspected houses. But in more modern books you will find only special warrants to search such and such houses specially named, in which the complainant has before sworn that he suspects his goods are concealed; and you will find it adjudged that special warrants only are legal. In the same manner I rely on it, that the writ prayed for in this petition, being general, is illegal. It is a power, that places the liberty of every man in the hands of every petty officer. I say I admit that special writs of assistance, to search special

places, may be granted, to certain persons on oath; but I deny that the
writ now prayed for can be granted, for I beg leave to make some observations on the writ itself, before I proceed to other acts of Parliament. In the first place, the writ is universal, being directed 'to all and
singular Justices, Sheriffs, Constables, and all other officers and subjects:' so, that, in short, it is directed to every subject in the King's
dominions. Every one with this writ may be a tyrant; if this commission be legal, a tyrant in a legal manner also may control, imprison, or murder any one within the realm. In the next place, it is
perpetual; there is no return. A man is accountable to no person for
his doings. Every man may reign secure in his petty tyranny, and
spread terror and desolation around him. In the third place, a person
with this writ, in the daytime, may enter all houses, shops, &c. at will,
and command all to assist him. Fourthly, by this writ not only
deputies, &c., but even their menial servants, are allowed to lord it
over us. Now one of the most essential branches of English liberty is
the freedom of one's house. A man's house is his castle; and whilst he
is quiet, he is as well guarded as a prince in his castle. This writ, if
it should be declared legal, would totally annihilate this privilege.
Custom-house officers may enter our houses, when they please; we
are commanded to permit their entry. Their menial servants may
enter, may break locks, bars, and every thing in their way; and
whether they break through malice or revenge, no man, no court, can
inquire. Bare suspicion without oath is sufficient. . . .

Again, these writs are not returned. Writs in their nature are
temporary things. When the purpose for which they are issued are
answered, they exist no more; but these live forever; no one can be
called to account. Thus reason and the constitution are both against
this writ. Let us see what authority there is for it. Not more than one
instance can be found of it in all our law-books; and that was in the
zenith of arbitrary power, namely, in the reign of Charles II., when
star-chamber powers were pushed to extremity by some ignorant
clerk of the exchequer. But had this writ been in any book whatever,
it would have been illegal. All precedents are under the control of the
principles of law. Lord Talbot says it is better to observe these than
any precedents, though in the House of Lords, the last resort of the
subject. No Acts of Parliament can establish such a writ; though it
should be made in the very words of the petition, it would be void.
An act against the constitution is void. (vid. Viner.) But these prove

no more than what I before observed, that special writs may be granted *on oath and probable suspicion.* The act of 7 & 8 William III. that the officers of the plantations shall have the same powers, &c. is confined to this sense; that an officer should show probable ground; should take his oath of it; should do this before a magistrate; and that such magistrate, if he think proper, should issue a special warrant to a constable to search the places. That of 6 Anne can prove no more.

Otis lost his case. After reserving judgment until fall, the Court renewed the writs. But the issue was not dead. When the Townshend Act of 1767 reaffirmed the legality of such general writs, similar controversies erupted in nearly all the colonies and continued until the outbreak of hostilities. Otis had put forth, and helped to popularize, the view that the colonists had rights that Parliament could not lawfully transgress. And increasingly the colonists would resist any statute that they believed violated these rights.

The next major challenge on constitutional grounds to British authority came as an outgrowth of the disallowance by the Privy Council in 1759 of the Virginia Two-penny Act. In 1748, the Virginia General Assembly had provided that each parish should pay the local Anglican minister an annual salary of sixteen thousand pounds of tobacco. Then in 1758, when drought brought a severe tobacco shortage, the General Assembly passed a law authorizing for one year the payment of all debts and taxes figured on a tobacco basis in local currency at the rate of two pence for each pound of tobacco—a rate which was about one-third the prevailing market price. Although this was a general act not directed against the clergy alone, they suffered a serious financial blow. Sending the Reverend John Camm to London as their spokesman, they protested the injustice of the law. The Privy Council disallowed the law in August, 1759, and the Virginia clergy thereupon sought redress for their losses in the local courts. The most famous of these suits by the clergy to recover their salaries was that instituted by the Reverend James Maury. The court ruled the law null and void, but the amount of damages was to be settled by the jury. The jury trial was held on December 1, 1763, and the attorney for the parish rate collectors, a rising young lawyer named Patrick Henry, delivered an eloquent challenge to the constitutionality of the action by the Privy Council in annulling the Two-penny Act. The following account, understandably not sympathetic to Henry, was written by Maury to John Camm, December 12, 1763:

Printed: John P. Kennedy, ed., *Journals of the House of Burgesses of Virginia, 1761–1765* (Richmond, 1907), pp. li-liii.

December 12th, 1763

To the Rev. John Camm.

Dear Sir:—

Now that I am somewhat at leisure, than when I wrote to you by Major *Winston*, from *Hanover*, some few days ago, I have sat down to give you the best account I can of the most material passages in the trial of my cause against the Collectors in that Court, both to satisfy your own curiosity, and to enable the lawyer, by whom it is to be managed in the General Court, to form some judgment of its merits. I believe, sir, you were advised from *Nov'r* Court, that the Bench had adjudged the twopenny act to be no law; and that, at the next, a jury, on a writ of inquiry, were to examine whether the Plaintiff had sustained any damages, and what. Accordingly, at *December* Court, a select jury was ordered to be summoned; but, how far they who gave the order, wished or intended it to be regarded, you may judge from the sequel. The Sheriff went into a public room, full of gentlemen, and told his errand. One excused himself (*Peter Robinson* of *King William*) as having already given his opinion in a similar case. On this, as a person then present told me, he immediately left the room, without summoning any one person there. He afterwards met another gentleman (*Richard Sq. Taylor*) on the green, and, on his saying he was not fit to serve, being a churchwarden, he took upon himself to excuse him, too, and, as far as I can learn, made no further attempts to summon gentlemen. These, You'll say, were but feeble endeavors to comply with the directions of the Court in that particular. Hence, he went among the vulgar herd. After he had selected and set down upon his list about eight or ten of these, I met him with it in his hand, and on looking over it, observed to him that they were not such jurors as the Court had directed him to get, being people of whom I had never heard before, except one, whom, I told him, he knew to be a party in the cause, as one of the Collector's Securities, and, therefore, not fit for a juror on that occasion. Yet this man's name was not erased. He was even called in Court, and, had he not excused himself, would probably have been admitted. For, I cannot recollect, that the Court expressed either surprise or dislike that a more proper jury had not been summoned. Nay, though I objected against them, yet, as *Patrick Henry* (one of the Defendant's lawyers) insisted they were honest men, and, therefore, unexception-able, they were immediately called to the book and sworn. Three of them, as I was afterwards told, nay, some said four, were Dissenters of that denomination called *New Lights*, which the Sheriff, as they were all his acquaintance, must have known. Messrs. *Gift* and *Mc-Dowall*, the two most considerable purchasers in that county, were now called in to prove the price of tobacco, and sworn. The testimony of the former imported, that, during the months of *May* and *June*, 1759, tobacco had currently sold at 50s. per hundred, and that himself, at or about the latter end of the last of those months, had sold some hundreds of hhds. at that price, and, amongst the rest, one hundred to be delivered in the month of *August*, which, however, were not delivered till *September*. That of the latter only proved, "That 50s. was the current price to tobacco that season." This was the sum of the evidence for the Plaintiff. Against him, was produced a receipt to the Collector, to the best of my remembrance in these words: "Received of *Thomas Johnson*, Jun'r, at this and some former payments, £144, current money, by *James Maury*." After the lawyers on both sides had displayed the force and weight of the evidence, pro and con to their Honors, the jurors, and one of those who appeared for the Defendants had observed to them that they must find, (or if they must find, I am not sure which, but think the former) for the Plaintiff, but need not find more than one farthing; they went out, and, according to instruction (though whether according to evidence or not, I leave you to judge), in less than five minutes brought in a verdict for the Plaintiff, one penny damages. *Mr. Lyons* urged, as the verdict was contrary to evidence, the jury ought to be sent out again. But no notice was taken of it, and the verdict admitted without

hesitation by the Bench. He then moved to have the evidence of
Messrs. *Gift* and *McDowell* recorded, with as little effect. His next
motion, which was for a new trial shared the same fate. He then
moved it might be admitted to record, "that he had made a motion
for a new trial, because he considered the verdict contrary to evidence, and that the motion had been rejected;" which, after much
altercation, was agreed to. He lastly moved for an appeal, which, too,
was granted. This, sir, as well as I can remember, is a just and
impartial narrative of the most material occurences in the trial of that
cause. One occurrence more, tho' not essential to the cause, I can't
help mentioning, as a striking instance of the loyalty, impartiality and
attachment of the Bench to the Church of *England* in particular, and
to religion at large. *Mr. Henry,* mentioned above (who had been
called in by the Defendants, as we suspected, to do what I some time
ago told you of), after *Mr. Lyons* had opened the cause, rose and
harrangued the jury for near an hour. This harangue turned upon
points as much out of his own depths, and that of the jury, as they
were foreign from the purpose; which it would be impertinent to
mention here. However, after he had discussed those points, he
labored to prove "that the act of 1758 had every characteristic of a
good law; that it was a law of general utility, and could not, consistently with what he called the original compact between King and
people, stipulating protection on the one hand and obedience on the
other be annulled." Hence, he inferred, "that a King, by disallowing
Acts of this salutary nature, from being the father of his people,
degenerated into a Tyrant and forfeits all right to his subjects' obedience." He further urged, "that the only use of an Established Church
and Clergy in society, is to enforce obedience to civil sanctions, and
that the observance of those which are called duties of imperfect
obligation; that, when a Clergy ceases to answer these ends, the
community have no further need of their ministry, and may justly
strip them of their appointments; that the Clergy of *Virginia*, in this
particular instance of their refusing to acquiesce in the law in question, had been so far from answering, that they had most notoriously
counteracted, those great ends of their institution; that, therefore,
instead of useful members of the state, they ought to be considered
as enemies of the community; and that, in the case now before them,
Mr. *Maury*, instead of countenance, and protection and damages,
very justly deserved to be punished with signal severity." And then he

perorates to the following purpose, "that excepting they (the jury) were disposed to rivet the chains of bondage on their own necks, he hoped they would not let slip the opportunity which now offered, of making such an example of him as might, hereafter, be a warning to himself and his brethren, not to have the temerity, for the future, to dispute the validity of such laws, authenticated by the only authority, which, in his conception, could give force to laws for the government of this Colony, the authority of a legal representative of a Council, and of a kind and benevolent and patriot Governor." You'll observe I do not pretend to remember his words, but take this to have been the sum and substance of this of his labored oration. When he came to that part of it where he undertook to assert, "that a King, by annulling or disallowing acts of so salutary a nature, from being the Father of his people degenerated into a Tyrant, and forfeits all right to his subjects' obedience;" the more sober part of the audience were struct with horror. Mr. *Lyons* called out aloud, and with an honest warmth, to the Bench, "That the gentleman had spoken treason," and expressed his astonishment "that their worship could hear it without emotion, or any mark of dissatisfaction." At the same instant, too, amongst some gentlemen in the crowd behind me, was a confused murmur of Treason, Treason! Yet Mr. *Henry* went on in the same treasonable and licentious strain, without interruption from the Bench, nay, even without receiving the least exterior notice of their disapprobation. One of the jury, too, was so highly pleased with these doctrines, that, as I was afterwards told, he every now and then gave the traitorous declaimer a nod of approbation. After the Court was adjourned, he apologised to me for what he had said, alleging that his sole view in engaging in the cause, and in saying what he had, was to render himself popular. You see, then, it is so clear a point in this person's opinion, that the ready road to popularity here, is, to trample under foot the interests of religion, the rights of the church, and the perogative of the crown. If this be not pleading for the "assumption of a power to bind the King's hands," if it be asserting "such supremacy in provincial Legislatures" as is inconsistent with the dignity of the Church of *England*, and manifestly tends to draw the people of these plantations from their allegiance to the King, tell me, my dear sir, what is so, if you can. Mr. *Cootes*, merchant on *James* River, after Court said "he would have given a considerable sum out of his own pocket, rather than his friend *Patrick* should have been guilty of a crime, but little, if any thing inferior to that which brought *Simon* Lord *Lovatt* to the block;" and justly observed that he exceeded the most seditious and inflammatory harangues of the Tribunes of old *Rome*.

My warmest wishes and prayers ever attend you. And besides these there is little else in the power of, my dear *Camm*,

Your affectionate,

J. MAURY

The jury returned a verdict of one penny—and the "Parsons' Cause" marked a chapter in the still-inchoate challenge to British supremacy. The case made Patrick Henry a popular hero and carried him to the House of Burgesses where he would take the lead in a future crisis of authority between the colonies and the mother country.

This crisis was not long in coming. With the signing of the Treaty of Paris on February 10, 1763, a new phase began in the relations between colonies and the mother country. On the one hand, the conquest of Canada and the removal of the French and Indian menace gave freer play to colonial separatist impulses. On the other hand, the war had revealed serious weaknesses in imperial administration while the acquisition of vast additional territories raised new problems demanding a solution by the new ministry headed by George Grenville.

The accession of George III to the throne in October, 1760, marked a watershed in British politics. The youthful new king was determined to take his rightful place as the active chief executive of the kingdom and break the captivity which he believed the "Old Whigs," in Charles Ritcheson's phrase, had imposed upon his grandfather. His target was "party" or "faction," against any attempt by a parliamentary faction to "give him the law." He, therefore, engineered the downfall first of the great war minister, William Pitt, and then of the leader of the Old Whigs, the Duke of Newcastle, and in May, 1761, he brought in as chief minister, his personal favorite, the Earl of Bute. The Bute ministry concluded the Treaty of Paris with the French to end the Great War for the Empire. But his personal unpopularity led Bute to give up leadership of the ministry in April, 1763, to his protege, George Grenville. Grenville, in Eric Robson's apt description, "unimaginative, obstinate, stiff, arrogant," and yet far from unintelligent, had to deal with the manifold problems arising in the aftermath of the war.

One was the question of relations with the Indians in the trans-Appalachian region. Some historians have claimed that the British government was animated in its western policy by a desire to restrict on mercantilist grounds the colonists to the seaboard. But the main objective appeared to have been preservation of peace on the frontier, and that meant safeguarding the Indians from the encroachments of white settlers and speculators as well as from unscrupulous traders. This problem became the more acute with the outbreak of Pontiac's Rebellion in May, 1763. The Grenville ministry's solution took the form of the Proclamation of October 7, 1763:

Printed: Clarence Brigham, ed., *British Royal Proclamations Relating to America, 1603–1783* (American Antiquarian Society *Transactions*, vol. XII, Worcester, Mass., 1911), pp. 212-218.

. . . Whereas it is just and reasonable, and essential to Our Interest and the Security of Our Colonies, that the several Nations or Tribes of Indians, with whom We are connected, and who live under Our Protection, should not be molested or disturbed in the Possession of such Parts of Our Dominions and Territories as, not having been ceded to, or purchased by Us, are reserved to them, or any of them, as their Hunting Grounds; We do therefore, with the Advice of Our Privy Council, declare it to be Our Royal Will and Pleasure, that no Governor or Commander in Chief in any of Our Colonies of Quebec, East Florida, or West Florida, do presume, upon any Pretence whatever, to grant Warrants of Survey, or pass any Patents for Lands beyond the Bounds of their respective Governments, as described in their Commissions; as also, that no Governor or Commander in Chief in any of Our other Colonies or Plantations in America, do presume,

for the present, and until Our further Pleasure be known, to grant
Warrants of Survey, or pass Patents for any Lands beyond the Heads
or Sources of any of the Rivers which fall into the Atlantick Ocean
from the West and North-West, or upon any Lands whatever, which,
not having been ceded to, or purchased by Us as aforesaid, are
reserved to the said Indians, or any of them.

And We do further declare it to be Our Royal Will and Pleasure,
for the present as aforesaid, to reserve under Our Sovereignty, Protection, and Dominion, for the Use of the said Indians, all the Lands
and Territories not included within the Limits of Our said Three New
Governments, or within the Limits of the Territory granted to the
Hudson's Bay Company, as also all the Lands and Territories lying
to the Westward of the Sources of the Rivers which fall into the Sea
from the West and North West, as aforesaid; and We do hereby
strictly forbid, on Pain of Our Displeasure, all Our loving Subjects
from making any Purchases or Settlements whatever, or taking Possession of any of the Lands above reserved, without Our especial
Leave and Licence for that Purpose first obtained.

And We do further strictly enjoin and require all Persons whatever,
who have either wilfully or inadvertently seated themselves upon any
Lands within the Countries above described, or upon any other
Lands, which, not having been ceded to, or purchased by Us, are still
reserved to the said Indians as aforesaid, forthwith to remove themselves from such Settlements.

And whereas great Frauds and Abuses have been committed in
the purchasing Lands of the Indians, to the great Prejudice of Our
Interests, and to the great Dissatisfaction of the said Indians; in order
therefore to prevent such Irregularities for the future, and to the End
that the Indians may be convinced of Our Justice, and determined
Resolution to remove all reasonable Cause of Discontent. We do, with
the Advice of Our Privy Council, strictly enjoin and require, that
no private Person do presume to make any Purchase from the said
Indians of any Lands reserved to the said Indians, within those Parts
of Our Colonies where We have thought proper to allow Settlement;
but that if, at any Time, any of the said Indians should be inclined to
dispose of the said Lands, the same shall be purchased only for Us,
in Our Name, at some publick Meeting or Assembly of the said
Indians to be held for that Purpose by the Governor or Commander
in Chief of Our Colonies respectively, within which they shall lie: and

in case they shall lie within the Limits of any Proprietary Government, they shall be purchased only for the Use and in the Name of such Proprietaries, conformable to such Directions and Instructions as We or they shall think proper to give for that Purpose: And We do, by the Advice of Our Privy Council, declare and enjoin, that the Trade with the said Indians shall be free and open to all our Subjects whatever; provided that every Person, who may incline to trade with the said Indians, do take out a Licence for carrying on such Trade from the Governor or Commander in Chief of any of Our Colonies respectively, where such Person shall reside; and also give Security to observe such Regulations as We shall at any Time think fit, by Ourselves or by Our Commissaries to be appointed for this Purpose, to direct and appoint for the Benefit of the said Trade; And We do hereby authorize, enjoin, and require the Governors and Commanders in Chief of all Our Colonies respectively, as well Those under Our immediate Government as those under the Government and Direction of Proprietaries, to grant such Licences without Fee or Reward, taking especial Care to insert therein a Condition, that such Licence shall be void, and the Security forfeited, in Case the Person, to whom the same is granted, shall refuse or neglect to observe such Regulations as We shall think proper to prescribe as aforesaid. . . .

The purpose underlying the Proclamation was to take regulation of Indian affairs out of the hands of the individual colonies and place it under royal officers. But this plan ran into two obstacles: the expense and the opposition of the colonists. Although the boundary line delineated was merely a temporary arrangement and was not intended as a permanent barrier to westward expansion, the Proclamation antagonized influential speculators while the frontiersmen paid no heed. British policy regarding the trans-Appalachian region would act as a continuing irritant in the years that followed; but the leadership of the colonial resistance to the mother country after 1763 came from the seaboard rather than the frontier. The western question was but one aspect of the larger problem of imperial administration facing the British government.

The crux of the problem was money. The government proposed to station an army of 10,000 men in North America to implement the program of imperial regulation envisaged in the Proclamation of 1763, to prevent any attempt by France and Spain to regain their lost possessions, and to "retain the Inhabitants of Our ancient Provinces in a State of Constitutional Dependence upon Great Britain." That cost was estimated at more than £220,000 annually; moreover, new responsibilities arising from the new acquisitions meant additional expenses. While Parliament had reimbursed a major share of the colonies' wartime expenditures, the war had left Britain itself burdened with a debt amounting to over £125,000,000 and taxes in the mother country had reached an excessively high level. Thus the major problem facing Grenville was to find new sources of revenue—and faced with this difficulty, he thought it just and proper that the American colonists should contribute to the cost of maintaining the troops needed for their security.

One possible source of revenue was through stricter enforcement of the laws of trade and navigation. A report by the Board of Trade in 1763 indicated that whereas the annual revenue from the mainland colonies was about £1,800, the cost of maintaining the customs service there was £7,600 a year. Smuggling—especially between the northern colonies and the French West Indies—was widespread, even in the midst of war. Stricter enforcement of the customs would produce a sizeable revenue. The steps taken by Grenville to transform the regulatory acts into a revenue-producing source were outlined in the following memorial from the Treasury, approved by the Privy Council, October 5, 1763:

Printed: W. L. Grant and James Munro, eds., *Acts of the Privy Council of England, Colonial Series* (6 vols., London, 1908–1912), IV, pp. 569-572.

[The following memorial of 4 Oct. from the Treasury is approved, and the Earl of Halifax, Secretary of State, the Admiralty, and the Board of Trade instructed to give directions in accordance therewith:—] We the Commissioners of your Majestys Treasury beg leave

humbly to represent to your Majesty, that having taken into Consideration the present state of the Duties of Customs imposed on your
Majestys Subjects in America and the West Indies, We find, that the
Revenue arising therefrom is very small and inconsiderable having in
no degree increased with the Commerce of those Countries, and is
not yet sufficient to defray a fourth Part of the Expence necessary for
collecting it. We observe with concern that through Neglect, Con-
nivance and Fraud, not only the Revenue is impaired, but the Commerce of the Colonies is diverted from its natural Course and the
salutary Provisions of many wise Laws to secure it to the Mother
Country are in great Measure defeated: Attention to Objects of so
great Importance, we are sensible is at all times our Duty, but at this
it is more indispensable when the Military Establishment necessary
for maintaining these Colonies requires a large Revenue to support
it, and when their vast Increase in Territory and Population makes
the proper Regulation of their Trade of immediate Necessity, lest the
continuance and extent of the dangerous Evils abovementioned may
render all Attempts to remedy them hereafter infinitely more difficult,
if not utterly impracticable. We have endeavoured therefore to discover, and as far as the Power of our Department will allow, remove
the Causes, to which the Deficiency of this Revenue and the contraband Trade with other European Nations are owing. For this
Purpose We have ordered all the Officers belonging to the Customs in
America and the West Indies to be fully instructed in their Duty to
repair forthwith to their respective Stations and constantly to reside
there for the future; and where We find, that a sufficient number of
proper Officers are not yet established, it is intended to supply the
Deficiency by the appointment of others. We have directed that all
the Officers of the Revenue in your Majestys Plantations should be
furnished with new and ample Instructions, enforcing in the strongest
manner the strictest attention to their Duty, and requiring that by
regular and constant correspondence, they give an Account as well
of their own Proceedings, as of the conduct of the Officers under
them, and inform Us likewise of any Obstructions they may meet
with in discharging the Business of their respective Offices. We have
ordered them to transmit exact Accounts of the Imports and Exports
in their several Districts, of the state of the Revenue, and of the
illicit Commerce with other European States from time to time in
consequence of these directions, with such Observations as may

occurr to them in regard either to the Efficacy and Inefficacy of any
subsisting regulations or to such Alterations as they may judge conducive to the farther Improvement of the Revenue to the prevention
of those Frauds by which it is impaired, and to the Suppression of
the contraband Trade which has been hitherto carried on with too
much Impunity: and We have directed the Commissioners of your
Majesty's Customs immediately to dismiss every Officer, that shall
fail to pay obedience to these Instructions or be any way deficient in
his Duty. But as the Restraint and Suppression of Practices which
have unhappily prevailed too long will certainly be encountered with
great difficulties in such distant Parts of your Majestys Dominions,
We apprehend that these Our Regulations will not fully answer the
end for which they are designed, unless, in consequence of your
Majestys Commands, the other Departments of Your Government
afford their utmost Assistance in support of them. With this View,
We thought it became us thus to lay Our Proceedings before your
Majesty, and further humbly to represent, that it appears to Us of
the highest Importance, that strict Orders should be given to the
Governors of all the Colonies, to make the Suppression of the clandestine and prohibited Trade with foreign Nations, and the Improvement of the Revenue, the constant and immediate Objects of their
Care, and by a vigorous discharge of the duty required of them by
several Acts of Parliament and a due exertion of their legal Authority,
to give the Officers of the Revenue the necessary Protection and
Support, and that they from time to time transmit such Observations
as occur to them on the state of the Illicit and Contraband Trade, and
on the conduct of all Persons, whose duty it is to prevent the same,
in order that the necessary Directions may be given for punishing
such Persons, as shall appear to be guilty of any Misbehaviour and
correcting all abuses for the future.—We are further humbly of
opinion that it will greatly contribute to the same salutary ends, and
to the carrying of the several Laws and Regulations into execution
with Success, if all Officers both Civil and Military are strictly commanded to give their Assistance upon all proper Occasions, and if
the Commanders in Chief of Your Majestys Ships and Troops in
America and the West Indies are directed to attend to this object
with the utmost care, and to make such a Disposition of the Force
under their respective Commands as will be most serviceable in suppressing these dangerous Practices, and in protecting the Officers of

the Revenue from the violence of any desperate and lawless Persons, who shall attempt to resist the due execution of the Laws in the same manner as is practiced in England.—The Advantages of a Sea Guard more especially in those Parts are sufficiently obvious. We depend upon it as the likeliest means for accomplishing these great Purposes: and the good Effects, that have already been experienced from the Measures lately taken for that purpose at Home, make us earnestly wish, that the same may not only be continued, but even extended and strengthened as far as the Naval Establishment will allow.— And lastly it appears to Us highly necessary that there should be established by Law a new and better method of condemning Seizures made in the Colonies; The Commissioners of the Customs have reported to Us, that they have received various Complaints of great Difficulties and Partialities in the Trials on these Occasions, and the several Statutes in force from the 12th of Charles the Second to the third of Your Majesty vary so much both as to the Mode and Place of Trial, that the Officers of the Revenue when they have made a Seizure cannot but be under great doubt and Uncertainty, in what manner they should proceed to the condemnation of it. It is therefore humbly submitted to Your Majesty whether from the Importance of this Object it would not be of the greatest Public Utility, that an Uniform Plan be prepared for establishing the Judicature of the Courts of Admiralty in that Country under Persons qualified for so important a Trust, in order that Justice may hereafter in all Cases be diligently and impartially administered and that such Regulations, as Parliament may think proper to make, may be duly carried into Execution.

The most flagrantly violated of the laws of trade was the Molasses Act of 1733. That act had imposed a duty of six pence a gallon on colonial imports of foreign molasses, not for purposes of revenue but to guarantee the British West Indian sugar interests a monopoly of the market. The mainland colonists protested that the duty was prohibitively high, and complained that its strict enforcement would be economically ruinous. The molasses was mainly distilled into rum, for domestic consumption as well as the African slave trade, but the British West Indies could not supply the demand of the mainland colonies, nor could they absorb all the surplus lumber, fish, and produce the mainlanders had to sell. Protesting that strict enforcement of the duty "will give a mortal wound to the Trade of these Colonies," the Boston merchants, organized as the Society for Encouraging Trade and Commerce, drew up in December, 1763, the following "Statement of Trade and Fisheries of Massachusetts" as part of their plea against renewal of the Act of 1733:

Printed: *Fitch Papers. Correspondence and Documents during Thomas Fitch's Governorship of the Colony of Connecticut, 1754–1766* (2 vols., ed., Albert Bates, Connecticut Historical Society *Collections,* vols. XVII and XVIII, Hartford, Conn., 1918–1920), iI, pp. 261-273.

As the Act, commonly called the Sugar Act, has been passed upwards of thirty Years without any Benefit to the Crown, the Duties arising from it, having never been appropriated by Parliament to any particular use; and as this Act will expire this Winter, the following Considerations are offered as Reasons why it should not be renewed.

First, It is apprehended, that the Trade is so far from being able to bear the high Duties imposed by this Act, that it will not bear any Duty at all. The Price of Molasses at present, is but 12^d Sterling per Gallon, at which Price it will barely answer to distil it into Rum for Exportation: Should this Duty be added, it would have the Effect of an absolute Prohibition on the Importation of Molasses and Sugar from the foreign Islands; and consequently the same Effect on the Exportation of Fish, Lumber and other Commodities from hence to those Islands; as the French, Dutch and other Foreigners whom we supply with those Articles, will not permit us to bring away their money; so that unless we can take their ordinary Sugars and Molasses in Return, this Trade will be lost. As we do not import any Rum from the foreign Islands, the Duty on that Commodity is of little consequence, and Great Britain would finally pay much more than the Duty on Sugars, if an End should be put to our Trade to the foreign Islands. For should the Colonies be obliged to take from our own Islands all the West India Produce that they consume, the Price in Great-Britain must necessarily advance more than double this Duty. If we are permitted to import foreign Sugars and Molasses into the

Northern Colonies, more of our West-India Produce will be carried to Great-Britain, where the Consumption is supposed to be equal to the whole Produce of our Islands.

Secondly, The Loss of the Trade to the foreign Islands on which great Part of our other Trade depends, must greatly affect all the Northern Colonies, and entirely destroy the Fishery in this Province, and at Newfoundland likewise; as our own Islands are not capable of taking off above one Third of our West-India Cod-Fish, nor one Quarter of the Mackrell, Shad, Alewives and other small Fish exported from hence. . . .

Thirdly, A Prohibition on the Trade to foreign Islands will greatly promote the French Fishery. . . .

Fourthly, The Fishery being a great Nursery of Seamen for his Majesty's Navy, the Destruction thereof must very much weaken the Naval Power of Great Britain. . . .

Fifthly, The Destruction of the Fishery will be very prejudicial to the Trade of Great-Britain, by lessening the Demand for her Manufactures. . . .

Sixthly, The Destruction of the Fishery will not only lessen the Importation of Goods from Great-Britain, but must greatly prejudice the whole Trade of the Province. The Trade to the foreign Islands is become very considerable: Surinam, and the other Dutch Settlements, are wholly supplied with Provisions, Fish, Lumber, Horses, Onions and other Articles exported from the Northern Colonies; for which we receive Molasses in Return; this is distilled into Rum for the Fishery, and to export to the Southern Colonies for Naval Stores, which we send to Great-Britain, and for Grain; and to Africa to purchase Slaves for our own Islands in the West Indies: If this Trade is destroyed, the Distillery on the Continent must be broken up, as all our own Islands do not export Molasses sufficient to supply the Northern Colonies. . . .

Seventhly, The Destruction of the Fishery will be the Ruin of those concerned in that Business, and that are dependent on it. . . .

Ninthly, This Act was procured by the Interest of the West-India Planters, with no other View than to enrich themselves, by obliging the northern Colonies to take their whole Supply from them; and they still endeavour the Continuance of it under a Pretence, that they can supply Great-Britain and all her Colonies with West-India Goods, which is perfectly chimerical: Take their own Accounts of the Exportation of their Produce from their several Islands, (which by the way, from some would be one half more than is really their own Produce, it being foreign Produce run among them, and then cleared out as English,) then take the natural Demand of Great-Britain for their Sugar, and the Demand of the Colonies for Rum, Sugar and Molasses; and it will appear that their Produce is by no Means sufficient to supply even the bare Necessities of the English. . . .

Upon the whole, It is plain that our Islands are able neither to supply us with what we want from them nor to take from us what Lumber and Fish we are obliged to export: And they will be still less able to do either; for our Demands will be growing faster than their Produce, and our Fishery which has been increasing, will continue still to increase, if not obstructed, while their Demands have not increased in any Proportion, and never can.

Grenville had no wish to destroy the New England economy. But he was desperately in need of new sources of revenue and had to keep in mind the powerful influence wielded by the West Indian planters in Parliament. Early in 1764, he therefore, introduced the American Revenue Act, popularly known as the Sugar Act, which continued and made perpetual the duty on colonial imports of foreign molasses, but reduced the rate to what Grenville believed was the more reasonable figure of three pence per gallon. The act passed with little opposition, and was signed by the king on April 5, 1764. Although in the form of a measure regulating colonial trade, its main purpose, explicitly stated in the preamble, was to raise a revenue.

To prevent smuggling, the act overhauled and strengthened the enforcement machinery. Shippers had to fill out an elaborate set of papers for every cargo; this requirement applied even to intercolonial coastal shipping. The burden of proof in trials under the act was placed upon the accused; while other provisions, in effect, freed customs officers from liability for damages for illegal seizures. As the capstone to this machinery of enforcement, the act provided for the trial of violators in any common law court, any provincial vice-admiralty court, or "any Court of Vice-

Admiralty which may or shall be appointed over all America
. . . at the election of the informer or prosecutor":

Printed: 4 George III, c. 15, Danby Pickering, ed., *The
Statutes at Large* (46 vols., Cambridge, 1762–1807),
XXVI, pp. 33-52.

An act for granting certain duties in the British *colonies and
plantations in* America, *for continuing, amending, and making perpetual, an act passed in the sixth year of the reign of his late majesty
King* George *the second,* (*intituled,* An act for the better securing and
encouraging the trade of his Majesty's sugar colonies in *America;*)
*for applying the produce of such duties, and of the duties to arise by
virtue of the said act, towards defraying the expences of defending,
protecting, and securing the said colonies and plantations; . . . and
more effectually preventing the clandestine conveyance of goods to
and from the said colonies and plantations, and improving and securing the trade between the same and* Great Britain.

Whereas *it is expedient that new provisions and regulations should
be established for improving the revenue of this kingdom, and for
extending and securing the navigation and commerce between* Great
Britain *and your Majesty's dominions in* America, *which, by the
peace, have been so happily enlarged: and whereas it is just and
necessary, that a revenue be raised, in your Majesty's said dominions
in* America, *for defraying the expences of defending, protecting, and
securing the same, we, your Majesty's most dutiful and loyal subjects,
the commons of* Great Britain, *in parliament assembled, being desirous to make some provision, in this present session of parliament,
towards raising the said revenue in* America, *have resolved to give
and grant unto your Majesty the several rates and duties herein after-
mentioned;* and do most humbly beseech your Majesty that it may be
enacted; and be it enacted by the King's most excellent majesty, by
and with the advice and consent of the lords spiritual and temporal,
and commons, in this present parliament assembled, and by the
authority of the same, That . . . from the twenty ninth day of *September,* one thousand seven hundred and sixty four, the said act [the
Molasses Act] subject to such alterations and amendments as are

herein after contained, shall be, and the same is hereby made perpetual.

V. And be it further enacted by the authority aforesaid, That in lieu and instead of the rate and duty imposed by the said act upon molasses and syrups, there shall, from and after the said twenty ninth day of *September*, one thousand seven hundred and sixty four, be raised, levied, collected, and paid, unto his Majesty, his heirs and successors, for and upon every gallon of molasses or syrups, being the growth, product, or manufacture, of any colony or plantation in *America*, not under the dominion of his Majesty, his heirs or successors, which shall be imported or brought into any colony or plantation in *America*, which now is, or hereafter may be, under the dominion of his Majesty, his heirs or successors, the sum of three pence. . . .

XI. And it is hereby further enacted by the authorities aforesaid, That all the monies which . . . shall arise by the several rates and duties herein before granted . . . shall be paid into the receipt of his Majesty's Exchequer, and shall be entered separate and apart from all other monies paid or payable to his Majesty, his heirs or successors: and shall be there reserved, to be, from time to time disposed of by parliament, towards defraying the necessary expenses of defending, protecting, and securing, the *British* colonies and plantations in *America*. . . .

XLI. And it is hereby further enacted and declared, . . . that all the forfeitures and penalties inflicted by this or any other act or acts of parliament relating to the trade and revenues of the said *British* colonies or plantations in *America*, which shall be incurred there, shall and may be prosecuted, sued for, and recovered in any court of record, or in any court of admiralty, in the said colonies or plantations where such offence shall be committed, or in any court of vice admiralty which may or shall be appointed over all *America* (which court of admiralty or vice admiralty are hereby respectively authorized and required to proceed, hear, and determine the same) at the election of the informer or prosecutor.

XLII. And it is hereby further enacted, That all penalties and forfeitures so recovered there, under this or any former act of parliament, shall be divided, paid, and applied, as follows; that is to say, after deducting the charges of prosecution from the gross produce thereof, one third part of the net produce shall be paid into the hands of the collector of his Majesty's customs at the port or place where such penalties or forfeitures shall be recovered, for the use of his Majesty, his heirs and successors; one third part to the governor or commander in chief of the said colony or plantation; and the other third part to the person who shall seize, inform, and sue for the same. . . .

XLV. And it is hereby further enacted by the authority aforesaid, That from and after the twenty ninth day of *September*, one thousand seven hundred and sixty four, if any ship or goods shall be seized for any cause of forfeiture, and any dispute shall arise whether the customs and duties for such goods have been paid, or the same have been lawfully imported or exported, or concerning the growth, product, or manufacture, of such goods, or the place from whence such goods were brought, then, and in such cases, the proof thereof shall lie upon the owner or claimer of such ship or goods, and not upon the officer who shall seize or stop the same; any law, custom, or usage, to the contrary notwithstanding.

XLVI. And be it further enacted by the authority aforesaid, That from and after the twenty ninth day of *September*, one thousand seven hundred and sixty four, in case any information shall be commenced and brought to trial in *America*, on account of any seizure of any ship or goods as forfeited by this or any other act of parliament relating to his Majesty's customs, wherein a verdict or sentence shall be given for the claimer thereof; and it shall appear to the judge or court before whom the same shall be tried, that there was a probable cause of seizure, the judge or court before whom the same shall be tried shall certify on the record or other proceedings, that there was a probable cause for the prosecutors seizing the said ship or goods; and, in such case, the defendant shall not be intitled to any costs of suit whatsoever; nor shall the persons who seized the said ship or goods, be liable to any action, or other suit or prosecution, on account of such seizure: and in case any action, or other suit or prosecution, shall be commenced and brought to trial against any person or persons whatsoever, on account of the seizing any such ship or goods, where no information shall be commenced or brought to trial to condemn the same, and a verdict or sentence shall be given upon such action or prosecution against the defendant or defendants, if the court or judge before whom such action or prosecution, shall certify in like manner as aforesaid that there was a probable cause for

such seizure, then the plaintiff, besides his ship or goods so seized, or
the value thereof, shall not be intitled to above two pence damages,
nor to any costs of suit; nor shall the defendant in such prosecution
be fined above one shilling.

XLVII. And be it further enacted by the authority aforesaid, That
if any action or suit shall be commenced, either in *Great Britain* or
America, against any person or persons for any thing done in pursuance of this or any other act of parliament relating to his Majesty's
customs, the defendant or defendants in such action or suit may plead
the general issue . . . that the same was done in pursuance and by
the authority of such act; and if it shall appear so to have been done,
the jury shall find for the defendant or defendants; and if the plaintiff
shall be nonsuited, or discontinue his action after the defendant or
defendants shall have appeared, or if judgment shall be given upon
verdict or demurrer against the plaintiff, the defendant or defendants
shall recover treble costs. . . .

Along with the Sugar Act, Grenville introduced a resolution
declaring that "toward defraying the said Expenses, it may be
proper to charge certain Stamp Duties in said Colonies and Plantations." The House of Commons approved the resolution in March,
1764; but Grenville announced that he would postpone action
until the following session. One reason for the delay was to gather
the necessary information about what items to tax. Another was
that he wished to give the colonies the opportunity to present an
alternative plan to raise the needed money. Historians have debated his sincerity: whether he did, in fact, intend to give the
colonies an option, or whether he was decided upon the stamp
tax and was simply making a false show of reasonableness. Sincere or not, Grenville did make the offer—and in a conference
with the colonial agents on May 17, 1764, he reiterated his desire
to raise the money "by means the most easy and least exceptionable to the Colonies." He warned, however, that if the colonies
failed to present a satisfactory alternative, and he was pessimistic
about that possibility, then he would ask Parliament to act. He
even expressed the hope that colonial assemblies would assent in
advance to such a tax. The following report of the conference

was sent by the agent for South Carolina, Charles Garth, to the committee of correspondence of the South Carolina Commons House, June 5, 1764:

Printed: Lewis Namier, "Charles Garth, Agent for South Carolina," *English Historical Review*, No. CCXVI (October, 1939), 646-648.

Gentlemen,

Since I wrote last, the several Agents for the Colonies in America have had a meeting to consider of the steps proper on their part to be taken, in consequence of the Stamp Bill being postpon'd to the next Sessions of Parliament: in duty to our constituents to procure the best intelligence possible and as a mark of respect for the candour shown in not hurrying a measure so interesting to the subject in America, we came to a resolution of waiting upon Mr. Grenville.

On the 17th of May we attended him, and after expressing our thanks for waving the intended bill in the last session, upon the principle of giving the Colonies the opportunity of knowing the intention of Government that they might be able to remit their several objections for the consideration of Parliament, we acquainted him with our wishes that he should be pleased to let us have copies of the Bill to transmit to America, in order that our respective constituents might have the whole, both substance and form under their deliberation, when they would be far better able to determine whether or how far, to approve or disapprove.—Mr. Grenville told us it was impossible for him to comply with our request, as the Bill was not yet thoroughly digested, and assured us that his motive for deferring it sprang from a desire of shewing his regard to the subjects in America, by previously consulting them on a measure, that if the principle upon which it was grounded should appear fair and just in itself, he believed could have the fewest objections of any that could be proposed:—the expence of maintaining, protecting and defending America, it was but natural for America to bear at a time when the revenue of the Mother Country stands in need of every relief and assistance to be had, in order to lessen and diminish as much as possible the immense load of debt upon the nation, that it may be able to exert itself upon every necessary occasion with that vigour, which the Colonies have happily experienced, and will at all times find essential to their immediate interest and welfare. The method of raising this relief from America had employ'd much of his attention, from a desire of doing it by means the most easy and least exceptionable to the Colonies; the raising it within themselves and appropriating it would have been attended with very many difficulties even if it could be suppos'd that 26 colonies (including the Continent and West India Islands) would all have adopted such a recommendation, and which in case of refusal to enforce the power of Parliament must have been had recourse to, whereas his intention by this delay was to have the sense of the Colonies themselves upon the matter, and if they could point out any system or plan as effectual and more easy to them, he was open to every proposition to be made from the Colonies, but when the subject had been fully considered by them upon its proper grounds and principles, and no other method should upon the whole be suggested so proper for America in general, it would be a satisfaction to him to carry it into the House with their concurrence and approbation. Objections of inability might possibly come from some Colonies, but, he believed, would have very little weight with Parliament; and with regard to the power of Parliament, the sense of the House of Commons had been sufficiently declaratory thereof, even if there had been no precedent of a revenue from America granted to the Crown by Act of Parliament, meaning the Act establishing a Post Office at New York.—We then took the liberty of asking him (upon supposition of concurrence in the Colonies to the mode) if he had either determined in his mind what things he should make subject to this Stamp Duty, and whether the stamps, to be directed, were to be as high as are by law imposed in Great Britain, or what proportion they would bear, as it seemed to us to be unreasonable that if stamps were to be as great as in England, they should be so high, the object of Government being nothing more than as it were a reimbursement for the expence annually incurred on account of the American Dominions, which £400,000 would amply satisfy, and towards raising the same the Duty Bill last Sessions must not be forgot, the Legislature having so appropriated the income that redounds to the revenue from the duties therein impos'd: Mr. Grenville believed upon the plan thought of the objects for the Stamp Duty would be as extensive, but what the rate of the stamps might be, was not determin'd, and added he should be, very ready to consult with us before the meeting of Parliament thereon to receive any propositions we might in the mean time be instructed upon by our respective constituents with regard to these points, if our Assemblies should, as he could not doubt, upon a due consideration they would, transmit us instructions with their assent to the plan for levying this money in the American Dominions. . . .

Grenville's hopes for colonial assent were in vain. The colonies were in the midst of a post-war depression, and the Sugar Act threatened to make their plight worse. The passage close upon the heels of the Sugar Act of an act prohibiting the colonies from making paper money legal tender aggravated the situation. The colonists had depended for their supply of hard money largely upon the West Indies trade; with the Sugar Act curtailing that traffic, the Currency Act of 1764 threatened to leave them without a medium of exchange for carrying on business. As Philadelphia merchant Samuel Rhoads, Jr., complained to his London correspondents: "If you will deprive us of all Medium of Trade among ourselves . . . & if we are not on any Terms allow'd a Trade to get Money, from abroad, we shall have none to pay for Goods, & then unless you will send them Gratis our Dealings must end."

These economic grievances were coupled with alarm over the vice-admiralty courts. Such courts, which operated without juries, were, as Carl Ubbelohde has shown, no innovation in the colonies. The Navigation Act of 1696 had granted such courts a concurrent jurisdiction with the common-law courts in trade and revenue cases; there were in 1763 eleven vice-admiralty courts in North America and customs officials could bring cases before the common-law or vice-admiralty courts as they so chose. Since the war had revealed many of the judges of the provincial vice-admiralty courts in collusion with the merchants to violate the law, the Sugar Act provided for a new vice-admiralty court whose jurisdiction would cover all of North America. This was not a court of appeal; it was a court of first instance having concurrent jurisdiction with the provincial vice-admiralty courts. Violations committed in any colony could be taken to this new court—established at Halifax—for trial "at the election of the informer or prosecutor," and the thought of having to plead their cases before so far-off a tribunal alarmed many merchants.

This new prominence given the vice-admiralty courts by the Sugar Act raised questions of constitutional principle in the minds of the colonists. In England, violations of the trade laws were tried before a jury in the common-law courts; in America, however, a single judge, acting without a jury and following civil law, could decide the issue. Was not the extensive jurisdiction granted to these vice-admiralty courts subversive of the colonists' sacred right to trial by jury?

But the colonists directed their fire first and foremost against what appeared to be a more ominous threat to their constitutional rights. The Sugar Act was an avowed revenue measure, and the proposed stamp tax hung over their heads. Boston took the lead. On May 15, 1764, the Boston town meeting appointed a committee, including an ambitious political wire-puller named Samuel Adams, to draw up instructions for the town's representatives in the Massachusetts House of Representatives. The instructions, approved May 24, instructed the representatives to protest the new measures as not simply economically burdensome but a threat to colonial rights:

Printed: Harry A. Cushing, ed., *The Writings of Samuel Adams* (4 vols., New York and London, 1904–1908), I, pp. 1-7.

. . . Our Trade has for a long time labored under great Discouragements; it is with the deepest Concern that we see such further Difficultys coming upon it as will reduce it to the lowest Ebb, if not totally obstruct & ruin it. We cannot help expressing our Surprize, that when so early Notice was given by the Agent of the Intentions of the Ministry to burthen us with new Taxes, so little Regard was had to this most interesting Matter, that the Court was not even called together to consult about it till the latter end of y° Year; the

Consequence of which was, that Instructions could not be sent to the Agent, tho sollicited by him, till the Evil had got beyond an easy Remedy. There is now no Room for further Delay: We therefore expect that you will use your earliest Endeavors in the Gen¹ Assembly, that such Methods may be taken as will effectually prevent these Proceedings against us. By a proper Representation we apprehend it may easily be made to appear that such Severitys will prove detrimental to Great Brittain itself; upon which Account we have Reason to hope that an Application, even for a Repeal of the Act, should it be already passd, will be successfull. It is the Trade of the Colonys, that renders them beneficial to the Mother Country: Our Trade, as it is now, & always has been conducted, centers in Great Brittain, & in Return for her Manufactures affords her more ready Cash, beyond any Comparison, than can possibly be expected by the most sanguine Promoters of these extraordinary Methods. We are in short ultimately yielding large Supplys to the Revenues of the Mother Country, while we are laboring for a very moderate Subsistence for ourselves. But if our Trade is to be curtaild in its most profitable Branches, & Burdens beyond all possible Bearing, laid upon that which is sufferd to remain, we shall be so far from being able to take off the manufactures of Great Brittain, that it will be scarce possible for us to earn our Bread.—But what still heightens our apprehensions is, that these unexpected Proceedings may be preparatory to new Taxations upon us: For if our Trade may be taxed why not our Lands? Why not the Produce of our Lands & every thing we possess or make use of? This we apprehend annihilates our Charter Right to govern & tax ourselves —It strikes at our Brittish Privileges, which as we have never forfeited them, we hold in common with our Fellow Subjects who are Natives of Brittain: If Taxes are laid upon us in any shape without our having a legal Representation where they are laid, are we not reducd from the Character of free Subjects to the miserable State of tributary Slaves?

We therefore earnestly recommend it to you to use your utmost Endeavors, to obtain in the Gen¹ Assembly all necessary Instructions & Advice to our Agent at this most critical [Juncture]; that while he is setting forth the unshaken Loyalty of this Province & this Town— its unrivald Exertions in supporting His Majestys Governmᵗ & Rights in this part of his Dominions—its acknowlegd Dependence upon & Subordination to Great Brittain, & the ready Submission of its Mer-

chants to all just & necessary Regulations of Trade, he may be able
in the most humble & pressing Manner to remonstrate for us all
those Rights & Privileges which justly belong to us either by Charter
or Birth. . . .

In October, the Massachusetts House adopted a remonstrance
strongly denying Parliament's right of taxation, but the more
conservatively inclined Council, led by Lieutenant-Governor
Thomas Hutchinson, insisted upon a milder statement. The re-
vised petition protested against the Sugar Act as economically
burdensome; assailed "the extension of the powers of the courts
of vice-admiralty"; but then merely claimed freedom from "internal taxes"—a distinction later to plague the colonists—as a
matter of privilege rather than right. Although this final statement was a mild one, the joint committee of the House and
Council that drew up the petition explained to the colony's
London agent, Jasper Mauduit, that they had toned down their
protest solely for reasons of policy:

Printed: Alden Bradford, ed., *Speeches of the Governors
of Massachusetts from 1765 to 1775; And the Answers of
the House of Representatives*. . . (Boston, 1818), pp. 24-25.

. . . We have endeavored to avoid giving offence, and have touched
upon our rights in such a manner, as that no inference can be drawn,
that we have given them up, on the one hand, nor that we set up in
opposition to the Parliament, nor deny that we are bound to the
observance of acts of Parliament, on the other. But in a letter to you,
we may be more explicit on this point—a right, the people of the
colonies have undoubtedly by charter and commissions to tax themselves. So far as the Parliament shall lay taxes on the colonies, so far
they will deprive them of this right. If the first settlers of the colonies
had not imagined that they were as secure of the enjoyment of this
right as of their titles to their lands, in all probability they would
never have left England, and no one colony could have been settled.
    Acts of Parliament, it will be said, are above charters, and can
annihilate them. It is true. So one act of Parliament may infringe

upon them. And, perhaps, there would be no greater reason for complaint in that case, than when the rights of a corporation in England, or in the colonies are infringed: to be sure not greater, than when what are deemed the fundamentals of the English constitution are changed, with respect to any considerable part of the subjects. Such fundamentals, we deem the right of being taxed by our own representatives only; and the rights to trials by juries. Upon the latter, we have said the less in our petition, because, by the charter, the power of appointing courts of admiralty, where no juries are in use, and which are the only occasions of our complaints upon that head, is reserved to the Crown. But then it must be remembered, that all seizures for illicit trade are tried in the exchequer in England by juries; and that we have no reason to suppose, that our ancestors, when they accepted the charter, imagined the powers of courts of admiralty would be extended beyond what they are in England—and as for the newly constituted court of admiralty, if the judge takes cognizance of all maritime matters and all offences which have been usually tried by courts of admiralty in America, and which may arise in any part of the colonies, it may bring such oppression upon the subjects as will be insupportable.

In point of equity, we think we may well claim an exemption from taxes by Parliament. Our ancestors, and we believe the first settlers of every colony, except Nova Scotia and Georgia, occasioned but little, some of them, no expense, and yet have brought an amazing addition of wealth, territory and subjects, to the nation. They are burdened with the support of government within themselves: they are under restraints in their trade, which the subjects of Great Britain are not; and what the colonies lose by that, Britain gains. The colonies find more employment for the manufactures in Britain, we believe, than all the world besides. And this is a matter which is not to be lightly considered. . . . In point of policy, it will certainly prove a mistake to lay further burdens on the colonies. You have now all we can spare from our necessary support, and the expense of clearing and cultivating a new country, and by this means increasing the dominions of Britain. In this way, the people pay to you cheerfully. In the other, it will ever be paid with grief and reluctance. . . .'

The protests were not confined to New England. The Pennsylvania Assembly instructed its London agent, Richard Jackson, to oppose the proposed stamp tax as violation of "their most essential Rights as British subjects" and raised the cry no taxation without representation. The most populous and influential of the colonies, Virginia, joined in the outcry. Declaring that the colonists "are not, and indeed cannot, constitutionally be represented" in Parliament, the Virginia petition of December 18, 1764, to the House of Commons—a petition approved by the appointed Council as well as the popularly elected House of Burgesses—demanded, in effect, complete local autonomy in matters of taxation:

Printed: Kennedy, *Journals of the House of Burgesses of Virginia, 1761–1765*, pp. 303-305.

To the Honourable the Knights, Citizens, and Burgesses of *Great Britain*, in Parliament assembled:
   The Remonstrance of the Council and Burgesses of *Virginia*.
   It appearing by the printed Votes of the House of Commons of *Great Britain* in Parliament assembled that in a Committee of the whole House, the 17th Day of *March* last, it was resolved that towards defending, protecting, and securing the *British* Colonies and Plantations in *America*, it may be proper to charge certain Stamp Duties in the said Colonies and Plantations; and it being apprehended that the same Subject, which was then declined, may be resumed and further pursued in a succeeding Session, the Council and Burgesses of *Virginia*, met in General Assembly, judge it their indispensable Duty, in a respectful Manner, but with decent Firmness, to remonstrate against such a Measure, that at least a Cession of those Rights, which in their Opinion must be infringed by that Procedure, may not be inferred from their Silence, at so important a Crisis.
   They conceive it is essential to *British* Liberty that Laws imposing Taxes on the People ought not to be made without the Consent of Representatives chosen by themselves; who, at the same Time that they are acquainted with the Circumstances of their Constituents, sustain a Proportion of the Burthen laid on them. This Privilege, inherent in the Persons who discovered and settled these Regions, could not be renounced or forfeited by their Removal hither, not as

Vagabonds or Fugitives, but licensed and encouraged by their Prince and animated with a laudable Desire of enlarging the *British* Dominion, and extending its Commerce: On the contrary, it was secured to them and their Descendents, with all other Rights and Immunities of *British* Subjects, by a Royal Charter, . . . and the Remonstrants do not discern by what Distinction they can be deprived of that sacred Birthright and most valuable Inheritance by their Fellow Subjects, nor with what Propriety they can be taxed or affected in their Estates by the Parliament, wherein they are not, and indeed cannot, constitutionally be represented.

And if it were proper for the Parliament to impose Taxes on the Colonies at all, which the Remonstrants take Leave to think would be inconsistent with the fundamental Principles of the Constitution, the Exercise of that Power at this Time would be ruinous to *Virginia*, who exerted herself in the late War it is feared beyond her Strength, insomuch that to redeem the Money granted for that Exigence her People are taxed for several Years to come: This, with the large Expenses incurred for defending the Frontiers against the restless *Indians*, who have infested her as much since the Peace as before, is so grievous that an Increase of the Burthen will be intolerable; especially as the People are very greatly distressed already from the Scarcity of circulating Cash amongst them, and from the little Value of their Staple at the *British* Markets.

And it is presumed that adding to that Load which the Colony now labours under will not be more oppressive to her People than destructive of the Interest of *Great Britain:* For the Plantation Trade, confined as it is to the Mother Country, hath been a principal Means of multiplying and enriching her Inhabitants; and, if not too much discouraged, may prove an inexhaustable Source of Treasure to the Nation. For Satisfaction in this Point, let the present State of the *British* Fleets and Trade be compared with what they were before the Settlement of the Colonies; and let it be considered that whilst Property in Land may be acquired on very easy Terms, in the vast uncultivated Territory of *North America*, the Colonists will be mostly, if not wholly, employed in Agriculture; whereby the Exportation of their Commodities [to] *Great Britain*, and the Consumption of their Manufactures supplied from thence, will be daily increasing. But this most desirable Connexion between *Great Britain* and her Colonies, supported by such a happy Intercourse of reciprocal Bene-

fits as is continually advancing the Prosperity of both, must be interrupted, if the People of the latter, reduced to extreme Poverty, should
be compelled to manufacture those Articles they have been hitherto
furnished with from the former.

From these Considerations, it is hoped that the Honourable House
of Commons will not prosecute a Measure which those who may
suffer under it cannot but look upon as fitter for Exiles driven from
their native Country after ignominiously forfeiting her Favours and
Protection, than for the Prosperity of *Britons* who have at all Times
been forward to demonstrate all due Reverence to the Mother Kingdom, and are so instrumental in promoting her Glory and Felicity;
and that *British* Patriots will never consent to the Exercise of anti-
constitutional Power, which even in this remote Corner may be dangerous in its Example to the interiour Parts of the *British* Empire,
and will certainly be detrimental to its Commerce.

By far the boldest action was taken by the New York Assembly. Whereas the other colonies had attacked the Sugar Act
simply on economic grounds, the New York Assembly bluntly
assailed parliamentary taxation of any kind—internal or external
—as a violation of colonial rights. Although continuing to recognize Parliament's authority to regulate trade, the New York
petition of October 18, 1764, repudiated any attempt to use such
regulations as a cover for taxation in one of the most uncom-
promising statements of colonial rights of the pre-revolutionary
period:

Printed: *Journals of the Votes and Proceedings of the
General Assembly of the Colony of New York* [1691–1765]
(2 vols., New York, 1764–1766), II, pp. 776-779.

*To the Honourable the Knights, Citizens and Burgesses, repre-
senting the Commons of* Great-Britain, *in Parliament assembled.*
*The Representation and Petition of the General-Assembly of the
Colony of* New-York.
Most humbly Shew,
That from the Year 1683, to this Day, there have been three

Legislative Branches in this Colony; consisting of the Governor and Council appointed by the Crown, and the Representatives chosen by the People, who, besides the Power of making Laws for the Colony, have enjoyed the Right of Taxing the Subject for the Support of the Government.

Under this Political Frame, the Colony was settled by Protestant Emigrants from several Parts of *Europe*, and more especially from *Great-Britain* and *Ireland*: And as it was originally modelled with the Intervention of the Crown, and not excepted to by the Realm of *England* before, nor by *Great-Britain*, since the Union, the Planters and Settlers conceived the strongest Hopes, that the Colony had gained a civil Constitution, which, so far at least as the Rights and Privileges of the People were concerned, would remain permanent, and be transmitted to their latest Posterity.

It is therefore with equal Concern and Surprize, that they have received Intimations of certain Designs lately formed, if possible, to induce the Parliament of *Great-Britain*, to impose Taxes upon the Subjects *here*, by Laws to be passed *there*; and as we who have the Honour to represent them, conceive that this Innovation, will greatly affect the Interest of the Crown and the Nation, and reduce the Colony to absolute Ruin; it became our indispensible Duty, to trouble you with a seasonable Representation of the Claim of our Constituents, to an Exemption from the Burthen of all Taxes not granted by themselves, and their Foresight of the tragical Consequences of an Adoption of the contrary Principle, to the Crown, the Mother Country, themselves and their Posterity. . . .

. . . An Exemption from the Burthen of ungranted, involuntary Taxes, must be the grand Principle of every free State.—Without such a Right vested in themselves, exclusive of all others, there can be no Liberty, no Happiness, no Security; it is inseparable from the very Idea of Property, for who can call that his own, which may be taken away at the Pleasure of another? . . . [T]he People of this Colony, inspired by the Genius of their Mother Country, nobly disdain the thought of claiming that Exemption as a *Privilege*.—They found it on a Basis more honourable, solid and stable; they challenge it, and glory in it as their Right. That Right their Ancestors enjoyed in *Great-Britain* and *Ireland*; their Descendants returning to those Kingdoms, enjoy it again: And that it may be exercised by his Majesty's Subjects at Home, and justly denied to those who submitted to

Poverty, Barbarian Wars, Loss of Blood, Loss of Money, personal Fatigues, and ten Thousand unutterable Hardships, to enlarge the Trade, Wealth, and Dominion of the Nation; or, to speak with the most unexceptionable Modesty, that when *as Subjects*, all have equal Merit; a Fatal, nay the most odious Discrimination should nevertheless be made between them, no Sophistry can recommend to the Sober, impartial Decision of Common Sense.

. . . No History can furnish an Instance of a Constitution to permit one Part of a Dominion to be taxed by another, and that too in Effect, but by a Branch of that other Part; who in all Bills for public Aids, suffer not the least Alteration.—And if such an absurd and unequal Constitution should be adopted, who, that considers the natural Reluctance of Mankind to burthens, and their Inclination to cast them upon the Shoulders of others, cannot foresee, that while the People on one Side of the *Atlantic*, enjoy an Exemption from the Load, those on the other, must submit to the most unsupportable Oppression and Tyranny.

Against these Evils, the Indulgence of the present Parliament, of which we have had such large Experience, cannot provide, if the grant Right to tax ourselves is invaded. Depressed by the Prospect of an endless Train of the most distressing Mischiefs, naturally attendant upon such an Innovation, his Majesty's *American* Subjects, will think it no inconsiderable Augmentation of their Misery, that the Measure itself implies the most severe and unmerited Censure, and is urged, as far as they are acquainted, by no good Reasons of State.

They are unconscious of any Conduct, that brings the least Imputation upon their Love and Loyalty, and whoever has accused them, has abused both the Colonies and their Mother Country; more faithful Subjects his Majesty has not, in any Part of his Dominions, nor *Britain* more submissive and affectionate Sons.

And if our Contributions to the Support of the Government upon this Continent, or for the Maintenance of an Army, to awe and subdue the Savages should be thought necessary, why shall it be presumed, without a Trial, that we more than others, will refuse to hearken to a just Requisition from the Crown? To Requisitions for Aids salutary to our own Interests? Or why should a more incorrigible and unreasonable Spirit be imputed to us, than to the Parliament of *Ireland*, or any other of his Majesty's Subjects?

Left to the Enjoyment of our antient Rights, the Government will be truly informed when a Tax is necessary, and of the Abilities of the People; and there will be an equitable Partition of the Burthen. And as the publick Charges will necessarily increase with the Increase of the Country, and the Augmentation or Reduction of the Force kept up, be regulated by the Power and Temper of our barbarian Enemy, the Necessity for continuing the present Model must appear to be most strongly inforced.—At the remote Distance of the *British* Commons from the sequestered Shades of the interior Parts of this Desart, false Intelligence of the State of the *Indians* may be given; whereas the Vicinity of the Colonies will enable them, not only, to detect all false Alarms, and check all fraudulent Accounts, but urge them by the never failing Motive of Self-Preservation, to oppose any hostile Attempts upon their Borders.

Nor will the Candour of the Commons of *Great-Britain*, construe our Earnestness to maintain this Plea, to arise from a Desire of Independency upon the supreme Power of the Parliament. Of so extravagant a Disregard to our own Interests we cannot be guilty.—From what other Quarter can we hope for Protection? We reject the Thought with the utmost Abhorrence; and a perfect knowledge of this Country will afford the fullest Proof, that nothing in our Temper can give the least Ground for such a Jealousy.

The peaceable and invariable Submission of the Colonies, for a Century past, forbids the Imputation, or proves it a Calumny.—What can be more apparent, than that the State which exercises a Sovereignty in Commerce, can draw all the Wealth of its Colonies into its own Stock? And has not the whole Trade of *North-America*, that growing Magazine of Wealth, been, from the Beginning, directed, restrained, and prohibited at the sole Pleasure of the Parliament? And whatever some may pretend, his Majesty's American Subjects are far from a Desire to invade the just Rights of *Great-Britain*, in all commercial Regulations. They humbly conceive, that a very manifest Distinction presents itself, which, while it leaves to the Mother Country an incontestible Power, to give Laws for the Advancement of her own Commerce, will, at the same Time, do no Violence to the Rights of the Plantations.

The Authority of the Parliament of *Great-Britain*, to model the Trade of the whole Empire, so as to subserve the Interest of her own, we are ready to recognize in the most extensive and positive Terms. Such a Preference is naturally founded upon her Superiority, and indissolubly connected with the Principle of Self-Preservation.—And therefore, to assign one Instance, instead of many, the Colonies cannot, would not ask for a Licence to import woolen Manufactures from *France*; or to go into the most lucrative Branches of Commerce, in the least Degree incompatible with the Trade and Interest of *Great-Britain*.

But a Freedom to drive all Kinds of Traffick in a Subordination to, and not inconsistent with, the *British* Trade; and an Exemption from all Duties in such a Course of Commerce, is humbly claimed by the Colonies, as the most essential of all the Rights to which they are intitled, as Colonists from, and connected, in the common Bond of Liberty, with the uninslaved Sons of *Great-Britain*.

For, with Submission, since all Impositions, whether they be internal Taxes, or Duties paid, for what we consume, equally diminish the Estates upon which they are charged; what avails it to any People, by which of them they are impoverished? Every Thing will be given up to preserve Life; and though there is a Diversity in the Means, yet, the whole Wealth of a Country may be as effectually drawn off, by the Exaction of Duties, as by any other Tax upon their Estates.

And therefore, the General Assembly of *New-York*, in Fidelity to their Constituents, cannot but express the most earnest Supplication, that the Parliament will charge our Commerce with no other Duties, than a necessary Regard to the particular Trade of *Great-Britain*, evidently demands; but leave it to the legislative Power of the Colony, to impose all other Burthens upon it's own People, which the publick Exigences may require.

Latterly, the Laws of Trade seem to have been framed without an Attention to this fundamental Claim.

Permit us, also, in Defence of our Attachment to the Mother Country, to add, what your Merchants (to whom we boldly make the Appeal) know to be an undoubted Truth; that this Continent contains some of the *most useful* of her Subjects.—Such is the Nature of our Produce, that all we acquire is less than sufficient to purchase what we want of your Manufactures; and, be the Policy of your Commerce what it will, all our Riches must flow into *Great-Britain*.— Immense have been our Contributions to the National Stock.—Our Staple, Industry, Trade and Wealth, all conduce to the particular Advantage of our fellow Subjects there.—The natural State of this

Country, necessarily forms the Ballance of Trade in her Favour.— Her growing Opulence must elevate her above all Fear and Jealousy of these Dependences. How much stronger then the Reasons for leaving us free from ungranted Impositions? Whoever will give full Scope to his Meditations on this Topic, will see it the Interest of *Great-Britain*, to adopt the Maxim, that her own Happiness is most intimately connected with the Freedom, Ease and Prosperity of her Colonies: The more extensive our Traffick, the Greater her Gains; we carry all to her Hive, and consume the Returns; and we are content with any constitutional Regulation that inriches her, though it impoverishes ourselves. . . .

The honourable House will permit us to observe next, that the Act of the last Session of Parliament, inhibiting all Intercourse between the Continent and the foreign Sugar Colonies, will prove equally detrimental to us and *Great-Britain.*—*That* Trade, gave a value to a vast, but now alas unsaleable Staple, which being there converted into Cash and Merchandize, made necessary Remittances for the *British* Manufactures we consumed: . . . And when we consider the Wisdom of our Ancestors in contriving Trials by Juries, we cannot stifle our Regret, that the Laws of Trade in general, change the Current of Justice from the common Law, and subject Controversies of the utmost Importance to the Decisions of the Vice-Admiralty Courts, who proceed not according the old wholesom Laws of the Land, nor are always filled with Judges of approved Knowledge and Integrity.— To this Objection, the aforementioned Statute will at first View appear to be so evidently open, that we shall content ourselves with barely suggesting, that the amazing Confidence it reposes in the Judges, gives great Grief to his Majesty's *American* Subjects. . . .

The General Assembly of this Colony have no desire to derogate from the Power of the Parliament of *Great-Britain*; but they cannot avoid deprecating the Loss of such Rights as they have hitherto enjoyed, Rights established in the first Dawn of our Constitution, founded upon the most substantial Reasons, confirmed by invariable Usage, conducive to the best Ends; never abused to bad Purposes, and with the Loss of which Liberty, Property, and all the Benefits of Life, tumble into Insecurity and Ruin: Rights, the Deprivation of which, will dispirit the People, abate their Industry, discourage Trade, introduce Discord, Poverty and Slavery; or, by depopulating the Colonies, turn a vast, fertile, prosperous Region, into a dreary Wilderness; impoverish *Great-Britain*, and shake the Power and Independancy of the most opulent and flourishing Empire in the World. All which your Petitioners (who repose the highest Confidence in your Wisdom and Justice) humbly pray, may be now taken into your seasonable Consideration, and such Measures pursued, as the Event may prove to have been concerted for the Common-Weal, of all the Subjects of *Great-Britain*, both at home and abroad.

But these colonial protests failed to deter the British ministry. Despite his professed willingness to allow the colonists to suggest an alternative method of raising the needed money, Grenville appeared never to have regarded that as a serious possibility. Even while the colonial assemblies were drawing up their protests, he had Thomas Whately, secretary to the Treasury, start work preparing the legislation. Whately finished his task by December. By this time, news of the colonial remonstrances had begun to reach the mother country. But the near-unanimity with which the petitions had denied the right of Parliament to tax the colonies stiffened the determination in British political circles to do so. To challenge the right of Parliament to tax the colonies appeared to threaten that due subordination of the colonies to the mother country that nearly all politically conscious Britons believed necessary and just.

Early in 1765 there appeared an anonymous pamphlet entitled *The Regulations Lately Made concerning the Colonies and the Taxes Imposed upon Them, considered* (London) defending the ministry's policies. Authorship was widely attributed to Grenville himself; the author was, in fact, Thomas Whately, and his views reflected Grenville's own. The pamphlet first defended the Sugar Act as a necessary and just measure to raise revenue; the most important part, however, was the rebuttal made to the colonial protests against the proposed stamp tax. Whately acknowledged that no subject could be taxed without his consent; but pointing out that Parliament had, in fact, taxed the colonists in the past, he denied any distinction between "internal" and "external" taxes. Answering the American cry of no taxation without representation, Whately contended that the colonists were "virtually represented" in Parliament just as non-voters in Britain itself were:

. . . The Circumstances of the Times, the Necessities of this Country, and the Abilities of the Colonies, concur in requiring an *American* Revenue; *Great Britain* strained to the utmost of her Strength, sinks under the Exertion, and will hardly recover by Rest alone, without the Aid of Remedy: her funded Debt increased by 65,061,960*l*. 7*s*. 10*d*. for the Expences of the last War, amounts now, the 1,000,000*l*. Civil List Debt being included, to the enormous Sum of 130,568,968*l*. 4*s*. 0¼. upon which 4,716,681*l*. 4*s*. 11½. Interest is annually paid. . . . Her Peace Establishment is at the same Time increased by the Necessity of keeping an Army in *America*, of augmenting her Fleet, and of providing for the many Expences of her additional Dominions. The whole Annual Revenue that is necessary to answer all these Demands, amounts to near 3,000,000*l*. and is raised by many, and some of them burthensome Taxes, which are imposed, not only upon the Luxuries of the Rich, but which all the Researches of Invention, and all the Resources of Finance, could not find Means to keep off from the Consumption of the Poor; and great Part of them are not meer Expedients for a present Exigency, but are entailed upon our Posterity perhaps to distant Generations. The whole of this vast Revenue is raised in *Great Britain* and is paid by the Inhabitants of *Great Britain*, excepting such Duties as are levied or retained upon Exportation to foreign Countries, or to the Colonies, and which after all Draw-backs and Bounties are allowed, make but a small Proportion of the whole; and even these, tho' produced on the Consumption of others, are still a Burthen upon the Trade of *Great Britain*; while the Colonies in *North America*, near two Million of *British* Subjects, an opulent, commercial, thriving people, and who have been enabled by the Patronage of their Mother Country to extend their Trade and their Cultivation over that fertile Continent, supported by her Wealth, protected by her Power, and blessed with her Laws, contribute to the national Expence by Taxes raised there, no more than seven or eight Hundred Pounds *per Ann*. and the Colonies in the *West-Indies*, where, tho' their Numbers are less, their Riches are greater, have remitted no more than eleven or twelve Hundred Pounds *per Ann*. to *England*: The whole Remittance from

all the Colonies at an Average of thirty Years has not amounted to
1900*l.* a year, and to make it still more ridiculous, the Establishment
of Officers necessary to collect this 1900*l.* amounts to 7600*l. per
Annum.*

There is no Occasion to accompany this Account with any Observations; only to state it, is to prove the Necessity of an additional
American Revenue; they can certainly bear more; they ought to raise
more: The Subjects and the Mode of new Impositions are therefore
the only Considerations; but to lay them on Subjects, and in such a
Manner as would not be oppressive to those who were to pay them,
would not be dangerous, in the delicate Situation of the Colonies,
with respect to their Trade, their Improvements, and their Connection with the Mother Country, and would at the same time apply
equally to all, in their different Stages of Progess from Infancy to
Maturity, was a Measure that required the utmost Caution, Circum-
spection, and Care: It came under the Deliberation of Parliament the
last Winter, and by their Wisdom an Act [the Sugar Act] was passed
to be the Foundation of an *American Revenue.* . . .

[By the Molasses Act of 1733] a Duty of Six-pence per Gallon was
laid upon all foreign Melasses; but such has been the Disregard of all
Revenue Laws in *America,* that this has produced hardly any Thing,
tho' the Commodity has been imported all the time in great Quantities. Instead of paying the Duty, a regular Course has been fallen into
of importing it free of any; and the Expence of such Smuggling has
been brought to a Certainty of about Three Half-pence a Gallon;
which was a Charge upon the raw Materials before it came to the
Manufacturer, amounting to one Fourth of the Duty, and destructive
of the whole: under this Charge the Distilleries of *North America*
have flourished to a surprizing Degree; and surely it is to be wished
that the Burthen now upon the Merchandize, should yield a Revenue
to the Publick instead of a Profit to Smugglers, or which is worse, to
Officers of the.Crown conniving at Smugglers: but it has been said
that the excessive high Duty, imposed by the 6 Geo. II. was the
Cause of the Smuggling, and that nothing will put a Stop to it but
reducing the Tax. The Fact is probable; the Legislature seem to have
thought that the Load was heavier than the Trade could bear; and
have therefore reduced it from Six-pence to Three-pence *per* Gallon:
this still is represented by some as too high; and indeed whatever
Rate is fixed, will in all Probability be censured by those whom it

affects; but so far is certain, that a Duty may always exceed the Expence of Smuggling; for no Man will expose his Character to Reflection, and his Property to Hazards, without the Temptation of Advantages over the fair Trader. And as Three Half-pence *per* Gallon was the Expence of Smuggling, while a general Relaxation of the Laws against it prevailed over all that Continent, now that these Laws are rigorously put into Execution, that Charge will be higher in Proportion to the additional Risque of Seizures; and at the same time the Temptation is less by the Difference between Three-pence and Six-pence. These Reasons concur to prove that a Duty considerably higher than Three Half-pence *per* Gallon may be imposed upon Melasses, without being, by its Excess, an Inducement to Smuggling. The next Question is, what the Trade can bear without being oppressed by it: It certainly can bear more now it is established, than it could in its Beginnings; it has thriven, it has increased, it continued to increase, under a Charge of Three Half-pence *per* Gallon; and as Experience has shewn that it can support such a Burthen, with Ease, the Presumption is from thence alone very strong, that it is equal to a greater without Inconvenience. The additional Charge upon the Commodity, by the Duty of Three-pence, is but Three Half-pence, so much only being the Difference between the former and the present Price of Importation: and as a Gallon of Melasses produces a Gallon of Rum, an addition of Three Half-Pence does not appear to us a severe Tax upon a Gallon of Rum. . . .

. . . As to the Revenue which the new Impositions will produce, I suppose it is very difficult, if not impossible to form any Calculation of its Amount: I will not even hazard a Conjecture upon it, as I cannot presume that I should be right; and I should be sorry to be wrong. Thus far however may be safely affirmed, that Duties so low, and now first laid, will not at present contribute largely to the Exigencies of the Public; for inconsiderable as they are, the Payment of them will be often avoided by Frauds and Subtilties, which no Penetration can foresee, and Experience only can discover and prevent. On the other hand, they will be an improving Revenue; because they are laid upon numerous Articles of general Consumption among an encreasing People; and if not productive of a great Fund immediately, will be at least a wide Foundation for a considerable future Revenue; but upon no Calculation can it be supposed to be equal to the Demand that must be made upon the Colonies; and therefore a further Tax has been proposed; it has been even resolved by a Vote of the House of Commons, that *it may be proper to charge certain Stamp Duties in the Plantations*; and here the Legislature stoped last Sessions out of Tenderness to the Colonies. A Stamp Duty, tho' often used in the Plantations for the Purposes of their own Government, has never been imposed there by Authority of Parliament, and time has been therefore very properly allowed, to enquire whether it will be attended with any Inconveniences, and to provide Expedients of Prevention or Remedy; but I believe the more it is examined, so much the more clearly will it appear, that this Mode of Taxation is the easiest, the most equal and the most certain that can be chosen: The Duty falls chiefly upon Property; but it is spread lightly over a great Variety of Subjects, and lies heavy upon none: The Act executes itself by annulling the Instruments that have not paid the small Sums they are charged with; and the Tax thus supported and secured, is collected by few Officers, without Expence to the Crown, or Oppression on the People.

The Revenue that may be raised by the Duties which have been already, or by these if they should be hereafter imposed, are all equally applied by Parliament, *towards defraying the necessary Expences of defending, protecting, and securing, the British Colonies and Plantations in America:* Not that on the one hand an *American* Revenue might not have been applied to different Purposes; or on the other, that *Great Britain* is to contribute nothing to these: The very Words of the Act of Parliament and of the Resolution of the House of Commons imply, that the whole of the Expence is not to be charged upon the Colonies. . . . [But] the Inhabitants of their Mother-Country would justly and loudly complain, if after all their Efforts for the Benefit of the Colonies, when every Point is gained, and every wish accomplished, they, and they alone should be called upon still to answer every additional Demand, that the Preservation of these Advantages, and the Protection of the Colonies from future Dangers, may occasion: *Great Britain* has a Right at all Times, she is under a Necessity, upon this Occasion, to demand their Assistance; but still she requires it in the Manner most suitable to their Circumstances; for by appropriating this Revenue towards the Defence and Security of the Provinces where it is raised, the Produce of it is kept in the Country, the People are not deprived of the Circulation of what Cash they have amongst themselves, and thereby the severest Oppression of an *American* Tax, that of draining the Plantations of Money which they can so ill spare, is avoided. What Part they ought to bear of the national Expence, that is necessary for their Protection, must depend upon their Ability, which is not yet sufficiently known: to the whole they are certainly unequal, that would include all the military and all the naval Establishment, all Fortifications which it may be thought proper to erect, the Ordnance and Stores that must be furnished, and the Provisions which it is necessary to supply; but surely a Part of this great Disbursement, a large Proportion at least of some particular Branches of it, cannot be an intolerable Burthen upon such a Number of Subjects, upon a Territory so extensive, and upon the Wealth which they collectively possess. As to the Quota which each Individual must pay, it will be difficult to persuade the Inhabitants of this Country, where the neediest Cottager pays out of his Pittance, however scanty, and how hardly soever earned, our high Duties of Customs and Excise in the Price of all his Consumption; it will be difficult I say, to persuade those who see, who suffer, or who relieve such Oppression; that the *West Indian* out of his Opulence, and the *North American* out of his Competency, can contribute no more than it is now pretended they can afford towards the Expence of Services, the Benefit of which, as a Part of this Nation they share, and as Colonists they peculiarly enjoy. They have indeed their own civil Governments besides to support; but *Great Britain* has her civil Government too; she has also a large Peace Establishment to maintain; and the national Debt, tho' so great a Part, and that the heaviest Part of it has been incurred by a War undertaken for the Protection of the Colonies, lies solely still upon her.

The Reasonableness, and even the Necessity of requiring an *American* Revenue being admitted, the Right of the Mother Country to impose such a Duty upon her Colonies, if duly considered, cannot be questioned: they claim it is true the Privilege, which is common to all *British* Subjects, of being taxed only with their own Consent, given by their Representatives, and may they ever enjoy the Privilege in all its Extent: May this sacred Pledge of Liberty be preserved inviolate, to the utmost Verge of our Dominions, and to the latest Page of our History! but let us not limit the legislative Rights of the *British* People to Subjects of Taxation only: No new Law whatever can bind us that is made without the Concurrence of our Representatives. The Acts of Trade and Navigation, and all other Acts that relate either to ourselves or to the Colonies, are founded upon no other Authority; they are not obligatory if a Stamp Act is not, and every Argument in support of an Exemption from the Superintendance of the *British* Parliament in the one Case, is equally applicable to the others. The Constitution knows no Distinction; the Colonies have never attempted to make one; but have acquiesced under several parliamentary Taxes. The 6 *Geo.* II. c. 13. which has been already refered to, lays heavy Duties on all foreign Rum, Sugar, and Melasses, imported into the *British* Plantations: the Amount of the Impositions has been complained of; the Policy of the Laws has been objected to; but the Right of making such a Law, has never been questioned. These however, it may be said, are Duties upon Imports only, and there some imaginary Line has been supposed to be drawn; but had it ever existed, it was passed long before, for by 25 *Charles* II. c. 7. enforced by 7 and 8 *Wil.* and *Mary*, c. 22. and by 1 *Geo.* I. c. 12. the Exports of the *West Indian* Islands, not the Merchandize purchased by the Inhabitants, nor the Profits they might make by their Trade, but the Property they had at the Time, the Produce of their Lands, was taxed, by the Duties then imposed upon Sugar, Tobacco, Cotton, Indigo, Ginger, Logwood, Fustick, and Cocoa, exported from one *British* Plantation to another.

It is in vain to call these only Regulations of Trade; the Trade of *British* Subjects may not be regulated by such Means, without the Concurrence of their Representatives. Duties laid for these Purposes, as well as for the Purposes of Revenue, are still Levies of Money upon the People. The Constitution again knows no Distinction between Impost Duties and internal Taxation; and if some speculative Difference should be attempted to be made, it certainly is contradicted by Fact; for an internal Tax also was laid on the Colonies by the Establishment of a Post Office there. . . . The Act treats this and the *British* Postage upon exactly the same Footing, and expresly calls them both a *Revenue*. . . .

The Instances that have been mentioned prove, that the Right of the Parliament of *Great Britain* to impose Taxes of every kind on the Colonies, has been always admitted; but were there no Precedents to support the Claim, it would still be incontestable, being founded on the Principles of our Constitution; for the Fact is, that the Inhabitants of the Colonies are represented in Parliament: they do not indeed chuse the Members of that Assembly; neither are Nine Tenths of the People of *Britain* Electors; for the Right of Election is annexed to certain Species of Property, to peculiar Franchises, and to Inhabitancy in some particular Places; but these Descriptions comprehend only a very small Part of the Land, the Property, and the People of this Island: all Copyhold, all Leasehold Estates, under the Crown, under the Church, or under private Persons, tho' for Terms ever so long; all landed Property in short, that is not Freehold, and all monied Property whatsoever are excluded: the Possessors of these have no Votes in the Election of Members of Parliament; Women and Persons under Age be their Property ever so large, and all of it Freehold, have none. The Merchants of *London*, a numerous and respectable Body of Men, whose Opulence exceeds all that *America* could collect; the Proprietors of that vast Accumulation of Wealth, the public Funds; the Inhabitants of *Leeds*, of *Halifax*, of *Birmingham*, and of *Manchester*, Towns that are each of them larger than the Largest in the Plantations; many of less Note that are yet incorporated; and that great Corporation the *East India* Company, whose Rights over the Countries they possess, fall little short of Sovereignty, and whose Trade and whose Fleets are sufficient to constitute them a maritime Power, are all in the same Circumstances; none of them chuse their Representatives; and yet are they not represented in Parliament? Is their vast Property subject to Taxes without their Consent? Are they all arbitrarily bound by Laws to which they have not agreed? The Colonies are in exactly the same Situation: All *British* Subjects are really in the same; none are actually, all are virtually represented in Parliament; for every Member of Parliament sits in the House, not as Representative of his own Constituents, but as one of that august Assembly by which all the Commons of *Great Britain* are represented. Their Rights and their Interests, however his own Borough may be affected by general Dispositions, ought to be the great Objects of his Attention, and the only Rules for his Conduct; and to sacrifice these to a partial Advantage in favour of the Place where he was chosen, would be a Departure from his Duty; if it were otherwise, *Old Sarum* would enjoy Privileges essential to Liberty, which are denied to *Birmingham* and to *Manchester*; but as it is, they and the Colonies and all *British* Subjects whatever, have an equal Share in the general Representation of the Commons of *Great Britain*, and are bound by the Consent of the Majority of that House, whether their own particular Representatives consented to or opposed the Measures there taken, or whether they had or had not particular Representatives there.

The Inhabitants of the Colonies however have by some been supposed to be excepted, because they are represented in their respective Assemblies. So are the Citizens of *London* in their Common Council; and yet so far from excluding them from the national Representation, it does not impeach their Right to chuse Members of Parliament: it is true, that the Powers vested in the Common Council of *London*, are not equal to those which the Assemblies in the Plantations enjoy; but still they are legislative Powers, to be exercised within their District, and over their Citizens; yet not exclusively of the general Superintendance of the great Council of the Nation: The Subjects of a By-law and of an Act of Parliament may possibly be the same; yet it never was imagined that the Privileges of *London* were incompatible with the Authority of Parliament; and indeed what Contradiction, what Absurdity, does a double Representation imply? What difficulty is there in allowing both, tho' both should even be vested with equal legislative Powers, if the one is to be exercised for local, and the other for general Purposes? and where is the Necessity that the Subordinate Power must derogate from the superior Authority? It would be a singular Objection to a Man's Vote for a Member of Parliament, that being represented in a provincial, he cannot be represented in a national Assembly; and if this is not sufficient Ground for an Objection, neither is it for an Exemption, or for any Pretence of an Exclusion.

The Charter and the proprietary Governments in *America*, are in this Respect, on the same Footing with the Rest. The comprehending them also, both in a provincial and national Representation, is not necessarily attended with any Inconsistency, and nothing contained in their Grants can establish one; for all who took those Grants were *British* Subjects, inhabiting *British* Dominions, and who at the Time of taking, were indisputably under the Authority of Parliament; no other Power can abridge that Authority, or dispense with the Obedience that is due to it: those therefore, to whom the Charters were originally given, could have no Exemption granted to them: and what the Fathers never received, the Children cannot claim as an Inheritance; nor was it ever in Idea that they should; even the Charters themselves, so far from allowing guard against the Supposition.

And after all, does any Friend to the Colonies desire the Exemption? he cannot, if he will reflect but a Moment on the Consequences. We value the Right of being represented in the national Legislature as the dearest Privilege we enjoy; how justly would the Colonies complain, if they alone were deprived of it? They acknowledge Dependance upon their Mother Country; but that Dependance would be Slavery not Connection, if they bore no Part in the Government of the whole: they would then indeed be in a worse Situation than the Inhabitants of *Britain*, for these are all of them virtually, tho' few of them are actually represented in the *House of Commons*; if the Colonies were not, they could not expect that their Interests and their Privileges would be any otherwise considered there, than as subservient to those of *Great Britain*; for to deny the Authority of a Legislature, is to surrender all Claims to a Share in its Councils; and if this were the Tenor of their Charters, a Grant more insidious and more replete with Mischief, could not have been invented: a permanent Title to a Share in national Councils, would be exchanged for a precarious Representation in a provincial Assembly; and a Forfeiture of their Rights would be couched under the Appearance of Privileges; they would be reduced from Equality to Subordination, and be at the same Time deprived of the Benefits, and liable to the Inconveniences, both of Independency and of Connection. Happily for them, this is not their Condition. They are on the contrary a Part, and an important Part of the Commons of *Great Britain*: they are represented in Parliament, in the same Manner as those Inhabitants of *Britain* are, who have not Voices in Elections; and they enjoy, with the Rest of their Fellow-subjects, the inestimable Privilege of not being bound by any Laws, or subject to any Taxes, to which the Majority of the Representatives of the Commons have not consented.

If there really were any Inconsistency between a national and a provincial Legislature, the Consequence would be the Abolition of the latter; for the Advantages that attend it are purely local: the District it is confined to might be governed without it, by means of the national Representatives; and it is unequal to great general Operations; whereas the other is absolutely necessary for the Benefit and Preservation of the whole: But so far are they from being incompatible, that they will be seldom found to interfere with one another: The Parliament will not often have occasion to exercise its Power over the Colonies, except for those purposes, which the Assemblies cannot provide for. A general Tax is of this Kind; the Necessity for it, the Extent, the Application of it, are Matters which Councils limited in their Views and in their Operations cannot properly judge of; and when therefore the National Council determine these Particulars, it does not encroach on the other, it only exercises a Power which that other does not pretend to, never claimed, or wished, nor can ever be vested with: The latter remains in exactly the same State as it was before, providing for the same Services, by the same Means, and on the same Subjects; but conscious of its own Inability to answer great Purposes than those for which it was instituted, it leaves the care of more general Concerns to that higher Legislature, in whose Province alone the Direction of them always was, is, and will be. The Exertion of that Authority which belongs to its universal Superintendance, neither lowers the Dignity, nor depreciates the Usefulness of more limited Powers: They retain all that they ever had, and are really incapable of more.

The Concurrence therefore of the provincial Representatives cannot be necessary in great public Measures to which none but the national Representatives are equal: The Parliament of *Great Britain* not only may but must tax the Colonies, when the public Occasions require a Revenue there: The present Circumstances of the Nation require one now; and a Stamp Act, of which we have had so long an Experience in this, and which is not unknown in that Country, seems an eligible Mode of Taxation. From all these Considerations, and from many others which will occur upon Reflexion and need not be suggested, it must appear *proper to charge certain Stamp Duties in the Plantations to be applied towards defraying the necessary Expences of defending, protecting, and securing the British Colonies and Plantations in America.* This Vote of the House of Commons closed the Measures taken last Year on the Subject of the Colonies: They appear to have been founded upon true Principles of Policy, of Commerce, and of Finance; to be wise with respect to the Mother-Country; just and even beneficial to the Plantations; and therefore it may reasonably be expected that either in their immediate Operations, or in their distant Effects, they will improve the Advantages we possess, confirm the Blessings we enjoy, and promote the public welfare.

Seeing the drift of events, the colonial agents called upon Grenville on February 2, 1765, in a last minute attempt to forestall action. The four agents who called on Grenville were Charles

Garth, agent for South Carolina and an M.P. himself; Richard Jackson, agent for Connecticut, Pennsylvania, and Massachusetts and another M.P.; and Benjamin Franklin and Jared Ingersoll of Connecticut, both of whom had recently arrived in London on private business. But Grenville was unbending, and in his budget message of February 6, formally called for adoption of the stamp tax proposal. In the debate that followed, only William Beckford, a wealthy London merchant and spokesman for the West Indian interests, denied the authority of Parliament to tax the colonies; the other opponents of the measure—including the most eloquent champion of the colonists, Colonel Isaac Barré, a veteran of the French and Indian Wars—merely assailed the expediency of the tax. Charles Townshend—to figure prominently in the worsening conflict between colonies and mother country in a few years— spoke strongly in favor of the proposal, and the House, by an overwhelming majority, approved the measure. The following account of the debate was sent by Jared Ingersoll to Governor Thomas Fitch of Connecticut, February 11, 1765:

Printed: *Fitch Papers* (Connecticut Historical Society *Collections,* XVIII), II, pp. 312-326.

London 11ᵗʰ Feb: 1765

Sʳ

Since my last to you, I have been honoured with yours of the 7th of December, in which you inform me that the Genˡ Assembly have been pleased to desire my Assistance while here in any Matters that may concern the Colony. Be so good, Sʳ, in return as to Assure the Assembly that I have not only a Due Sense of the honour they have done me by placing this Confidence in me, but that I have ever since my arrival here, from Motives of Inclination, as well as Duty, done every thing in my Power to promote the Colony's Interests.

The principal Attention has been to the Stamp bill that has been preparing to Lay before Parliament for taxing America. The Point of the Authority of Parliament to impose such Tax I found on my Arrival here was so fully and Universally yielded, that there was not the least hopes of making any impressions that way. Indeed it has appeared since that the House would not suffer to be brought in, nor would any one Member Undertake to Offer to the House, any Petition from the Colonies that held forth ye Contrary of that Doctrine. I own I advised the Agents if possible to get that point Canvassed that so the Americans might at least have the Satisfaction of having the point Decided upon a full Debate, but I found it could not be done, and here before I proceed to acquaint you with the Steps that have been taken, in this Matter, I beg leave to give you a Summary of the Arguments which are made Use of in favour of such Authority.

The House of Commons, say they, is a branch of the supreme legislature of the Nation, & which in its Nature is supposed to represent, or rather to stand in the place of, the Commons, that is, of the great body of the people, who are below the dignity of peers; that this house of Commons Consists of a certain number of Men Chosen by certain people of certain places, which Electors, by the Way, they Insist, are not a tenth part of the people, and that the Laws, rules and Methods by which their number is ascertained have arose by degrees & from various Causes & Occasions, and that this house of Commons, thefore, is now fixt and ascertained & is a part of the Supreme unlimited power of the Nation, as in every State there must be some unlimited Power and Authority; and that when it is said they represent the Commons of England, it cannot mean that they do so because those Commons choose them, for in fact by far the greater part do not, but because by their Constitution they must themselves be Commoners, and not Peers, and so the Equals, or of the same Class of Subjects, with the Commons of the Kingdom. They further urge, that the only reason why America has not been heretofore taxed in the fullest Manner, has been merely on Account of their Infancy and Inability; that there have been, however, not wanting Instances of the Exercise of this Power, in the various regulations of the American trade, the Establishment of the post Office &c, and they deny any Distinction between what is called an internal & external Tax as to the point of the Authority imposing such taxes. And as to the Charters in the few provinces where there are any, they say, in the first place, the King cannot grant any that shall exempt them from the Authority of one of the branches of the great body of Legislation, and in the second place say the King has not done, or attempted to do it. In that of Pensilvania the Authority of Parliament to impose taxes is expressly mentioned & reserved; in ours tis said, our powers are generally such as are *According to the Course of other Corporations in England* (both which Instances by way of Sample were mentioned & referred to by Mr Grenville in the House); in short they say a Power to tax is a necessary Part of every Supreme Legislative Authority, and that if they have not that Power over America, they have none, & then America is at once a Kingdom of itself.

On the other hand those who oppose the bill say, it is true the Parliament have a supreme unlimited Authority over every Part & Branch of the Kings dominions and as well over Ireland as any other place, yet we believe a British parliament will never think it prudent to tax Ireland. Tis true they say, that the Commons of England & of the british Empire are all represented in and by the house of Commons, but this representation is confessedly on all hands by Construction & Virtually only as to those who have no hand in choosing the representatives, and that the Effects of this implied Representation here & in America must be infinitely different in the Article of Taxation. Here in England the Member of Parliament is equally known to the Neighbour who elects & to him who does not; the Friendships, the Connections, the Influences are spread through the whole. If by any Mistake an Act of Parliament is made that prove injurious and hard the Member of Parliament here sees with his own Eyes and is moreover very accessible to the people, not only so, but the taxes are laid equally by one Rule and fall as well on the Member himself as on the people. But as to America, from the great distance in point of Situation, from the almost total unacquaintedness, Especially in the more northern Colonies, with the Members of Parliament, and they with them, or with the particular Ability & Circumstances of one another, from the Nature of this very tax laid upon others not Equally & in Common with ourselves, but with express purpose to Ease ourselves, we think, say they, that it will be only to lay a foundation of great Jealousy and Continual Uneasiness, and that to no purpose, as we already by the Regulations upon their trade draw from the Americans all that they can spare, at least they say this Step should not take place untill or unless the Americans are allowed to send Members to Parliament; for *who of you*, said Coll Barre Nobly in his Speech in the house upon this Occasion, *who of you reasoning upon this Subject feels warmly from the Heart* (putting his hand to his own breast) *for the Americans as they would for themselves or as you would for the people of your own native Country?* and to this point Mr Jackson produced Copies of two Acts of Parliament granting the priviledge of having Members to the County Palitine of Chester & the Bishoprick of Durham upon Petitions preferred for that purpose in the Reign of King Henry the Eighth and Charles the first, the preamble of which Statutes counts upon the Petitions from those places as setting forth that being in their general Civil Jurisdiction Exempted from the Common Law Courts &c, yet being Subject to the general Authority of Parliament, were taxed in Common with the rest of ye Kingdom, which taxes by reason of their having no Members in Parliament to represent their Affairs, often proved hard and injurious &c and upon that ground they had the priviledge of sending Members granted them —& if this, say they, could be a reason in the case of Chester and Durham, how much more so in the case of America.

Thus I have given you, I think, the Substance of the Arguments on both sides of that great and important Question of the right & also of the Expediency of taxing America by Authority of Parliament. I cannot, however, Content myself without giving you a Sketch of what the aforementioned Mr Barre said in Answer to some remarks made by M^r Ch. Townsend in a Speech of his upon this Subject. I ought here to tell you that the Debate upon the American Stamp bill came on before the house for the first time last Wednesday, when the same was open'd by Mr Grenville the Chanceller of the Exchequer, in a pretty lengthy Speech, & in a very able and I think in a very candid manner he opened the Nature of the Tax, Urged the Necessity of it, Endeavoured to obviate all Objections to it—and took Occasion to desire the House to give ye bill a most Serious and Cool Consideration & not suffer themselves to be influenced by any resentments which might have been kindled from any thing they might have heard out of doors—alluding I suppose to the N. York and Boston Assemblys' Speeches & Votes—that this was a matter of revenue which was of all things the most interesting to ye Subject &c. The Argument was taken up by several who opposed the bill (viz) by Alderman Beckford, who, and who only, seemed to deny ye Authority of Parliament, by Col. Barre, Mr Jackson, Sr William Meredith and some others. Mr Barre, who by the way I think, & I find I am not alone in my Opinion, is one of the finest Speakers that the House can boast of, having been some time in America as an Officer in the Army, & having while there, as I had known before, contracted many Friendships with American Gentlemen, & I believe Entertained much more favourable Opinions of them than some of his profession have done, Delivered a very handsome & moving Speech upon the bill & against the same, Concluding by saying that he was very sure that Most who Should hold up their hands to the Bill must be under a Necessity of acting very much in the dark, but added, perhaps as well in the Dark as any way.

After him Mr Charles Townsend spoke in favour of the Bill—took Notice of several things Mr Barre had said, and concluded with the following or like Words:—And now will these Americans, Children planted by our Care, nourished up by our Indulgence untill they are grown to a Degree of Strength & Opulence, and protected by our Arms, will they grudge to contribute their mite to releive us from the heavy weight of that burden which we lie under? When he had done, Mr Barre rose and having explained something which he had before said & which Mr Townsend had been remarking upon, he then took up the beforementioned Concluding words of Mr Townsend, and in a most spirited & I thought an almost inimitable manner, said—

"They planted by your Care? No! your Oppressions planted em in America. They fled from your Tyranny to a then uncultivated and unhospitable Country—where they exposed themselves to almost all the hardships to which human Nature is liable, and among others to the Cruelties of a Savage foe, the most subtle and I take upon me to say the most formidable of any People upon the face of Gods Earth. And yet, actuated by Principles of true english Lyberty, they met all these hardships with pleasure, compared with those they suffered in their own Country, from the hands of those who should have been their Friends.

"They nourished by *your* indulgence? they grew by your neglect of Em:—as soon as you began to care about Em, that Care was Excercised in sending persons to rule over Em, in one Department and another, who were perhaps the Deputies of Deputies to some Member of this house—sent to Spy out their Lyberty, to misrepresent their Actions & to prey upon Em; men whose behaviour on many Occasions has caused the Blood of those Sons of Liberty to recoil within them; men promoted to the highest Seats of Justice, some, who to my knowledge were glad by going to a foreign Country to Escape being brought to the Bar of a Court of Justice in their own.

"They protected by *your* Arms? they have nobly taken up Arms in your defence, have Exerted a Valour amidst their constant & Laborious industry for the defence of a Country, whose frontier, while drench'd in blood, its interior Parts have yielded all its little Savings to your Emolument. And beleive me, remember I this Day told you so, that same Spirit of freedom which actuated that people at first, will accompany them still.—But prudence forbids me to explain myself further. God knows I do not at this Time speak from motives of party Heat, what I deliver are the genuine Sentiments of my heart; however superiour to me in general knowledge and Experience the reputable body of this house may be, yet I claim to know more of America than most of you, having seen and been conversant in that Country. The People I beleive are as truly Loyal as any Subjects the King has, but a people Jealous of their Lyberties and who will vindicate them, if ever they should be violated—but the Subject is too delicate & I will say no more."

These sentiments were thrown out so intirely without premeditation, so forceably and so firmly, and the breaking off so beautifully abrupt, that the whole house sat awhile as Amazed, intently Looking and without answering a Word.

I own I felt Emotions that I never felt before & went the next Morning & thank'd Coll Barre in behalf of my Country for his noble and spirited Speech.

However, S^r after all that was said, upon a Division of the house upon the Question, there was about 250 to about 50 in favour of the Bill.

The truth is I beleive some who inclined rather against the Bill voted for it, partly because they are loth to break the Measures of the Ministry, and partly because they dont undertake to inform themselves in the fullest manner upon the Subject. The Bill comes on to a second Reading tomorrow, when ours and the Massachusetts Petitions will be presented & perhaps they may be some further Debate upon the Subject, but to no purpose I am very sure, as to the Stopping or preventing the Act taking Place. . . . .

The bill—scheduled to go into effect on November 1, 1765— became law March 22. The act levied stamp duties on a long list of colonial legal documents as well as on newspapers, newspaper advertising, pamphlets, and playing cards. The money raised was to be used to defray "the necessary expenses of defending, protecting, and securing, the said colonies and plantations." Violations were made punishable in the local vice-admiralty courts or at the new vice-admiralty court at Halifax "at the election of the informer or prosecutor":

Printed: 5 George III, c. 12, Pickering, *The Statutes at Large*, XXVI, pp. 179-204.

An act for granting and applying certain stamp duties, and other duties, in the British *colonies and plantations in* America, *towards further defraying the expences of defending, protecting, and securing the same.* . . .

WHEREAS *by an act made in the last session of parliament, several duties were granted, continued, and appropriated, towards defraying the expences of defending, protecting, and securing, the* British *colonies and plantations in* America: *and whereas it is just and necessary, that provision be made for raising a further revenue within your Majesty's dominions in America, towards defraying the said expences:* we, your Majesty's most dutiful and loyal subjects, the commons of *Great Britain* in parliament assembled, have therefore resolved to give and grant unto your Majesty the several rates and duties herein after mentioned; and do most humbly beseech your Majesty that it may be enacted, and be it enacted by the King's most excellent majesty, by and with the advice and consent of the lords spiritual and temporal, and commons, in this present parliament assembled, and by the authority of the same, That from and after the first day of *November*, one thousand seven hundred and sixty five, there shall be raised, levied, collected, and paid unto his Majesty, his heirs, and successors throughout the colonies and plantations in *America* which now are, or hereafter may be, under the dominion of his Majesty, his heirs and successors. . . .

[There follows a detailed schedule of the stamp duties levied upon an extensive list of business and legal documents, including: court pleadings and actions, admissions to the bar, bills of lading, export clearances, appointments to public office, liquor licenses, wills, bonds for securing the payment of money, land grants and conveyances, and "any indenture, lease, conveyance, contract, stipulation, bill of sale, charter party, protest, articles of apprenticeship, or covenant."]

And for and upon every pack of playing cards, and all dice, which shall be sold or used within the said colonies and plantations, the several stamp duties following (that is to say)

For every pack of such cards, the sum of one shilling.

And for every pair of such dice, the sum of ten shillings.

And for and upon every paper, commonly called a *pamphlet*, and upon every news paper, containing publick news, intelligence, or occurrences, which shall be printed, dispersed, and made publick, within any of the said colonies and plantations, and for and upon such advertisements as are herein after mentioned, the respective duties following. . . .

XV. And be it further enacted by the authority aforesaid, That if any person or persons shall sign, ingross, write, print, or sell, or expose to sale, or cause to be signed, ingrossed, written, printed, or sold, or exposed to sale, in any of the said colonies or plantations, or in any other part of his Majesty's dominions, any matter or thing, for which the vellum, parchment, or paper, is hereby charged to pay any duty, before the same shall be marked or stamped with the marks or stamps to be provided as aforesaid, or upon which there shall not be some stamp or mark resembling the same; or shall sign, ingross, write, print, or sell, or expose to sale, or cause to be signed, ingrossed, written, printed, or sold, or exposed to sale, any matter or thing upon any vellum, parchment, or paper, that shall be marked or stamped for any lower duty than the duty by this act made payable in respect thereof; every such person so offending shall, for every such offence, forfeit the sum of ten pounds. . . .

XXI. And be it further enacted by the authority aforesaid, That if any register, publick officer, clerk, or other person in any court, registry, or office within any of the said colonies or plantations, shall, at any time after the said first day of *November*, one thousand seven hundred and sixty five, enter, register, or inroll, any matter or thing hereby charged with a stamp duty, unless the same shall appear to be duly stamped; in every such case such register, publick officer, clerk, or other person, shall for every such offence, forfeit the sum of twenty pounds. . . .

LIV. And be it further enacted by the authority aforesaid, That all the monies which shall arise by the several rates and duties hereby granted (except the necessary charges of raising, collecting, recovering, answering, paying, and accounting for the same, and the necessary charges from time to time incurred in relation to this act, and the execution thereof) shall be paid into the receipt of his Majesty's exchequer, and shall be entered separate and apart from all other monies, and shall be there reserved to be from time to time disposed of by parliament, towards further defraying the necessary expences of defending, protecting, and securing, the said colonies and plantations. . . .

LVII. And be it further enacted by the authority aforesaid, That all forfeitures and penalties incurred after the twenty ninth day of *September*, one thousand seven hundred and sixty five, for offences committed against an act passed in the fourth year of the reign of his present Majesty [the Sugar Act of 1764] . . . and for offences committed against any other act or acts of parliament relating to the trade or revenues of the said colonies or plantations; shall and may be prosecuted, sued for, and recovered, in any court of record, or in any court of admiralty, in the respective colony or plantation where the offence shall be committed, or in any court of vice admiralty appointed or to be appointed, and which shall have jurisdiction within such colony, plantation, or place, (which courts of admiralty or vice admiralty are hereby respectively authorized and required to proceed, hear, and determine the same) at the election of the informer or prosecutor. . . .

III. America Resists

WOULD the colonies resist or not? The answer was not long in coming. The Parson's Cause had catapulted Patrick Henry to the forefront of Virginia politics. Elected to the House of Burgesses in 1765, he immediately became leader of the up-country members against the dominant tidewater oligarchy led by Speaker of the House John Robinson. On May 29, 1765—his twenty-ninth birthday—Henry introduced a set of resolutions into the House of Burgesses. At his death Henry left a copy of these resolutions:

Printed: Kennedy, *Journals of the House of Burgesses of Virginia, 1761–1765*, pp. lxiv-lxv.

[1.] *Resolved,* That the first adventurers and settlers of this his Majesty's colony and dominion brought with them, and transmitted to their posterity, and all other his Majesty's subjects since inhabiting in this his Majesty's said colony, all the privileges, franchises, and immunities that have at any time been held, enjoyed, and possessed by the people of *Great Britain.*

[2.] *Resolved,* That by two royal charters, granted by King *James* the First the colonists aforesaid are declared entitled to all the privileges, liberties, and immunities of denizens and natural-born subjects, to all intents and purposes as if they had been abiding and born within the realm of *England.*

[3.] *Resolved,* That the taxation of the people by themselves, or by persons chosen by themselves to represent them, who [can] only know what taxes the people are able to bear, and the easiest mode of raising them, and are equally affected by such taxes themselves, is the distinguishing characteristick of *British* freedom, and without which the ancient Constitution cannot subsist.

[4.] *Resolved,* That his Majesty's leige people of this most ancient colony have uninterruptedly enjoyed the right of being thus governed by their own Assembly in the article of their taxes and internal police, and that the same hath never been forfeited or in any other way given up, but hath been constantly recognized by the kings and people of *Great Britain.*

[5.] *Resolved, therefore,* That the General Assembly of this colony have the only and sole exclusive right and power to lay taxes and impositions upon the inhabitants of this colony, and that every attempt to vest such power in any person or persons whatsoever, other then the General Assembly aforesaid, has a manifest tendency to destroy *British* as well *American* freedom.

The resolutions as printed in the newspapers included a preamble as well as two additional inflammatory resolves. The following appeared in the *Newport Mercury* of June 24, and were reprinted in the *Boston Gazette* of July 2, 1765:

Printed: Kennedy, *Journals of the House of Burgesses of Virginia, 1761–1765,* pp. lxvi-lxvii.

Whereas, the Honorable House of Commons, in *England,* have of late draw[n] into question how far the General Assembly of this colony hath power to enact laws for laying of taxes and imposing duties payable by the people of this, his Majesty's most ancient colony; for settling and ascertaining the same to all future times, the House of Burgesses of this present General Assembly have come to the following resolves.

*   *   *   *

[6.] *Resolved,* That his Majesty's leige people, the inhabitants of this colony, are not bound to yield obedience to any law or ordinance whatever, designed to impose any taxation whatsoever upon them, other than the laws or ordinances of the General Assembly aforesaid.

[7.] *Resolved,* That any person who shall by speaking or writing, assert or maintain that any person or persons, other than the General Assembly of this colony, have any right or power to impose or lay any taxation on the people here, shall be deemed an enemy to his Majesty's colony.

What exactly happened remains unknown. The manuscript records of the House of Burgesses have disappeared; the printed record shows only the first four resolves adopted by the House on May 30. One of the spectators watching in the lobby was young Thomas Jefferson. In later years, Jefferson recalled the scene:

Printed: Kennedy, *Journals of the House of Burgesses of Virginia, 1761–1765*, pp. lxv-lxvi.

Mr *Henry* moved and Mr *Johnston* seconded these resolutions successively. They were opposed by Messrs. Randolph, Bland, Pendleton, Wythe, and all the old members, whose influence in the House had, till then, been unbroken. They did it, not from any question of our rights, but on the ground that the same sentiments had been, at their preceding session, expressed in a more conciliatory form, to which the answers were not yet received. But torrents of sublime eloquence from *Henry,* backed by the solid reasoning of *Johnston,* prevailed. The last, however, and strongest resolution was carried but by a single vote. The debate on it was most bloody. I was then but a student, and stood at the door of communication between the House and the lobby (for as yet there was no gallery) during the whole debate and vote; and I will remember that, after the members on the division were told and declared from the chair, *Peyton Randolph* (the Attorney-General) came out at the door where I was standing, and said as he entered the lobby: 'By God, I would have given 500 guineas for a single vote'; for one would have divided the House, and *Robinson,* was in the chair, who he knew would have negatived the resolution. Mr Henry left town that evening. . . . In the meantime, some of the timid members, who had voted for the strongest resolution, had become alarmed; and as soon as the House met, a motion was made and carried to expunge it from the journal. . . .

The last resolution to which Jefferson referred was the fifth. The account sent by Governor Francis Fauquier to the Board of

Trade, June 5, 1765, reported that Henry had not even offered the sixth and seventh resolutions because of the closeness of the vote on the fifth:

Printed: Kennedy, *Journals of the House of Burgesses of Virginia, 1761–1765*, pp. lxvii–lxviii.

Williamsburg June 5th 1765.

My Lords,

On *Saturday* the 1st instant I dissolved the Assembly after passing all the Bills, except one, which were ready for my assent. The four Resolutions which I have now the honor to inclose to your Lordships, will shew Your Lordships the reason of my conduct, and I hope justify it. I will relate the whole proceeding to Your Lordships in as concise a manner as I am able.

On *Wednesday* the 29th of May, just at the end of the Session when most of the members had left the town, there being but 39 present out of 116 of which the House of Burgesses now consists, a motion was made to take into consideration the Stamp Act, a copy of which had crept into the House, and in a Committee of the whole House five resolutions were proposed and agreed to, all by very small majorities. On *Thursday* the 30th they were reported & agreed to by the House, the numbers being as before in the Committee; the greatest majority being 22 to 17; for the 5th Resolution, 20 to 19 only. On *Friday* the 31st there having happened a small alteration in the House there was an attempt to strike all the Resolutions off the Journals. The 5th which was thought the most offensive was accordingly struck off, but it did not succeed as to the other four. I am informed the gentlemen had two more resolutions in their pocket, but finding the difficulty they had in carrying the 5th which was by a single voice, and knowing them to be more virulent and inflammatory; they did not produce them. The most strenuous opposers of this rash heat were the late Speaker, the King's Attorney and Mr. *Wythe*; but they were overpowered by the young hot and giddy members. In the course of the debates I have heard that very indecent language was used by a Mr. *Henry* a young lawyer who had not been a month a Member of the House; who carryed all the young Members with him; so that I hope I am authorised in saying there is cause at least to doubt whether this would have been the sense of the Colony if more of their Representatives had done their duty by attending to the end of the Session. . . .

What the "indecent language" used by Henry was remains equally uncertain. The classic account is by William Wirt in his biography of Henry published in 1807: ". . . he exclaimed, in a voice of thunder, and with the look of a god, 'Caesar had his Brutus—Charles the first, his Cromwell, and George the third— ('Treason!' cried the speaker—'treason, treason,' echoed from every part of the house. . . . Henry faltered not an instant; but rising to a loftier attitude, and fixing on the speaker an eye of the most determined fire, he finished his sentence with the firmest emphasis)—*may profit by their example*. If *this* be treason, then make the most of it.' "

This heroic version was based on recollections forty years after the event. A contemporary eye-witness account by an unknown French traveler diminishes Henry's daring; it also indicates that the seventh resolution was, in fact, introduced and debated on May 31, but that the governor's hasty dissolution of the assembly prevented formal action from being taken:

Printed: "A French Traveller in the Colonies," I, *American Historical Review*, XXVI, No. 4 (July, 1921), pp. 745-746.

May the 30th. Set out Early from halfway house in the Chair and broke fast at York, arived at williamsburg at 12. . . . I went imediately to the assembly which was seting, where I was entertained with very strong Debates Concerning Dutys that the parlement wants to lay on the american Colonys, which they Call or Stile stamp Dutys. Shortly after I Came in one of the members stood up and said he had read that in former times tarquin and Julus had their Brutus, Charles had his Cromwell, and he Did not Doubt but some good american would stand up, in favour of his Country, but (says he) in a more moderate manner, and was going to Continue, when the speaker of the house rose and Said, he, the last that stood up had spoke traison, and was sorey to see that not one of the members of the house was loyal Enough to stop him, before he had gone so far. upon which the Same member stood up again (his name is henery) and said that if he had afronted the speaker, or the house, he was ready to ask pardon, and he would shew his loyalty to his majesty King G. the third, at the Expence of the last Drop of his blood, but what he had said must be atributed to the Interest of his Countrys Dying liberty which he had at heart, and the heat of passion might have lead him to have said something more than he intended, but, again, if he said any thing wrong, he beged the speaker and the houses pardon. some other Members stood up and backed him, on which that afaire was droped.

May the 31th. I returned to the assembly today, and heard very hot Debates stil about the Stamp Dutys. the whole house was for Entering resolves on the records but they Differed much with regard the Contents or purport therof. some were for shewing their resentment to the highest. one of the resolves that these proposed, was that any person that would offer to sustain that the parlement of Engl'd had a right to impose or lay any tax or Dutys whats'r on the american Colonys, without the Consent of the inhabitants therof, Should be looked upon as a traitor, and Deemed an Enemy to his Country. there were some others to the same purpose, and the majority was for Entring these resolves, upon which the Governor Disolved the assembly, which hinderd their proceeding.

Whatever did actually happen, the newspaper accounts led the colonists to believe that the Virginia House of Burgesses had boldly declared for resistance to the Stamp Act. Even before news of the resolutions reached Boston, the Massachusetts House of Representatives had voted, on June 8, 1765, to ask the assemblies of the other colonies to send delegates to a general congress in New York that October "to consider of a general and united, dutiful, loyal and humble representation of their conditions to his majesty and to the parliament, and to implore relief." The Stamp Act Congress met in New York beginning October 7, 1765, with delegates present from nine colonies. The majority of the twenty-seven delegates were moderates, and the conservative Timothy Ruggles of Massachusetts was named chairman. In the discussion over framing a declaration of the rights and grievances of the colonists, no one challenged the authority of

Parliament to regulate the trade of the colonies; but many opposed
an explicit declaration of Parliament's authority lest such a statement appear to justify the taxes levied under the Sugar Act. The
final version, drafted by John Dickinson of Pennsylvania, simply
reaffirmed that the colonists owed "all due subordination" to
Parliament; the declaration then went on to demand, in effect,
complete local autonomy in all matters of taxation.

Printed: Edmund S. Morgan, ed., *Prologue to Revolution:
Sources and Documents on the Stamp Act Crisis, 1764–
1766* (Chapel Hill, N.C., 1959), pp. 62-63.

The Members of this Congress, sincerely devoted, with the warmest
Sentiments of Affection and Duty to his Majesty's Person and Government, inviolably attached to the present happy Establishment of
the Protestant Succession, and with Minds deeply impressed by a
Sense of the present and impending Misfortunes of the *British* Colonies on this Continent; having considered as maturely as Time will
permit, the Circumstances of the said Colonies, esteem it our indispensable Duty, to make the following Declarations of our humble
Opinion, respecting the most Essential Rights and Liberties of the
Colonists, and of the Grievances under which they labour, by Reason
of several late Acts of Parliament.

I. That his Majesty's Subjects in these Colonies, owe the same
Allegiance to the Crown of *Great-Britain,* that is owing from his
Subjects born within the Realm, and all due Subordination to that
August Body the Parliament of *Great-Britain.*

II. That his Majesty's Liege Subjects in these Colonies, are entitled to all the inherent Rights and Liberties of his Natural born
Subjects, within the Kingdom of *Great-Britain.*

III. That it is inseparably essential to the Freedom of a People,
and the undoubted Right of *Englishmen,* that no Taxes be imposed
on them, but with their own Consent, given personally, or by their
Representatives.

IV. That the People of these Colonies are not, and from their
local Circumstances cannot be, Represented in the House of Commons in *Great-Britain.*

V. That the only Representatives of the People of these Colonies, are Persons chosen therein by themselves, and that no Taxes ever have been, or can be Constitutionally imposed on them, but by their respective Legislature.

VI.   That all Supplies to the Crown, being free Gifts of the People, it is unreasonable and inconsistent with the Principles and Spirit of the *British* Constitution, for the People of *Great-Britain,* to grant to his Majesty the Property of the Colonists.

VII.   That Trial by Jury, is the inherent and invaluable Right of every *British* Subject in these Colonies.

VIII.   That the late Act of Parliament, entitled, *An Act for granting and applying certain Stamp Duties, and other Duties, in the* British *Colonies and Plantations in* America, *&c.* by imposing Taxes on the Inhabitants of these Colonies, and the said Act, and several other Acts, by extending the Jurisdiction of the Courts of Admiralty beyond its ancient Limits, have a manifest Tendency to subvert the Rights and Liberties of the Colonists.

IX.   That the Duties imposed by several late Acts of Parliament, from the peculiar Circumstances of these Colonies, will be extremely Burthensome and Grievous; and from the scarcity of Specie, the Payment of them absolutely impracticable.

X.   That as the Profits of the Trade of these Colonies ultimately center in *Great-Britain,* to pay for the Manufactures which they are obliged to take from thence, they eventually contribute very largely to all Supplies granted there to the Crown.

XI.   That the Restrictions imposed by several late Acts of Parliament, on the Trade of these Colonies, will render them unable to purchase the Manufactures of *Great-Britain.*

XII.   That the Increase, Prosperity, and Happiness of these Colonies, depend on the full and free Enjoyment of their Rights and Liberties, and an Intercourse with *Great-Britain* mutually Affectionate and Advantageous.

XIII.   That it is the Right of the *British* Subjects in these Colonies, to Petition the King, or either House of Parliament.

Lastly, That it is the indispensable Duty of these Colonies, to the best of Sovereigns, to the Mother Country, and to themselves, to endeavour by a loyal and dutiful Address to his Majesty, and humble Applications to both Houses of Parliament, to procure the Repeal of the Act for granting and applying certain Stamp Duties, of all Clauses of any other Acts of Parliament, whereby the Jurisdiction of

the Admiralty is extended as aforesaid, and of the other late Acts
for the Restriction of *American* Commerce.

The delegates thereupon proceeded to adopt petitions to the
King, the House of Lords, and the House of Commons. The appeal was to the rights of Englishmen rather than to natural rights;
most importantly, the petition to the Commons made explicit
the distinction between legislation by Parliament—which the
colonists accepted—and taxation—which they rejected:

Printed: Morgan, *Prologue to Revolution,* pp. 66-69.

That the several late Acts of Parliament imposing divers Duties
and Taxes on the Colonies, and laying the Trade and Commerce
thereof under very Burthensome Restrictions, but above all the Act
for granting and applying certain Stamp Duties, &c. in *America,* have
fill'd them with the deepest Concern and Surprize; and they humbly
conceive the Execution of them will be attended with Consequences
very Injurious to the Commercial Interest of *Great-Britain* and her
Colonies, and must terminate in the eventual Ruin of the latter.
Your Petitioners therefore most ardently implore the Attention of
the Honourable House, to the united and dutiful Representation of
their Circumstances, and to their earnest Supplications for Relief,
from those Regulations which have already involv'd this Continent in
Anxiety, Confusion, and Distress.
We most sincerely recognize our Allegiance to the Crown, and
acknowledge all due Subordination to the Parliament of *Great-Britain,*
and shall always retain the most grateful Sense of their Assistance and
Protection. It is from and under the *English* Constitution, we derive
all our Civil and Religious Rights and Liberties: We Glory in being
Subjects of the best of Kings, and having been Born under the most
perfect Form of Government; but it is with most ineffable and humiliating Sorrow, that we find ourselves, of late, deprived of the
Right of Granting our own Property for his Majesty's Service, to
which our Lives and Fortunes are entirely devoted, and to which,
on his Royal Requisitions, we have ever been ready to contribute to
the utmost of our Abilities.

We have also the Misfortune to find, that all the Penalties and Forfeitures mentioned in the Stamp Act, and in divers late Acts of Trade extending to the Plantations, are, at the Election of the Informer, Recoverable in any Court of Admiralty in *America*. This, as the newly erected Court of Admiralty has a general Jurisdiction over all *British America,* renders his Majesty's Subjects in these Colonies, liable to be carried, at an immense Expence, from one End of the Continent, to the other.

It gives us also great Pain, to see a manifest Distinction made therein, between the Subjects of our Mother Country, and those in the Colonies, in that the like Penalties and Forfeitures recoverable there only in his Majesty's Courts of Record, are made cognizable here by a Court of Admiralty: By these Means we seem to be, in Effect, unhappily deprived of Two Privileges essential to Freedom, and which all *Englishmen* have ever considered as their best Birthrights, that of being free from all Taxes but such as they have consented to in Person, or by their Representatives, and of Trial by their Peers.

Your Petitioners further shew, That the remote Situation, and other Circumstances of the Colonies, render it impracticable that they should be Represented, but in their respective subordinate Legislature; and they humbly conceive, that the Parliament, adhering strictly to the Principles of the Constitution, have never hitherto Tax'd any, but those who were actually therein Represented; for this Reason, we humbly apprehend, they never have Tax'd *Ireland,* or any other of the Subjects without the Realm.

But were it ever so clear, that the Colonies might in Law, be reasonably deem'd to be Represented in the Honourable House of Commons, yet we conceive, that very good Reasons, from Inconvenience, from the Principles of true Policy, and from the Spirit of the *British* Constitution, may be adduced to shew, that it would be for the real Interest of *Great-Britain,* as well as her Colonies, that the late Regulations should be rescinded, and the several Acts of Parliament imposing Duties and Taxes on the Colonies, and extending the Jurisdiction of the Courts of Admiralty here, beyond their ancient Limits, should be Repeal'd.

We shall not Attempt a minute Detail of all the Reasons which the Wisdom of the Honourable House may suggest, on this Occasion, but would humbly submit the following Particulars to their Consideration.

That Money is already become very scarce in these Colonies, and is still decreasing by the necessary Exportation of Specie from the Continent, for the Discharge of our Debts to *British* Merchants.

That an immensly heavy Debt is yet due from the Colonies for *British* Manufactures, and that they are still heavily burthen'd with Taxes to discharge the Arrearages due for Aids granted by them in the late War.

That the Balance of Trade will ever be much against the Colonies, and in Favour of *Great-Britain,* whilst we consume her Manufactures, the Demand for which must ever Increase in Proportion to the Number of Inhabitants settled here, with the Means of Purchasing them. We therefore humbly conceive it to be the Interest of *Great-Britain,* to increase, rather than diminish, those Means, as the Profits of all the Trade of the Colonies ultimately center there to pay for her Manufactures, as we are not allowed to purchase elsewhere; and by the Consumption of which, at the advanced Prices the British Taxes oblige the Makers and Venders to set on them, we eventually contribute very largely to the Revenue of the Crown.

That from the Nature of *American* Business, the Multiplicity of Suits and Papers used in Matters of small Value, in a Country where Freeholds are so minutely divided, and Property so frequently transferr'd, a Stamp Duty must ever be very Burthensome and Unequal.

That it is extremely improbable that the Honourable House of Commons, shou'd at all Times, be thoroughly acquainted with our Condition, and all Facts requisite to a just and equal Taxation of the Colonies.

It is also humbly submitted, Whether there be not a material Distinction in Reason and sound Policy, at least, between the necessary Exercise of Parliamentary Jurisdiction in general Acts, for the Amendment of the Common Law, and the Regulation of Trade and Commerce through the whole Empire, and the Exercise of that Jurisdiction, by imposing Taxes on the Colonies.

That the several subordinate Provincial Legislatures have been moulded into Forms, as nearly resembling that of their Mother Country, as by his Majesty's Royal Predecessors was thought convenient; and their Legislatures seem to have been wisely and graciously established, that the Subjects in the Colonies might, under the due

Administration thereof, enjoy the happy Fruits of the *British* Government, which in their present Circumstances, they cannot be so fully and clearly availed of, any other Way under these Forms of Government we and our Ancestors have been Born or Settled, and have had our Lives, Liberties, and Properties, protected. The People here, as everywhere else, retain a great Fondness for their old Customs and Usages, and we trust that his Majesty's Service, and the Interest of the Nation, so far from being obstructed, have been vastly promoted by the Provincial Legislatures.

That we esteem our Connections with, and Dependance on *Great-Britain,* as one of our greatest Blessings, and apprehend the latter will appear to be sufficiently secure, when it is considered, that the Inhabitants in the Colonies have the most unbounded Affection for his Majesty's Person, Family, and Government, as well as for the Mother Country, and that their Subordination to the Parliament, is universally acknowledged.

We therefore most humbly entreat, That the Honourable House would be pleased to hear our Counsel in Support of this Petition, and take our distressed and deplorable Case into their serious Consideration, and that the Acts and Clauses of Acts, so grievously restraining our Trade and Commerce, imposing Duties and Taxes on our Property, and extending the Jurisdiction of the Court of Admiralty beyond its ancient Limits, may be repeal'd; or that the Honourable House would otherwise relieve your Petitioners, as in your great Wisdom and Goodness shall seem meet.

At about the same time as the Stamp Act Congress was meeting, an Annapolis printer published an anonymous pamphlet entitled *Considerations on the Propriety of Imposing Taxes in the British Colonies, For the Purpose of Raising a Revenue, by Act of Parliament.* The work was the answer of a leading Maryland lawyer and politician named Daniel Dulany to the arguments of Thomas Whately and other British writers justifying the Stamp Act. Dulany's main purpose was to refute the idea that colonists were "virtually represented" in Parliament. Arguing they were not so represented, he assailed parliamentary taxation of the colonists as contrary to the principles of the British constitution. Only their local assemblies could levy taxes. Yet this, he insisted, did not free the colonies from all dependence upon Parliament. Dulany reaffirmed the supreme legislative authority of Parliament —and in so doing, he elaborated the distinction between legislation and taxation. Parliament could regulate the trade of the empire, and the duties levied might produce an "incidental revenue," but Parliament could not levy taxes for revenue. If Parliament, however, did violate this principle, what then? Dulany was no revolutionist; he proposed no more than orderly protest and economic pressure:

Printed: *Maryland Historical Magazine*, VI, No. 4 (December, 1911), pp. 376-406; VII, No. 1 (March, 1912), pp. 26-59.

In the constitution of *England*, the three principal forms of government, monarchy, aristocracy, and democracy, are blended together in certain proportions; but each of these orders, in the exercise of the legislative authority, hath its peculiar department, from which the others are excluded. In this division, the *granting of supplies,* or *laying taxes,* is deemed to be the province of the house of commons, as the representative of the people.—All supplies are supposed to flow from their gift; and the other orders are permitted only to assent, or reject generally, not to propose any modification, amendment, or partial alteration of it.

THIS observation being considered, it will undeniably appear, that, in framing the late *Stamp Act,* the commons acted in the character of representative of the colonies. They assumed it as the principle of that measure, and the *propriety* of it must therefore stand, or fall, as the principle is true or false: for the preamble sets forth, That the commons of *Great Britain* had resolved to *give* and *grant* the several rates and duties imposed by the act; but what right had the commons of *Great Britain* to be thus munificent at the expence of the commons of *America?*—to give property, not belonging to the giver, and without the consent of the owner, is such evident and flagrant injustice, in *ordinary cases,* that few are hardy enough to avow it; and therefore, when it really happens, the fact is disguised and varnished over by the most plausible pretences the ingenuity of the giver can suggest. But it is alledged that there is a *virtual,* or *implied representation* of the colonies, springing out of the constitution of the *British* government; and it must be confessed on all hands, that, as the representation is not actual, it is virtual, or it doth not exist at all; for no third kind of representation can be imagined. The colonies claim the privilege, which is common to all *British subjects,* of being taxed *only* with their own consent given by their representatives; and all the advocates for the *Stamp Act* admit this claim. Whether, therefore, upon the whole matter, the imposition of the *Stamp Duties* is a *proper* exercise of constitutional authority, or not, depends upon the single question, Whether the commons of *Great Britain* are *virtually* the representatives of the commons of *America,* or not?

THE advocates for the *Stamp Act* admit, in express terms, that "the colonies do not choose members of parliament:" but they assert that "the colonies are *virtually* represented in the same manner with the non-electors resident in *Great Britain.*" . . .

Now this argument, which is all that their invention hath been able to supply, is totally defective; for it consists of facts not true, and of conclusions inadmissible. . . .

I SHALL undertake to disprove the supposed similarity of situation, whence the same kind of representation is deduced, of the inhabitants of the colonies, and of the *British* non-electors; and, if I succeed, the notion of a *virtual representation* of the colonies must fail, which, in truth, is a mere cob-web, spread to catch the unwary. . . .

. . . The security of the [British] non-electors against oppression, is, that their oppression will fall also upon the electors and the representatives. The one can't be injured, and the other indemnified.

FURTHER, if the non-electors should not be taxed by the *British* parliament, they would not be taxed *at all;* and it would be iniquitous as well as a solecism, in the political system, that they should partake of all the benefits resulting from the imposition, and application of taxes, and derive an immunity from the circumstance of not being qualified to vote. Under this constitution then, a double or virtual representation may be reasonably supposed. The electors, who are inseparably connected in their interests with the non-electors, may be justly deemed to be the representatives of the non-electors, at the same time they exercise their personal privilege in their right of election; and the members chosen, therefore, the representatives of both. This is the only rational explanation of the expression, *virtual representation*. . . .

THE situation of the non-electors in *England*—their capacity to become electors—their inseparable connection with those who are electors, and their representatives—their security against oppression resulting from this connection, and the necessity of imagining a double or virtual representation, to avoid iniquity and absurdity, have been explained—the inhabitants of the colonies are, *as such,* incapable of being electors, the privilege of election being exerciseable only in person; and therefore, if *every* inhabitant of *America* had the requisite freehold, not *one* could vote, but upon the supposition of his ceasing to be an inhabitant of *America,* and becoming a resident of *Great Britain;* a supposition which would be impertinent, because it shifts the question.—Should the colonies not be taxed by *Parliamentary impositions,* their respective legislatures have a regular, adequate, and constitutional authority to tax them, and therefore there would not necessarily be an iniquitous and absurd exemption, from their not being represented by *the house of commons.*

THERE is not that intimate and inseparable relation between the *electors of Great Britain* and the *Inhabitants of the colonies,* which must inevitably involve both in the same taxation: on the contrary, not a single *actual* elector in *England* might be immediately affected by a taxation in *America*, imposed by a statute which would have a general operation and effect, upon the properties of the inhabitants of the colonies. The latter might be oppressed in a thousand shapes, without any sympathy, or exciting any alarm in the former. More-over, even acts, oppressive and injurious to the colonies in an extreme degree, might become popular in *England,* from the promise or ex-pectation, that the very measures which depressed the colonies, would give ease to the inhabitants of *Great Britain.* It is indeed true, that the interests of *England* and the colonies are allied, and an injury to the colonies, produced into all its consequences, will eventually affect the mother country; yet these consequences being generally remote, are not at once foreseen; they do not immediately alarm the fears and engage the passions of the *English* electors: the connection between a freeholder of *Great Britain* and a *British American,* being deducible only thro' a train of reasoning, which few will take the trouble, or can have opportunity, if they have capacity, to investigate:

wherefore the relation between the *British American* and the *English electors,* is a knot too infirm to be relied on as a competent security, especially against the force of a present, counteracting, expectation of relief.

IF it would have been a just conclusion, that the *colonies* being exactly in the *same* situation with the *non-electors* of *England*, are *therefore* represented in the same manner, it ought to be allowed, that the reasoning is solid, which, after having evinced a total *dissimilarity* of situation, infers, that the representation is *different*.

IF the commons of *Great Britain* have no right by the constitution to GIVE AND GRANT property *not* belonging to themselves but to others, without their consent actually or virtually given; if the claim of the colonies, not to be taxed *without their consent,* signified by their representatives, is well founded; if it appears that the colonies are not actually represented by the commons of *Great Britain,* and that the notion of a double or virtual representation, doth not with any propriety apply to the people of *America*; then the principle of the *stamp act* must be given up as indefensible on the point of representation. . . .

BUT it has been objected, that if the inhabitants of *America,* because represented in their respective assemblies, are *therefore* exempted from a *parliamentary tax,* than the citizens of *London,* who are represented in their common council, may plead the *same immunity*. . . .

THE objection having been stated, the answer is obvious and clear.

THE colonies have a complete and adequate legislative authority, and are not only represented in their assemblies, but in *no other manner*. The power of making bye-laws vested in the common council is inadequate and incomplete, being bounded by a few particular subjects; and the common council are actually represented too, by having a choice of members to serve in parliament. How then can the reason of the exemption from internal parliamentary taxations, claimed by the colonies, apply to the citizens of *London*. . . .

BUT it has been alledged, that if the right to *give and grant* the property of the colonies by an internal taxation is denied by the house of commons, the subordination and dependence of the colonies, and the superintendence of the *British* parliament, can't be consistently establish'd;—that any supposed line of distinction between the two cases, is but "a whimsical imagination, a "chimerical speculation

against fact and experience."—Now, under favour, I conceive there
is more confidence than solidity in this assertion; and it may be satisfactorily and easily proved, that the subordination and dependence
of the colonies may be preserved, and the *supreme authority* of the
mother country be firmly supported, and yet the principle of representation, and the right of the *British* house of commons, flowing
from *it,* to *give and grant* the property of the commons of *America,*
be denied.

THE colonies are dependent upon *Great Britain;* and the supreme
authority vested in the king, lords, and commons, may justly be
exercised to secure, or preserve their dependence, whenever necessary for that purpose. This authority results from, and is implied
in the idea of the relation subsisting between *England* and her colonies; for, considering the nature of human affections, the inferior is
not to be trusted with providing regulations to prevent his rising to an
equality with his superior. But tho' the right of the superior, to use the
proper means for preserving the subordination of his inferior, is
admitted, yet it does not necessarily follow, that he has a right to
seize the property of his inferior when he pleases, or to command
him in every thing; since, in the degrees of it, there may very well
exist a *dependency* and *inferiority,* without absolute *vassalage* and
slavery. In what the superior may *rightfully* controul, or compel, and
in what the inferior ought to be at liberty to act without controul or
compulsion, depends upon the nature of the dependence and the
degree of the subordination; and these being ascertained, the measure
of obedience, and submission, and the extent of the authority and
superintendence, will be settled. When powers, compatible with the
relation between the superior and inferior, have, by express compact,
been granted to, and accepted by the latter, and have been, after that
compact, repeatedly recognized by the former;—when they may be
exercised effectually upon every occasion without any injury to that
relation, the authority of the superior can't properly interpose; for
by the powers vested in the inferior, is the superior limited.

BY their constitutions of government, the colonies are empowered
to impose internal taxes. This power is compatible with their dependence, and hath been expressly recognized by *British* ministers and the
British parliament upon many occasions; and it may be exercised
effectually without striking at, or impeaching, in any respect, the
superintendency of the *British* parliament. May not then the line be

distinctly and justly drawn between such acts as are necessary, or proper, for preserving or securing the dependency of the colonies, and such as are not necessary, or proper, for that very important purpose? . . .

A LITTLE examination will find how unfair and deceptive the representation is, that the colonies in *North America,* "two millions of *British* subjects, an opulent, thriving and commercial people, contribute to the national expense, no more than 7 or 800*l. per annum* by taxes raised *there*" . . . .

THE truth is, that a vast revenue arises to the *British* nation from taxes paid by the colonies in *Great Britain.* . . .

IN the article of tobacco, for instance, the planter pays a tax upon that produce of his land and labour consumed in *Great Britain,* more than six times the clear sum received by him for it, besides the expences of freight, commission and other charges, and double freight, commission and charges upon the tobacco re-exported, by which the *British* merchants, mariners, and other *British* subjects, are supported; —a tax, at least, equal to what is paid by any farmer of *Great Britain,* possessed of the same degree of property; and moreover the planter must contribute to the support of the expensive internal government of the colony, in which he resides.

Is it objected, that the duties charged upon tobacco, fall ultimately upon the consumers of this commodity in the consequential price set upon it? Be it so, and let the principle be established that all taxes upon a commodity, are paid by the consumers of it, and the consequence of this principle be fairly drawn, and equally applied.

THE *British* consumers therefore, ultimately pay the high duties laid upon tobacco, in proportion to the quality of that commodity which they consume.—The colonies therefore, in proportion to their consumption of *British* manufactures, pay also the high duties of customs and excise, with which the manufactures are charged in the consequential price set upon their consumptions. In their passage moreover, from the *British* manufactures to the *American* importers, the commodities go thro' a great many hands, by which their costs are enhanced; the factors, the carriers, the shop-keepers, the merchants, the brokers, the porters, the water-men, the mariners, and others, have their respective profits, from which they derive their subsistence, and the support of their families, and are enabled to pay the high duties of customs and excise, in the price of their consumptions.

THE policy of the late regulations of the colonies is of the same character with their justice and lenity. The produce of their lands, the earnings of their industry, and the gains of their commerce center in *Great Britain,* support the artificers, the manufactories, and navigation of the nation, and with them the *British* landholders too. . . .

THE right of exemption from all taxes *without their consent,* the colonies claim as *British* subjects. They derive this right from the common law, which their charters have declared and confirmed, and they conceive that when stripped of this right, whether by prerogative or by any other power, they are at the same time deprived of every privilege distinguishing free-men from slaves.

ON the other hand, they acknowledge themselves to be subordinate to the mother country, and that the authority vested in the supreme council of the nation, may be justly exercised to support and preserve that subordination.

GREAT and just encomiums have been bestowed upon the constitution of *England,* and their representative is deservedly the favourite of the inhabitants in *Britain.* But it is not because the supreme council is called *parliament,* that they boast of their constitution of government; for there is no particular magical influence from the combination of the letters which form the word; it is because they have a share in that council, that they appoint the members who constitute one branch of it, whose duty and interest it is to consult their benefit, and to assert their rights, and who are vested with an authority, to prevent any measures taking effect dangerous to their liberties, or injurious to their properties.

BUT the inhabitants in the colonies have no share in this great council. None of the members of it are, or can be of their appointment, or in any respect dependent upon them. There is no immediate connection, on the contrary, there may be an opposition of interest. . . .

WE claim an exemption from all *parliamentary* impositions, that we may enjoy those securities of our rights and properties, which we are entitled to by the constitution. For those securities are derived to the subject from the principle *that he is not to be taxed without his own consent;* and an inhabitant in *America* can give his consent in no other manner than in assembly. It is in the councils that exist there, and there *only,* that he hath a share, and whilst he enjoys it, his rights and privileges are as well secured as any elector's in *England,* who hath a share in the national councils there; for the words *parlia-*

ment and *assembly* are, in this respect, only different terms to express the same thing. . . .

. . . Tho' it hath been admitted, that the *stamp act* is the first statute that hath imposed an internal tax upon the colonies *for the single purpose of revenue,* yet the advocates for that law contend, that there are any instances of the parliament's exercising a supreme legislative authority over the colonies, and actually imposing *internal taxes* upon their properties,—that the duties upon any exports or imports are internal taxes,—that an impost on a foreign commodity is as much an internal tax, as a duty upon any production of the plantations,—that no distinction can be supported between one kind of tax and another, an authority to impose the one extending to the other. . . .

IT appears to me, that there is a clear and necessary distinction between an act imposing a tax for *the single purpose of revenue,* and those acts which have been made for the regulation of trade, and have produced some revenue *in consequence of their effect* and operation as *regulations of trade.*

THE colonies claim the privileges of *British* subjects;—it has been proved to be inconsistent with those privileges, to tax them *without their own consent,* and it hath been demonstrated that a tax imposed by parliament, is a tax *without their consent.*

THE subordination of the colonies, and the authority of the parliament to preserve it, hath been fully acknowledged. Not only the welfare, but perhaps the existence of the mother country, as an independent kingdom, may depend upon her trade and navigation, and these so far upon her intercourse with the colonies, that, if this should be neglected, there would soon be an end to that commerce, whence her greatest wealth is derived, and upon which her maritime power is principally founded. From these considerations, the right of the *British parliament* to regulate the trade of the colonies may be justly deduced; a denial of it would contradict the admission of the subordination, and of the authority to preserve it, resulting from the nature of the relation between the mother country and her colonies. It is a common, and frequently the most proper method to regulate trade by duties on imports and exports. The authority of the mother country to regulate the trade of the colonies being unquestionable, what regulations are the most proper, are to be of course submitted to the determination of the parliament; and, if an *incidental revenue* should be produced by such regulations, these are not therefore unwarrantable.

A RIGHT to impose an internal tax on the colonies, without their consent, *for the single purpose of revenue,* is denied, a right to regulate their trade without their consent is admitted. . . .

IT must be acknowledged that the balance of trade between *Great Britain* and her colonies is considerably against the latter, and that no gold or silver mines have yet been discovered in the old *American* settlements, or among the *treasures* of the new acquisitions. How then is this balance to be discharged? The former trade of the colonies, which enabled them to keep up their credit with *Great Britain,* by applying the balance they had gained against foreigners, is now so fettered with difficulties, as to be almost prohibited. In order therefore to reduce the balance against them upon the trade between the colonies and *Great Britain,* this trade must be contracted. . . .

. . . Let the manufacture of *America* be the symbol of dignity, the badge of virtue, and it will soon break the fetters of distress. A garment of linsey-wolsey, when made the distinction of real patriotism, is more honourable and attractive of respect and veneration, than all the pageantry, and the robes, and the plumes, and the diadem of an emperor without it. Let the emulation be not in the richness and variety of foreign productions, but in the improvement and perfection of our own.—Let it be demonstrated that the subjects of the *British* empire in *Europe* and *America* are the same, that the hardships of the latter will ever recoil upon the former.

IN theory it is supposed that each is equally important to the other, that all partake of the adversity and depression of any. The theory is just, and time will certainly establish it; but if another principle should be ever hereafter adopted in practice, and a violation deliberate, cruel, ungrateful, and attended with every circumstance of provocation, be offered to our fundamental rights, why should we leave it to the slow advances of time (which may be the great hope and reliance, probably, of the authors of the injury, whose view it may be to accomplish their selfish purposes in the interval) to prove what might be demonstrated immediately?—Instead of moping, and puling, and whining to excite compassion; in such a situation we ought with spirit, and vigour, and alacrity, to bid defiance to tyranny, by exposing its impotence, by making it as contemptible, as it would be detestable. By a vigorous application to manufactures, the consequence of oppression in the colonies to the inhabitants of *Great Britain,* would

strike home, and immediately. None would mistake it. Craft and
sublety would not be able to impose on the most ignorant and credulous; for if any should be so weak of sight as not to see, they would
not be so callous as not to feel it.—Such conduct would be the most
dutiful and beneficial to the mother country. It would point out the
distemper when the remedy might be easy, and a cure at once
effected by a simple alteration of regimen. . . .

NOT only, "as a friend to the colonies," but as an inhabitant having
my all at stake upon their welfare I desire an "exemption from taxes
imposed *without my consent,*" and I have reflected longer than "a
moment upon the consequences:" I value it as one of the dearest
privileges I enjoy: I acknowledge dependence on *G. Britain,* but I
can perceive a degree of it without slavery, and I disown all other.
I do not expect that the interests of the colonies will be considered by
some men, but in subserviency to other regards. The effects of
luxury, venality, and oppression, posterity may perhaps experience,
and SUFFICIENT FOR THE DAY WILL BE THE EVIL THEREOF.

Dulany's pamphlet became an immediate best seller. But his
appeal, as that of the Stamp Act Congress, had been to the principles of the British constitution. Yet was this not a weak reed
upon which to rest a defense of colonial rights? Lawyers could,
and did, differ over what were, in fact, the principles of the
British constitution. In advance of most of the colonists, Samuel
Adams was prepared to appeal to "the law of God and nature."
Under his leadership, the Massachusetts House of Representatives
adopted, on October 29, 1765, the following resolutions:

Printed: Cushing, *The Writings of Samuel Adams,* I, pp.
23-26.

Whereas the just rights of his Majesty's subjects of this Province,
derived to them from the British Constitution, as well as the royal
charter, have been lately drawn into question: in order to ascertain
the same, this House do unanimously come into the following resolves:—

1. *Resolved,* That there are certain essential rights of the British

Constitution of government, which are founded in the law of God and nature, and are the common rights of mankind;—therefore,

2. *Resolved,* That the inhabitants of this Province are unalienably entitled to those essential rights in common with all men: and that no law of society can, consistent with the law of God and nature, divest them of those rights.

3. *Resolved,* That no man can justly take the property of another without his consent; and that upon this original principle, the right of representation in the same body which exercises the power of making laws for levying taxes, which is one of the main pillars of the British Constitution, is evidently founded.

4. *Resolved,* That this inherent right, together with all other essential rights, liberties, privileges, and immunities of the people of Great Britain, have been fully confirmed to them by Magna Charta, and by former and by later acts of Parliament.

5. *Resolved,* That his Majesty's subjects in America are, in reason and common sense, entitled to the same extent of liberty with his Majesty's subjects in Britain. . . .

10. *Resolved,* That the inhabitants of this Province are not, and never have been, represented in the Parliament of Great Britain; and that such a representation there as the subjects in Britain do actually and rightfully enjoy *is impracticable* for the subjects in America. . . .

12. *Resolved,*—as a just conclusion from some of the foregoing resolves,—That all acts made by any power whatever, other than the General Assembly of this Province, imposing taxes on the inhabitants, are infringements of our inherent and unalienable rights as men and British subjects, and render void the most valuable declarations of our charter.

13. *Resolved,* That the extension of the powers of the Court of Admiralty within this Province is a most violent infraction of the right of trials by juries,—a right which this House, upon the principles of their British ancestors, hold most dear and sacred; it being the only security of the lives, liberties, and properties of his Majesty's subjects here. . . .

Even while voting resolutions denying Parliament's right to tax them, the colonialists were taking violent action to nullify the Stamp Act. The newspaper reports of Patrick Henry's resolutions in Virginia provided the needed spark, and Boston set the pace.

The lead was taken by the Loyal Nine, an organization made up of Boston shopkeepers and artisans and the forerunner of the Sons of Liberty. On the evening of August 14, a mob led by shoemaker Ebenezer McIntosh burned in effigy Andrew Oliver, the provincial secretary and the newly appointed stamp distributor for the colony, and wrecked his house:

Francis Bernard to the Board of Trade, August 15, 1765,
Huntington Library MSS., H.M. 1947, pp. 35-43.*

Castle William Augt 15, 1765.

My Lords,

I am Extreamly concerned that I am Obliged to give your Lordship that is to follow: as it will reflect disgrace upon this province, and bring the Town of Boston under great Difficulties. Two or three Months ago I thought that this people would have Submitted to the Stamp-Act, without Actual Opposition. Murmurs indeed were continually heard but they seemed to be such as in time would die away. But the publishing the Virginia Resolves, proved an Alarmed Bell to the Disaffected. From that time an Infamous Weekly paper which is printed here, has swarmed with Libels of the most attrocious Kind, these have been urged with so much Vehemence, and so industriously repeated that I have considered them as preludes to Action. But I did not know that it would have Commenced so early, or be Carried to such Lengths, as it has been.

Yesterday Morning at break of Day was discovered hanging upon a Tree in a Street of the Town an Effigy with Inscriptions showing that it was intended to represent Mr Oliver, the Secretary, who had lately accepted the Office of Stamp Distributor. Some of the neighbours offered to take it down, but they were given to know that would not be permitted. Many gent^n especially some of the Council, treated it as a Boyish Sport, that did not deserve the Notice of the Governor and Council. But I did not think [so]. However I contented myself with the Lieu^t Governor, as Chief Justice directing the Sheriff to order his Officers to take down the Effigy, and I appointed a Council to meet in the Afternoon, to consider what should be done, if the Sheriff's Officers were Obstructed in removing the Effigy.

---

* Punctuation slightly altered for readability.

Before the Council met The Sheriff reported that his Officers had endeavoured to take down the Effigy, but could not do it without Imminent Danger of their Lives. The Council met, I represented this Transaction to them, as the beginning in my Opinion, of much greater Commotions and Desired their Advice what I should do upon this Occasion. A Majority of the Council spoke in form against doing any thing, but upon very Different principles. Some said, that it was a triffling business which if let alone, would subside of itself but if taken Notice of would become a Serious Affair; others said that it was a Serious Affair already, that it was a preconcerted Business, in which the greatest part of the Town was Engaged, that we had no force to Oppose to it and making an Opposition to it, without a power to support the Opposition would only inflame the people and be a means of extending the mischief to persons not at the present the Objects of it. Tho the Council were almost unanimous in Advising that nothing should be done, they were averse to having such advice Entered upon the Council Book. But I insisted upon their giving me an answer to my Question and that it should be entered in the Book; when after a long altercation, it was avoided by their advising me to order the Sheriff to Assemble the Peace Officers, and preserve the Matter of Form rather than of real Significance.

It now grew dark when the Mob which had been gathering all the afternoon, came down to the Town House, bringing the Effigy, with them, and knowing that we were sitting in the Council Chamber, they gave three huzza's by way of Defiance, and passed on. From thence they went to a new Building lately Erected by Mr Oliver to let out for Shops and not quite finished. This [they] called the Stamp Office and pulled it down to the Ground in Two Minutes; from thence they went to Mr Olivers House, before which they beheaded the Effigy and broke all the Windows next the street. Then they carried the Effigy to Fort Hill near Mr Oliver's House where they burnt the Effigy in a Bonfire made of the Timber they had pulled down from the Building. Mr Oliver had removed his Family from his house and remained himself with a few Friends where the Mob returned to Attack the House. Mr Oliver was prevailed upon to retire, and his Friends kept possession of the House. The Mob finding the Doors Barricaded broke down the whole Fence of the Garden towards Fort Hill, and coming on beat in all the Doors and Windows of the Garden Front, and entered the House, the Gentlem^n there Retiring. As soon as they

got possession they searched about for Mr Oliver Declaring they
would kill him. Finding that he had left the House, a party set out to
search two neighbouring Houses, in one of which Mr Oliver was; but
happily they were diverted from this pursuit by a Gentleman telling
them that Mr Oliver was gone with the Governor to the Castle, otherwise he would certainly have been murdered. After Eleven o'clock
the mob seeming to grow quiet the (Lieu^t Gov.) Chief Justice and the
Sheriff ventured to go to Mr Oliver's house to endeavour to persuade
them to disperse. As soon as they began to speak, a Ring Leader cries
out, "the Governor and the Sheriff; to Your Arms my Boys." Presently after a Volley of Stones followed and the two Gentlemen nar-
rowly escaped thro favour of the Night, not without some Bruises.
I should have mentioned before that I sent a Written Order to the
Colonel of the Regiment of Militia to beat an Alarm; he Answered
that it would signify nothing; for as soon as the Drum was heard the
Drummer would be knocked down and the Drum broke: he added
that probably all the Drummers of the Regiment were in the Mob.
Nothing more being to be done, the Mob were left to disperse at their
own Time which they did about Twelve o'clock. . . .

The next day, faced with threats of further violence, Oliver
agreed to resign the stamp distributorship. But this did not halt the
disturbances. On August 26, the mob marched again. The local
customs officials were the first target; then the mob proceeded
to plunder and demolish the house of Thomas Hutchinson, the
lieutenant-governor and chief justice of the province, who was
the leader of the small group of wealthy and influential families
that had in the past largely dominated the politics of the colony:

Francis Bernard to the Board of Trade, August 31, 1765,
Huntington Library MSS., H.M. 1947, pp. 72-92.*

Castle William Aug. 31, 1765.
My Lords.
It is with the Utmost Concern that I am Obliged to Continue the
Subject of my last Letters of the 15th & 16th [and] of the 22^d Instant;

---

* Punctuation slightly altered for readability.

the Disorders of the Town having been carried to much greater Lengths than what I have before informed your Lordship of.

After the Demolition of Mr Olivers House was found so practible and easy, that the Government was Obliged to look on without being able to take any one Step to prevent it, and the principle people of the Town publickly avowed and Justifyed the act, the Mob, both great and small, became highly elated, and all kinds of Ill humours were set on float. Everything that for Years past had been the Cause of any popular discontent, was received and private Resentments against persons in office revoked themselves in and endeavoured to execute themselves under the Mask of Public Cause. . . .

On Monday August 26th there was some small Rumour, that Mischief would be done that Night, but it was in general disregarded. Towards Evening some Boys began to light a Bonfire before the Town House which is an Usual Signal for a Mob. Before it was quite dark a great Company of people gathered together Crying Liberty and property which is the usual Notice of their Intention to plunder and pull down an House. They went first to Mr Paxton's House; (who is Marshall of the Court of Admiralty and Surveyor of the Port) and finding before it the owner of the House (Mr Paxton being only a Tenant) he assured them that Mr Paxton had quitted the House with his best Effects, that the House was his, that he had never injured them, and finally invited them to go to the Tavern, and drink a Barrel of punch. The Offer was Accepted and so that House was saved. As soon as they had drinked the Punch they went to the house of Mr Storey Register-deputed of the Admiralty, broke into it and broke it all to pieces and took out all the Books and Papers among which were all the Records of the Court of Admiralty and carried them to the Bonfire and there burnt them. They also looked about for him with an Intention to kill him. From thence they went to Mr. Hallowell's, Comptroller of the Customs, broke into his House, and Destroyed and carryed off everything of Value with about Thirty pounds Sterling in Cash. This House was lately built by himself, and fitted and finished with great Elegance. But the Grand Mischief was to Come.

The Lieu^t Governor had been apprized that there was an evil spirit gone forth against him but being Conscious, that he had not in the least deserved to be made a party in regard to the Stamp Act or the Custom House, he rested in full Security, that the Mob would not Attack him and he was at Supper with his family when he received Advice, that the Mob were coming to him. He immediately sent away his Children and determined to Stay in the House himself but happily his eldest Daughter returned and Declared she would not Stir from the House unless he went with her by which m̃eans she got him away, which was then Undoubtedly the Occasion of saving his Life. For as soon as the Mob had got into the House with a most Inestimable Fury they immediately looked about for him to murder him and even made diligent Enquiry whither he was gone. They went to work with a Rage scarce to be Exemplifyed by the most Savage People. Everything moveable was destroyed in the Most Minute Manner except such things of value as were worth carrying off among which was near £1000 in specie besides a great quantity of family plate &c. But the Loss to be most Lamented is that there was in one Room kept for that purpose a large and Valuable Collection of Manuscripts and Original papers which he had been gathering all his Lifetime and to which all persons who had been in possession of Valuable Papers of a Publick Kind had been contributing as to a Publick Museum. As these related to the History and Policy of the Country from the Time of its Settlement to the present and was the only Collection of its Kind, the Loss to the Publick is great and Irretrievable as it is to himself the Loss of the papers of a Family which had made a figure in this province for 130 years. As for the House which from its structure and inside finishing seemed to be from a design of Inigo Jones or his Successor, it appears that they were a long while resolved to level it to the Ground. They worked three Hours at the Cupola before they could get it down, and they uncovered part of the Roof. But I suppose that the Thickness of the Walls which were of very fine Brick Work adorned with Ionick Pilasters worked into the Wall prevented their compleating their purpose though they work at it till day light. The next day the Streets were found Scattered with Money, plate, Rings &c. which had been dropt in carrying off. The whole Loss in this House is reckoned at 3000 Pounds Sterling.

As soon as I received Advice of this at the Castle I immediately sent an order to the Secretary to Summon a Council at Cambridge early in the afternoon not thinking Boston a safe Place out at. As I was going thither on the Road I received a letter from the Secretary

desiring I would hold the Council at Boston for that this Affair had
given such a Turn to the Town that all the Gentlemen in the place
were ready to Support the Government in Detecting and punishing
the Actors in the last horrid Scene and there was a Town Meeting
appointed to testify their Abhorrence of it. I accordingly went to the
Council and there Issued Orders to the Colonel of the Regiment of
Militia, the Captain of the Company of Cadet Guards, the Captains of
the Batteries and of the Companies of Militia in Charles Town,
Cambridge, and Roxbury to raise their several Corps and make Detachments therefrom to help a Constant Guard and I Recommended
to the Gentlemen of the Town who were Excused from Military Duty
to enroll themselves as Voluntiers in some of the Corps, many of
which did especially in the Cadets which were doubled upon this
Occasion [and] to whom I assigned the Guard of the Custom House
where there were several thousand pounds of the Kings Money. And
these measures were but just taken in time for otherwise a much
greater Mischief would have happened the Second Night than the
former. For it seems the Mob had set down no less than fifteen
Houses in or near the Town to be Attacked the next, among which
the Custom House and the Houses of some of the most respectable
persons in the Government. It was now becoming a War of Plunder
of generall levying and taking away the Distinction of Rich and Poor.
So that these gentlemen who had promoted and approved the Cruel
Treatment of Mʳ Oliver became now as fearful for themselves as the
most Loyal person in the town could be: they found as I told some of
them that they had raised the Devil and could not lay him again.
However by means of the Military Guard the Town was kept quiet
that night without anything happeng except that the Cadets were
Obliged once to present their pieces but did not fire.

After I had established these Guards which took up all that Day
I considered whether it would be proper to Call in Assistance from
without. By an instruction, I am directed to have the Advice of
Council Whenever I call for Military Aid. I know that the council
would never advise to call in the Kings Troops in cases more desperate than this; their own Situation and Dependance would make
them afraid of being answerable to the people for so disagreeable a
step: I therefore put the Question whether it was expedient to adver-
tize General Gage and Lord Colville of what had happened at Boston.
But they advised in the Negative, Saying that such Advertisements

would amount to a tacit request for Forces, and tho they expected such forces would be Ordered hither sometime or other they would not help to bring them here nor hasten them before the Time. I therefore Transmitted to General Gage a copy of this Resolution of Council, Copies of my Proclamations with Advice of the Intention of Lodging the Stamps in the Castle and Augmenting the Garrison for that purpose; from all which he will see the Restraint I am under. I then Accquainted the Council with the Various [reports] I had heard of the Castle being threatened if the Stamps were put in there, represented the present State of the Garrison and proposed that an Independant Company should be raised for Augmenting the Garrison, which they readily came into and Immediately Dispatched Orders for that purpose. I am also by all Means in my power Strengthening the Castle, so that if I can get the reinforcement here in Time I shant be afraid for the Castle against any Number, tho I cant think that any people will be Desperate enough to Attack it Notwithstanding what has been given out.

When first the Town took this new Turn I was in hopes that they would have disavowed all the riotous proceedings, that of the first night as well as the last. But it is no such thing; great pains are taken to seperate the two Riots, what was done against Mr Oliver is still approved of as a necessary Declaration of their resolution not to Submit to the Stamp Act and even the Cruel Treatment of him and his Family is Justifyed by its Consequences, the frightning him into a resignation and it has been publickly hinted that if a Line is not drawn between the first Riot and the last the Civil Power will not be supported by the principal People of the Town as it is Assumed it shall be now. And indeed if the last riot had been the only one the Civil Government would appear to be in full power; many people Concerned in the last Riot are daily taken up and Committed to Goal where a Constant Guard is kept by the militia and the Town Cries aloud for some of them to be made Examples of; And yet if one was to offer to take up one of the persons concerned in the first Riot only, things would again be flung into Confusion and the Civil power would become as weak as ever; So that the present Authority of the Government is only Exercised upon Condition and with presented limitations. . . .

McIntosh was arrested, but he knew far too much about the

investigators of the first riot. Under pressure from the leading men of property, the authorities were forced to release him, and no one was punished for the affair. All authority, Governor Francis Bernard lamented to General Thomas Gage, was at an end. "The Town of Boston is in the Possession of an incensed & implacable Mob."

The contagion spread rapidly. By November 1, 1765, the date on which the Stamp Act was to go into effect, mob violence had forced the resignation of the stamp distributors in nearly every colony. This resistance to the Stamp Act was spearheaded by a secret organization known as the "Sons of Liberty," which had spread to all the colonies. Who were these Sons of Liberty? The mobs were composed largely of shopkeepers, artisans, and mechanics in the towns, but all the reports indicate that the men who planned and inspired the riots were prominent and well-to-do lawyers and merchants. "The Lawyers are the Source from whence the Clamors have flowed in every Province," the British commander-in-chief in North America, General Thomas Gage, complained to Secretary of State Henry S. Conway. "The whole Body of Merchants in general, Assembly Men, Magistrates, &c. have been united in this Plan of Riots, and without the Influence and Instigation of these the inferior people would have been quiet. Very great Pains was taken to rouse them before they Stirred."

Without the stamps, no vessels could legally leave colonial ports; the courts could not sit in civil cases; no newspapers could be printed. But in colony after colony, mob action and threats of violence forced the customs officials to clear ships without the stamps and issue certificates stating that no stamps were available. Most printers continued issuing their newspapers; in some of the colonies, even the courts resumed sitting.

While thus nullifying the law in practice, the Sons of Liberty moved to bring pressure to bear upon Britain to repeal the obnoxious legislation. The most effective instrument was to boycott British goods. A gathering of New York merchants on October 31, 1765, the day before the Stamp Act was to go into force, took the lead:

Printed: Merrill Jensen, *American Colonial Documents to 1776* [English Historical Documents, IX] (New York, 1955), pp. 671-672.

AT A general meeting of the merchants of the city of New York, trading to Great Britain, at the house of Mr. George Burns, of the said city, innholder, to consider what was necessary to be done in the present situation of affairs with respect to the Stamp Act, and the melancholy state of the North American commerce, so greatly restricted by the impositions and duties established by the late acts of trade, they came to the following resolutions, viz.

First. That in all orders they send out to Great Britain for goods or merchandise of any nature, kind, or quality whatsoever, usually imported from Great Britain, they will direct their correspondents not to ship them unless the Stamp Act be repealed. It is nevertheless agreed that all such merchants as are owners of and have vessels already gone, and now cleared out for Great Britain, shall be at liberty to bring back in them, on their own accounts, crates and casks of earthen ware, grindstones, pipes, and such other bulky articles as owners usually fill up their vessels with.

Secondly. It is further unanimously agreed that all orders already sent home, shall be countermanded by the very first conveyance; and the goods and merchandise thereby ordered, not to be sent unless upon the condition mentioned in the foregoing resolution.

Thirdly. It is further unanimously agreed that no merchant will vend any goods or merchandise sent upon commission from Great Britain that shall be shipped from thence after the first day of January next, unless upon the condition mentioned in the first resolution.

Fourthly. It is further unanimously agreed that the foregoing resolutions shall be binding until the same are abrogated at a general meeting hereafter to be held for that purpose.

In witness whereof we have hereunto respectively subscribed our names.

[This was subscribed by upwards of two hundred principal merchants.]

In consequence of the foregoing resolutions the retailers of goods of the city of New York subscribed a paper in the words following, viz.

We, the underwritten, retailers of goods, do hereby promise and oblige ourselves not to buy any goods, wares, or merchandises of any person or persons whatsoever that shall be shipped from Great Britain after the first day of January next unless the Stamp Act shall be repealed—as witness our hands.

Similar agreements were entered into by the merchants of Philadelphia, Boston, and the smaller New England ports. The effectiveness of these non-importation agreements—a weapon made the sharper by the refusal of the Americans to pay debts owed to English firms—was attested by the following petition from the London merchants to the House of Commons, January 17, 1766:

Printed: T. C. Hansard, *Parliamentary History of England . . . to the Year 1803* (36 vols., London, 1806–1820), XVI, pp. 133-136.

That the petitioners have been long concerned in carrying on the trade between this country and the British colonies on the continent of North America; and that they have annually exported very large quantities of British manufactures, consisting of woollen goods of all kinds, cottons, linens, hardware, shoes, houshold furniture, and almost without exception of every other species of goods manufactured in these kingdoms, besides other articles imported from abroad, chiefly purchased with our manufactures and with the produce of our colonies; by all which, many thousand manufacturers, seamen, and labourers, have been employed, to the very great and increasing benefit of this nation; and that, in return for these exports, the petitioners have received from the colonies, rice, indico, tobacco, naval stores, oil, whale fins, furs, and lately pot-ash, with other commodities, besides remittances by bills of exchange and bullion, obtained by the colonists in payment for articles of their produce, not required for the British market, and therefore exported to other places; and that, from the nature of this trade, consisting of British manufactures exported, and of the import of raw materials from America, many of them used in our manufactures, and all of them tending to lessen our dependence on neighbouring states, it must be deemed of the highest importance in the commercial system of this nation; and that this commerce, so beneficial to the state, and so necessary for the support of multitudes, now lies under such difficulties and discouragement, that nothing less than its utter ruin is apprehended, without the immediate interposition of parliament; and that, in consequence of the trade between the colonies and the mother country, as established and as permitted for many years, and of the experience which the petitioners have had of the readiness of the Americans to make their just remittances to the utmost of their real ability, they have been induced to make and venture such large exportations of British manufactures, as to leave the colonies indebted to the merchants of Great Britain in the sum of several millions sterling; and that at this time the colonists, when pressed for payment, appeal to past experience, in proof of their willingness; but declare it is not in their power, at present, to make good their engagements, alledging, that the taxes and restrictions laid upon them, and the extension of the jurisdiction of vice admiralty courts established by some late acts of parliament, particularly by an act passed in the fourth year of his present Majesty, for granting certain duties in the British colonies and plantations in America, and by an act passed in the fifth year of his present Majesty, for granting and applying certain stamp duties, and other duties, in the British colonies and plantations in America, with several regulations and restraints, which, if founded in acts of parliament for defined purposes, are represented to have been extended in such a manner as to disturb legal commerce and harass the fair trader, have so far interrupted the usual and former most fruitful branches of their commerce, restrained the sale of their produce, thrown the state of the several provinces into confusion, and brought on so great a number of actual bankruptcies, that the former opportunities and means of remittances and payments are utterly lost and taken from them; and that the petitioners are, by these unhappy events, reduced to the necessity of applying to the House, in order to secure themselves and their families from impending ruin; to prevent a multitude of manufacturers from becoming a burthen to the community, or else seeking their bread in other countries, to the irretrievable loss of this kingdom; and to preserve the strength of this nation entire, its commerce flourishing, the revenues increasing, our navigation, the bulwark of the kingdom, in a state of growth and extension, and the colonies, from inclination, duty, and interest, firmly attached to the mother country; and therefore praying the consideration of the premises, and entreating such relief, as to the House shall seem expedient.

At the same time, the colonists prepared to resist by force of arms if events came to that juncture. This unbending resolve was sustained by the widespread belief among the colonists that the Stamp Act represented an opening wedge for further taxation that would reduce them to slavery. Irrational as this fear was, the Sons of Liberty did not hesitate to face the supreme test of a revolutionary movement. Meeting after meeting in the winter of 1765–1766 resolved to defend colonial rights, in the words of the Wallingford, Connecticut, Sons of Liberty, "to the last extremity, even to take the field." There was even an attempt to organize this resistance on an inter-colonial basis. "The following Narrative," Governor Bernard of Massachusetts wrote Secretary of State Conway, January 19, 1766. "I took from the Mouth of a Gentleman, who was present at the time & place":

Printed: *Fitch Papers* (Connecticut Historical Society *Collections*, XVIII), II, pp. 384-386.

On the 31st day of Decem^r 1765, two persons came to New London & went to a Tavern there: they said they came from New York; one of them called himself Hughes & said he was brother to Mr Hughes of Philadelphia appointed Distributor of Stamps there, the other called himself Mott. They sent for 6 or 7 Inhabitants of New London who were known to be most violent against the Stamp Act, & produced to them a letter from one Sears of New York a noted Captain of the Mob there, recommending them & their business to the people of Connecticut. They said they were sent by the People of New York to inform the People of Connecticut, that it was expected Troops would be sent from England to enforce their Submission to the Stamp Act; that it was necessary for them to unite in opposition to the

English Forces upon this occasion; that most probably New York would be attacked first, & therefore Connecticut ought to march in defence of New York; that they were therefore sent to learn what Number of Men from Connecticut might be depended upon to assist the People of New York to support themselves against the English Forces. They added that They were to go from thence to Norwich & from thence to Windham, at both places they were to make the same Enquiry; and they said that two other Persons were gone to Boston on the same Business. . . .

All the royal governors were prohibited by their instructions from calling for military aid without the consent of their councils, and none were able to obtain this required assent. But the British commander-in-chief in North America, General Thomas Gage, alarmed by the breakdown of regular government, moved on his own initiative to strengthen his forces for what he feared was the impending showdown. "There seems," Gage wrote Conway, February 22, 1766, "throughout the Provinces to be a Dissolution of all legal Authority, that Subordination is entirely destroyed, and that all coercive Powers in Government are annihalated, The People so accustomed to Excess and Riot without controul, that it is to be feared it would not be an easy Task to bring them back to their Duty, Should the Wisdom of Parliament even think proper to remove the present Cause of Clamor, by a Repeal of the Stamp Act. There has not however been any Requisition made for my Assistance, but it becomes my Duty when I see the King's Affairs in such a Situation, to do everything which depends upon me for the Support of his Service, and I must take my own Resolution; which is to draw in all the Force I can, and as soon as it can be done, into these Provinces."

By the time the news of American resistance reached England, the Grenville ministry had fallen. The reason for Grenville's downfall was not his American policy, but personal friction with the King. George III turned first to William Pitt to form a new cabinet, but Pitt refused. Wishing to be rid of Grenville at any price, George turned, in July, 1765, to the Marquis of Rockingham and the Old Whigs—the erstwhile followers of the Duke of Newcastle. The American crisis was the main problem facing the Rockingham ministry. Protests were pouring in from British merchants and manufacturers about the harm done by the American boycott. But counterbalancing these protests was the growing fear among politically conscious Britons that the colonial resistance to the Stamp Act was but a first step toward full independence. George Grenville and his influential ally, the Duke of Bedford, would bitterly assail any move to repeal the act; on the other hand, the still powerful Pitt refused to join the ministry or even make known his position. Caught in the crossfire, Rockingham temporized. The speech from the throne on January 14 was noncommittal—but the debate that followed was explosive.

William Pitt started off by attacking the Grenville Ministry; "every capital measure they have taken," he declared, "has been entirely wrong." He then went on to support the distinction made by the colonists between legislation and taxation:

Printed: Hansard, *Parliamentary History*, XVI, pp. 97-100.

. . . It is my opinion, that this kingdom has no right to lay a tax upon the colonies. At the same time, I assert the authority of this kingdom over the colonies, to be sovereign and supreme, in every circumstance of government and legislation whatsoever. They are the subjects of this kingdom, equally entitled with yourselves to all the natural rights of mankind and the peculiar privileges of Englishmen. Equally bound by its laws, and equally participating of the constitution of this free country. The Americans are the sons, not the bastards, of England. Taxation is no part of the governing or legislative power. The taxes are a voluntary gift and grant of the Commons alone. In legislation the three estates of the realm are alike concerned, but the concurrence of the peers and the crown to a tax, is only necessary to close with the form of a law. The gift and grant is of the Commons alone. In ancient days, the crown, the barons, and the clergy possessed the lands. In those days, the barons and the clergy gave and granted to the crown. They gave and granted what was their own. At present, since the discovery of America, and other circumstances permitting, the Commons are become the proprietors of the land. The crown has divested itself of its great estates. The church (God bless it) has but a pittance. The property of the Lords, compared with that of the Commons, is as a drop of water in the ocean: and this House represents those Commons, the proprietors of the lands; and those proprietors virtually represent the rest of the inhabitants. When, therefore, in this House we give and grant, we give and grant what is our own. But in an American tax, what do we do? We, your Majesty's Commons of Great Britain, give and grant to your Majesty, what? Our own property? No. We give and grant to your Majesty, the property of your Majesty's commons of America. It is an absurdity in terms.

The distinction between legislation and taxation is essentially necessary to liberty. The Crown, the Peers, are equally legislative powers with the Commons. If taxation be a part of simple legislation, the Crown, the Peers, have rights in taxation as well as yourselves: rights which they will claim, which they will exercise, whenever the principle can be supported by power.

There is an idea in some, that the colonies are virtually represented in this House. I would fain know by whom an American is represented here? Is he represented by any knight of the shire, in any county in this kingdom? Would to God that respectable representation was augmented to a greater number! Or will you tell him, that he is represented by any representative of a borough—a borough, which perhaps, its own representative never saw. This is what is called, 'the rotten part of the constitution.' It cannot continue the century; if it does not drop, it must be amputated. The idea of a virtual representation of America in this House, is the most contemptible idea that ever entered into the head of a man; it does not deserve a serious refutation.

The Commons of America, represented in their several assemblies, have ever been in possession of the exercise of this, their constitutional right, of giving and granting their own money. They would have been slaves if they had not enjoyed it. At the same time, this kingdom, as the supreme governing and legislative power, has always bound the colonies by her laws, by her regulations, and restrictions in trade, in navigation, in manufactures, in every thing, except that of taking their money out of their pockets without their consent.

Here I would draw the line,

'Quam ultra citraque nequit consistere rectum.'

Then Grenville rose in reply and insisted that the power to tax was an inseparable part of Parliament's supremacy over the colonies:

Printed: Hansard, *Parliamentary History*, XVI, pp. 101-103.

. . . I cannot understand the difference between external and internal taxes. They are the same in effect, and only differ in name. That this kingdom has the sovereign, the supreme legislative power over America, is granted. It cannot be denied; and taxation is a part of that sovereign power. It is one branch of the legislation. It is, it has been exercised, over those who are not, who were never represented. It is exercised over the India Company, the merchants of London, the proprietors of the stocks, and over many great manufacturing towns. It was exercised over the palatinate of Chester, and the bishopric of Durham, before they sent any representatives to parliament. . . . When I proposed to tax America, I asked the House, if any gentleman would object to the right; I repeatedly asked it, and no man would attempt to deny it. Protection and obedience are reciprocal. Great Britain protects America; America is bound to yield obedience. If not, tell me when the Americans were emancipated? When they want the protection of this kingdom, they are always very ready to ask it. That protection has always been afforded them in the most full and ample manner. The nation has run itself into an immense debt to give them their protection; and now they are called upon to contribute a small share towards the public expence, an expence arising from themselves, they renounce your authority, insult your officers, and break out, I might almost say, into open rebellion. The seditious spirit of the colonies owes its birth to the factions in this House. Gentlemen are careless of the consequences of what they say, provided it answers the purposes of opposition. We were told we trod on tender ground; we were bid to expect disobedience. What was this, but telling the Americans to stand out against the law, to encourage their obstinacy with the expectation of support from hence? Let us only hold out a little, they would say, our friends will soon be in power. Ungrateful people of America! . . .

Pitt spoke a second time in answer to Grenville and applauded American resistance. While reaffirming Parliament's supreme authority over the colonies, Pitt insisted that "there is a plain distinction between taxes levied for the purposes of raising a revenue, and duties imposed for the regulation of trade." His solution was simple: immediate repeal of the Stamp Act along with a declaratory act reaffirming "the sovereign authority of this country over the colonies":

Printed: Hansard, *Parliamentary History,* XVI, pp. 103-108.

Gentlemen, Sir, I have been charged with giving birth to sedition in America. They have spoken their sentiments with freedom, against this unhappy act, and that freedom has become their crime. Sorry I am to hear the liberty of speech in this House, imputed as a crime. But the imputation shall not discourage me. It is a liberty I mean to exercise. No gentleman ought to be afraid to exercise it. It is a liberty by which the gentleman who calumniates it might have profited. He ought to have profited. He ought to have desisted from his project. The gentleman tells us, America is obstinate; America is almost in open rebellion. I rejoice that America has resisted. Three millions of people, so dead to all the feelings of liberty, as voluntarily to submit to be slaves, would have been fit instruments to make slaves of the rest. . . .

. . . The gentleman tells us of many who are taxed, and are not represented—The India company, merchants, stock-holders, manufacturers. Surely many of these are represented in other capacities, as owners of land, or as freemen of boroughs. It is a misfortune that more are not actually represented. But they are all inhabitants, and, as such, are virtually represented. Many have it in their option to be actually represented. They have connexions with those that elect, and they have influence over them. . . .

. . . I am no courtier of America, I stand up for this kingdom. I maintain, that the parliament has a right to bind, to restrain America. Our legislative power over the colonies is sovereign and supreme. When it ceases to be sovereign and supreme, I would advise every gentleman to sell his lands, if he can, and embark for that country. When two countries are connected together, like England and her colonies, without being incorporated, the one must necessarily govern; the greater must rule the less; but so rule it, as not to contradict the fundamental principles that are common to both.

If the gentleman does not understand the difference between internal and external taxes, I cannot help it; but there is a plain distinction between taxes levied for the purposes of raising a revenue, and duties imposed for the regulation of trade, for the accommodation of the subject; although, in the consequences, some revenue might incidentally arise from the latter.

The gentleman asks, when were the colonies emancipated? But I desire to know, when they were made slaves? But I dwell not upon words. When I had the honour of serving his Majesty, I availed myself of the means of information, which I derived from my office: I speak, therefore, from knowledge. My materials were good. I was at pains to collect, to digest, to consider them; and I will be bold to affirm, that the profits to Great Britain from the trade of the colonies, through all its branches, is two millions a year. . . . This is the price that America pays you for her protection. And shall a miserable financier come with a boast, that he can fetch a pepper-corn into the exchequer, to the loss of millions to the nation! . . .

. . . The Americans have not acted in all things with prudence and temper. They have been wronged. They have been driven to madness by injustice. Will you punish them for the madness you have occasioned? Rather let prudence and temper come first from this side. I will undertake for America, that she will follow the example. There are two lines in a ballad of Prior's, of a man's behaviour to his wife, so applicable to you and your colonies, that I cannot help repeating them:

'Be to her faults a little blind:
'Be to her virtues very kind.'

Upon the whole, I will beg leave to tell the House what is really my opinion. It is, that the Stamp Act be repealed absolutely, totally, and immediately. That the reason for the repeal be assigned, because it was founded on an erroneous principle. At the same time, let the sovereign authority of this country over the colonies, be asserted in as strong terms as can be devised, and be made to extend to every point of legislation whatsoever. That we may bind their trade, confine their manufactures, and exercise every power whatsoever, except that of taking their money out of their pockets without their consent.

The weak Rockingham ministry could not survive without at least the benevolent neutrality of Pitt, and the cabinet took its cue from Pitt's speech. On January 17, the cabinet decided upon repeal of the Stamp Act. But whereas Pitt had called for a public declaration that the Stamp Act had been founded upon "an erroneous principle," Rockingham feared that Parliament would never swallow so bitter a pill as a clear-cut disavowal of its right to tax the colonists. To sweeten the dose, he misrepresented the colonists' position. The colonists had drawn the distinction between the power to tax and the power to make laws and claimed full power of taxation for their local assemblies. They accepted regulation of trade by Parliament even if the duties brought in an incidental revenue, but such duties for the purpose of revenue were another story. Unfortunately the colonial protests were not always as unambiguous on this question as they might have been, and the resulting confusion led many Englishmen to believe that the distinction was between "internal" and "external" taxation. The Rockingham ministry took advantage of this confusion to hide the true position of the colonists and let Parliament believe that the Americans were objecting merely to internal taxes. The ministry's trump card in this strategy was the carefully rehearsed testimony before the House of Commons given by Benjamin Franklin:

Printed: *Parliamentary History*, XVI, pp. 137-159.

. . . What was the temper of America towards Great Britain before the year 1763?—The best in the world. They submitted willingly to the government of the crown, and paid, in all their courts, obedience to acts of parliament. Numerous as the people are in the several old provinces, they cost you nothing in forts, citadels, garrisons or armies, to keep them in subjection. They were governed by this country at the expence only of a little pen, ink, and paper. They were led by a thread. They had not only a respect, but an affection for Great Britain, for its laws, its customs and manners, and even a fondness for its fashions, that greatly increased the commerce.

Natives of Britain were always treated with particular regard; to be an Old-England man was, of itself, a character of some respect, and gave a kind of rank among us.

And what is their temper now?—O, very much altered.

Did you ever hear the authority of parliament to make laws for America questioned till lately?—The authority of parliament was allowed to be valid in all laws, except such as should lay internal taxes. It was never disputed in laying duties to regulate commerce.

In what light did the people of America use to consider the parliament of Great Britain?—They considered the parliament as the great bulwark and security of their liberties and privileges, and always spoke of it with the utmost respect and veneration. . . .

And have they not still the same respect for parliament?—No; it is greatly lessened.

To what causes is that owing?—To a concurrence of causes; the restraints lately laid on their trade, by which the bringing of foreign gold and silver into the colonies was prevented; the prohibition of making paper money among themselves; and then demand a new and heavy tax by stamps; taking away at the same time, trials by juries, and refusing to receive and hear their humble petitions.

Don't you think they would submit to the Stamp Act, if it was modified, the obnoxious parts taken out, and the duty reduced to some particulars, of small moment?—No; they will never submit to it. . . .

What is your opinion of a future tax, imposed on the same principle with that of the Stamp Act, how would the Americans receive it?—Just as they do this. They would not pay it.

Have not you heard of the resolution of this House, and of the House of Lords, asserting the right of parliament relating to America, including a power to tax the people there?—Yes, I have heard of such resolutions.

What will be the opinion of the Americans on those resolutions?—They will think them unconstitutional and unjust.

Was it an opinion in America before 1763, that the parliament had no right to lay taxes and duties there?—I never heard any objection to the right of laying duties to regulate commerce; but a right to lay internal taxes was never supposed to be in parliament, as we are not represented there.

On what do you found your opinion, that the people in America

made any such distinction?—I know that whenever the subject has
occurred in conversation where I have been present, it has appeared
to be the opinion of every one, that we could not be taxed in a
parliament where we were not represented. But the payment of duties
laid by act of parliament, as regulations of commerce, was never
disputed. . . .

You say the colonies have always submitted to external taxes,
and object to the right of parliament only in laying internal taxes; now
can you shew that there is any kind of difference between the two
taxes to the colony on which they may be laid?—I think the difference is very great. An external tax is a duty laid on commodities
imported; that duty is added to the first cost, and other charges on
the commodity, and when it is offered to sale, makes a part of the
price. If the people do not like it at that price, they refuse it; they
are not obliged to pay it. But an internal tax is forced from the
people without their consent, if not laid by their own representatives.
The Stamp Act says, we shall have no commerce, make no exchange
of property with each other, neither purchase nor grant, nor recover
debts; we shall neither marry nor make our wills, unless we pay such
sums, and thus it is intended to extort our money from us, or ruin us
by the consequences of refusing to pay it. . . .

If the Stamp Act should be repealed, would not the Americans
think they could oblige the parliament to repeal every external tax
law now in force?—It is hard to answer questions what people at
such a distance will think.

But what do you imagine they will think were the motives of
repealing the Act?—I suppose they will think that it was repealed
from a conviction of its inexpediency; and they will rely upon it, that
while the same inexpediency subsists, you will never attempt to make
such another.

What do you mean by its inexpediency?—I mean its inexpediency
on several accounts; the poverty and inability of those who were to
pay the tax; the general discontent it has occasioned; and the impracticability of enforcing it. . . .

If the Stamp Act should be repealed, and the crown should make a
requisition to the colonies for a sum of money, would they grant it?—
I believe they would.

Why do you think so?—I can speak for the colony I live in; I
had it in instruction from the assembly to assure the ministry, that as

they always had done, so they should always think it their duty to grant such aids to the crown as were suitable to their circumstances and abilities, whenever called upon for the purpose, in the usual constitutional manner. . . .

But as to an internal tax, how small soever, laid by the legislature here on the people there, while they have no representatives in this legislature, I think it will never be submitted to.—They will oppose it to the last.—They do not consider it as at all necessary for you to raise money on them by your taxes, because they are, and always have been, ready to raise money by taxes among themselves, and to grant large sums, equal to their abilities, upon requisition from the crown.—They have not only granted equal to their abilities, but, during all the last war, they granted far beyond their abilities, and beyond their proportion with this country. . . . There was no occasion for this act, to force money from a willing people; they had not refused giving money for the purpose of the act; no requisition had been made: they were always willing and ready to do what could reasonably be expected from them, and in this light they wish to be considered. . . .

Don't you know that there is, in the Pennsylvania charter, an express reservation of the right of parliament to lay taxes there?— I know there is a clause in the charter, by which the King grants that he will levy no taxes on the inhabitants, unless it be with the consent of the assembly, or by an act of parliament.

How then could the assembly of Pennsylvania assert, that laying a tax on them by the Stamp Act was an infringement of their rights?— They understand it thus: by the same charter, and otherwise, they are entitled to all the privileges and liberties of Englishmen; they find in the Great Charters, and the Petition and Declaration of Rights, that one of the privileges of English subjects is, that they are not to be taxed but by their common consent; they have therefore relied upon it, from the first settlement of the province, that the parliament never would, nor could, by colour of that clause in the charter, assume a right of taxing them, till it had qualified itself to exercise such right, by admitting representatives from the people to be taxed, who ought to make a part of that common consent.

Are there any words in the charter that justify that construction?— The common rights of Englishmen, as declared by Magna Charta, and the Petition of Right, all justify it.

Does the distinction between internal and external taxes exist in the words of the charter?—No, I believe not.

Then may they not, by the same interpretation, object to the parliament's right of external taxation?—They never have hitherto. Many arguments have been lately used here to shew them that there is no difference, and that if you have no right to tax them internally, you have none to tax them externally, or make any other law to bind them. At present they do not reason so, but in time they may possibly be convinced by these arguments.

Do not the resolutions of the Pennsylvania assemblies say, all taxes?—If they do, they mean only internal taxes; the same words have not always the same meaning here and in the colonies. By taxes they mean internal taxes; by duties they mean customs; these are the ideas of the language. . . .

Dangerous as this distinction between internal and external taxation was, even more dangerous was the purposeful ambiguity of the Declaratory Act accompanying repeal. That resolution, presented by Secretary of State Henry S. Conway on February 3, affirmed that Parliament "had full power and authority to make laws and statutes of sufficient force to bind the colonies and people of America, subjects of the crown of Great Britain, in all cases whatsoever." But this vague phrase "in all cases whatsoever" left unanswered the vital question, Did Parliament's power to legislate include the power to tax? Most members believed that it did; most of the colonists as well as Pitt thought it did not. But the ambiguity enabled the ministry to keep its ranks intact and proceed with repeal. The great debate in the Committee of the Whole of the House of Commons over repeal was described by Charles Garth—a member of Parliament and London agent for Maryland and South Carolina—in the following letter of March 5, 1766 to the Maryland members of the Stamp Act Congress, Edward Tilghman, William Murdoch, and Thomas Ringgold:

Printed: "Stamp Act Papers," *Maryland Historical Magazine,* VI, No. 3 (September, 1911), 287-308.*

---

* Paragraphing slightly altered for readability.

. . . The 3d of Febry we went into a Debate to consider of Resolutions proper to be agreed upon, after the Information and Intelligence that had been communicated; when Mr Secretary Conway had proposed a Resolution Vizt "That the King's Majesty by and with the Consent of the Lords Spiritual & Temporal & Commons in Parliament assembled had, hath, and of Right ought to have full Power and Authority to make Laws and Statutes of sufficient Force & Validity to bind the People in America, Subjects of Great Britain, in all Cases whatsoever." Mr Conway and the Chancellor of the Exchequer said they were induced to offer the Proposition in this extensive Manner, not only as necessary to meet the Resolutions and Language of several of the Colonies, but because upon the fullest Enquiry into the Constitution of Great Britain, they were convinced that in Point of Law, the King, Lords and Commons were undoubtedly possessed of that Power, tho' in Point of Policy, Justice or Equity, it was a Power that they ought to exercise but in the most extraordinary Cases only.

Colo Barrie mov'd to have the Words "in all Cases whatsoever" left out, and he shou'd have no objection to the Resolution as it wou'd then stand, he was seconded by Mr Pitt. The Arguments in Support of this Motion imported among the Variety of Suggestions offer'd, that the Subjects in the Colonies, when first they emigrated from hence, went with License, carrying with them every Right the Crown could grant, and every Right of British Subjects, carrying with them the Common Law of the Land; that by the Common Law and Spirit of this Constitution no Man could be taxed without being represented, that the People of America could not with the smallest Propriety be said to be represented in the Parliament of Great Britain, and it was Representation that alone gave the Right and Power to the Commons of imposing Taxes, this was the Foundation of all Mr Locke's Arguments & Reasoning, greater Authority could not be produced: That the Principles of Taxation as distinguished from Legislation were as distinct Principles & Powers as any two Propositions under the Sun, had been considered uniformly such by our Ancestors thro' many Ages; . . . [That] it was plain we intended [the colonists] to be as free as ourselves, having given them a Constitution as nearly resembling our own as we can; They have the Power given them of raising and of granting their Money, a Power which constitutes the very Essence of Parliament, if this Power is taken from them, the very Existence the very Essence of Assemblies is destroy'd. Grievances then can never be redress'd, and Grievances they have had and will in all Probability have again, which ought always to take Place of Grants of Money, otherwise very material Grievances among those distant Subjects may sometimes (at least for a long Time) remain without Redress. Upon this Principle the Stamp Act cou'd not but be deemed a Grievance, and circumstanc'd as they are calls loudly for Redress, but at the same Time that you redress the Grievance, the Violence committed calls equally for the Hand of Resentment, and it greatly imported the Dignity of Parliament to see that the principal Offenders were brought to condign Punishment; The Claim of Contribution from the Colonies none can deny to be just, but the Mode of procuring it may be quite the reverse, Great Britain and the Colonies in the Article of Taxes may have very opposite Interests, and there may be a Probability of Alleviation to the Burthens of one at the Expense of Oppression to the other: Besides that the Circumstances and Abilities of the Colonies cannot be so justly and truly known to the Commons of England as to their own immediate Representatives in their several and Respective Assemblies; there they enjoy the Exercise of that fundamental Right, of having some one in the Case of Tallages to speak for them and to represent their Condition & Abilities, in Parliament it is an almost impracticable and impossible thing, and by that Means they lose a very important Privilege belonging to the Represented. The supreme Power wheresoever lodged is undoubtedly comptroulable, for it must and it will controul itself by the Powers of Reason, always should act upon the Principles of Humanity & Justice; Circumstanc'd then as the Colonists are in Point of Distance, Situation, Abilities & Rights, the greatest Caution cannot be too great in the Exercise of this great Supreme Power, as it is to affect the Subject there: It was Lenity, Humanity & Magnanimity that did more to preserve to Rome the Roman Colonies secure & dependent than all the Legions she ever was Mistress of or cou'd at any Time command: That shou'd it be the Sense of the House after all, that Parliament is in Possession of this *Summum Jus.* it will do well to remember, the *summa Injuria* is its well known Offspring.

On the other Hand, the Attorney General [Charles] York[e], the Chancellor of the Exchequer [William Dowdeswell], all the Gentlemen of the long Robe, and others express'd themselves in favour

of the Proposition, as offered by Mr Conway after approving the
Propriety of confining the Debate to the single Point of Power and
the Right in the Parliament, without intermingling therewith any
thing touching the Expediency of a Repeal of the Law so greatly
complained of, which wou'd become a fit and proper Subject for the
Consideration of another Day, they entered fully and at large into
the great Question; The Heads of the most material Arguments I
think were to the Effect following: That the Establishment of the
Colonies was originally by License from the Crown, who by Charter
gave them the *Jura regalia* and Powers of Government as necessary
for their Protection, Defence, and Support, of Civil Government
among them, being to be so far distant from the great executive
Power of the Realm, which Powers of Government so given by the
Crown were of a Nature with those granted to the East India Company and to great Cities and Corporations in England, each having
a Power of raising Money for their Support, but neither of which
cou'd by any Grant the King cou'd make, be exempt from the
supreme Authority of King, Lords & Commons. That the Crown
was but a Part of the supreme Power of the Realm, and therefore
cou'd give no more, indeed in some Instances seem'd to have granted
all that he had to grant, but by no Construction cou'd be deem'd to
have granted that which he had no Power to grant, that which
belonged to the supreme legislative Power, which in all Ages did
extend wheresoever the Sovereignty of the Crown did extend; That
the Colonists carried with them all the Subjection and Allegiance
they owed when resident in Great Britain, that no Time nor Distance cou'd terminate that Subjection and Allegiance, which by the
Law of the Land must descend to their own immediate Heirs, & to all
their Posterity; whatever Compact was stipulated between the Crown
and those his Subjects upon their Emigration no Condition whatever
was made or wou'd have been suffer'd between them and the supreme
Sovereign Power. That the Parliament had Power to alter and change
their Property, to enact Laws for Punishment of great Offences and
in particular of High Treason, by which the Property might be divested, Inheritance taken away etc. without their immediate Consent,
and yet not have a Power to impose a Tax upon their Property,
seem'd an extraordinary Proposition; . . . That in 1717 a Bill was
brought in to take away the Charters which had been granted to
the several Colonies, the Power of Parliament in any of those Cases

was never questioned, that if the Parliament had the Power to take
away those Charters, by Virtue of which the Colonists claim the
Right & Power of imposing and levying Taxes, it cou'd not but be
possessed of the Power of Taxation; . . . That the supreme Power
must be compleat and entire; in Legislation and Taxation coequal
and coextending, and tho' by Equity from Regard to Circumstances
and Situations Indulgence had been given either to come to Parliament or to raise Money in the Way of Taxation for the local Purposes
of subordinate Districts and Governments, yet that Indulgence cou'd
never abridge the Supremacy in any of its Powers and Authority;
Upon this Principle the Parliament of Great Britain alone could and
did, (Ireland having that Indulgence granted) absolve the People of
Ireland from Duties due to the Crown, impos'd by Acts pass'd in
their own Parliament; It was the Commons of England that directed
that the Charge of the Army, kept up for the Defence and Security
of that Kingdom, shou'd be provided for by the People of Ireland,
leaving the Provision to be made by the Irish Parliament, which if
not complied with, wou'd have been enforc'd by a Law of Great
Britain, and was so understood and known at that Time in both
Kingdoms: That in all the antient Subsidy Acts, the Form and Tenor
thereof runs that the Subsidies laid and impos'd are to be paid by his
Majesty's Subjects within the Realm and in all the King's Dominions,
particular Parts and Places were sometimes expressly excepted, as
Wales constantly before the Statute of H. 8. Ireland, the Counties
Palatine upon whom the Charge of defending the Northern Frontiers
fell by their Charters, Calais, Guienne, Gascony, and particular Corporations upon particular Accounts, which Exceptions, it was said,
prove that if they had not been particularly excepted, altho' not represented, they must have been comprised under the Act & within the
View thereof. . . .

That the Strength of the Empire in America depends upon an
entire and exact Obedience to the Supreme Authority in Great
Britain, which if infring'd in any Instance, no Man cou'd foresee the
Confusion that must inevitably follow, Cases might and undoubtedly
wou'd happen to puzzle the ablest Lawyers of the Time to distinguish
the Difference between Duties and Taxation, between the Right of
laying one & the other; That this was settled and established to be
one entire Power lodged in the Commons of England in the great
Conference in William the 3d's Time, between the House of Lords

and Commons, when the Lords were inclin'd to have establish'd a
Difference between Duties and Impositions upon Merchandize, and
the Grant of Taxes and Subsidies, with a View to confine the Power
of the Commons to the latter only, the Commons said it was the
Usage of Parliament the Uniformity of all Ages which limits the
Power of the Crown and the Power of both Houses of Parliament;
under this Sanction they claim'd the Power entire and in its full
Extent. . . . That all Government is founded in Trust, wherever the
Trust is placed, that Trust is absolute and entire, the Kingdom and
Colonies compose one great Mass of political Strength, and tho' the
jealous Language of Liberty cou'd not but approve itself to every
Lover of Liberty and Admirer of this Constitution, yet when that
Jealousy was carried so far as to tell the Sovereign Power they will
not trust you, unless you recede from your Power, it becomes too
alarming and calls for the Exertion of Spirit & of Wisdom. Ask
France what Occasion She wou'd wish for yr Destruction, she will
answer, let Divisions be kept up and fomented between you and your
Colonies, that a Departure from your Sovereign Power will be that
Diminution and Weakening of yr Authority, she wou'd be most
pleased to see as the surest Means to her of compassing the great
Object of her Ambition; this Sovereignty then is so necessary to be
compleat and entire for the Sake of Great Britain and America
equally, so essential for the Benefit and Happiness of the whole, that
if once broke into, the Depedency of the Colonies once given Way
to, your Power and Authority, as a great respected Kingdom in
Europe, is blasted, no Friend will trust you, no Enemy will fear you.
    The Debate ended about 4 in the Morning, when the Question was
put in Consequence of Colo. Barrie's Motion, "that the Words in all
Cases whatsoever stand Part of the Resolution"; I believe from the
Sound there were not more than ten dissenting Voices. . . .

This overwhelming defeat of the move by Pitt and his supporters to strike out the words "in all cases whatsoever" on the
ground that Parliament had no right to tax the colonies answered
for most members the question whether the resolution did or did
not cover the right of taxation. With this issue of right settled, the
ministry pushed for repeal of the Stamp Act on the ground of its
inexpediency. The supporters of repeal argued that enforcement
of the act would require large-scale military force, and they re-

minded the House of the damage inflicted upon British merchant and manufacturing interests by the colonial boycott. The two measures—repeal and the Declaratory Act—went through Parliament, in Charles Garth's apt phrase, "Hand in Hand," and received the royal assent on March 18, 1766. Repeal was justified on grounds of expediency: that "continuance of the said act would be attended with many inconveniencies, and may be productive of consequences greatly detrimental to the commercial interests of these kingdoms." The accompanying Declaratory Act stated:

Printed: 6 George III, c. 12, Pickering, *Statutes at Large*, XXXIII, pp. 19-20.

An act for the better securing the dependency of his Majesty's dominions in America *upon the crown and parliament of* Great Britain.

Whereas several of the houses of representatives in his Majesty's colonies and plantations in America, *have of late, against law, claimed to themselves, or to the general assemblies of the same, the sole and exclusive right of imposing duties and taxes upon his Majesty's subjects in the said colonies and plantations; and have, in pursuance of such claim, passed certain votes, resolutions, and orders, derogatory to the legislative authority of parliament, and inconsistent with the dependency of the said colonies and plantations upon the crown of* Great Britain: may it therefore please your most excellent Majesty, that it may be declared; and be it declared by the King's most excellent majesty, by and with the advice and consent of the lords spiritual and temporal, and commons, in this present parliament assembled, and by the authority of the same, That the said colonies and plantations in *America* have been, are, and of right ought to be, subordinate unto, and dependent upon the imperial crown and parliament of *Great Britain*; and that the King's majesty, by and with the advice and consent of the lords spiritual and temporal, and commons of *Great Britain*, in parliament assembled, had, hath, and of right ought to have, full power and authority to make laws and statutes of sufficient force and validity to bind the colonies and people of *America*, subjects of the crown of *Great Britain*, in all cases whatsoever.

II. And be it further declared and enacted by the authority aforesaid, That all resolutions, votes, orders, and proceedings, in any of the said colonies or plantations, whereby the power and authority of the parliament of *Great Britain*, to make laws and statutes as aforesaid, is denied, or drawn into question, are, and are hereby declared to be, utterly null and void to all intents and purposes whatsoever.

But repeal merely postponed the showdown between the colonies and the mother country. Despite the Declaratory Act, many Britons saw repeal as a fatal surrender of Parliament's authority. On the other hand, as the Morgans have shown, the colonists interpreted repeal to mean acceptance by Parliament of their claim to complete local autonomy in matters of taxation. Most Americans were not privy to the secret debates in the Committee of the Whole of the House of Commons, and they took the vague words in the Declaratory Act to accord with their own distinction between legislation and taxation. So the basic issue between the colonists and mother country remained unresolved—and the Stamp Act crisis had brought to the forefront men of more extreme views who would resist what they regarded as any further British encroachments.

IV. Townshend Rekindles the Flames

IN relaying the news of the repeal of the Stamp Act to the royal governors, Secretary of State Henry Conway expressed the ministry's hope that "the moderation, the forbearance, the unexampled levity and tenderness of Parliament" would restore the colonies to "cheerful obedience to the Laws and Legislative authority of Great Britain." The ministry made additional bows toward winning colonial good will: the duty on molasses was reduced from three pence to one penny per gallon—although this duty was now made to apply to British- as well as foreign-made molasses; free ports for foreign produce were opened in Jamaica and Dominica; and bounties were increased for colonial products. The most auspicious augury of improved relations between the colonists and the mother country was the replacement of the Rockingham ministry in August, 1766, by a new one headed by the colonists' hero William Pitt.

But the Stamp Act crisis had left its lasting mark. The election in the spring of 1766 in Massachusetts witnessed the triumph of the radical party led by James Otis and Samuel Adams. There followed a long conflict between the governor and the House over the resolution passed by the House of Commons calling upon the colonies to make compensation to victims of the Stamp Act riots. Finally, early in December, the Massachusetts House voted compensation, but tacked on to the bill a rider granting a "free and general Pardon and Indemnity and Oblivion to the offenders in the late Times." The act was thus a clear-cut usurpation of the right of the crown alone to grand pardons, and the Privy Council disallowed the law as unconstitutional. By that time, however, the compensation had been paid, and although the pardon granted to the rioters was legally void, no effort was made toward their apprehension or punishment.

An even more serious challenge to British authority came in New York. The dispute involved the Quartering Act of 1765. By that act, the colonies were required to provide barracks or other suitable accommodations for British troops as well as "fire, candles, vinegar and salt, bedding, utensils for dressing victuals, and small beer, cyder, or rum." Since New York was the headquarters of the British army in North America, the expense was a heavy one for that colony. When the New York Assembly met in the spring of 1766, the Assembly balked at appropriating any money for quartering the troops. After a long hassle with the governor, the Assembly finally agreed to provide barracks, fire wood, candles, and kitchen utensils, but claimed to do so in response to a royal requisition rather than in obedience to an act of Parliament—and underlined their defiance by refusing to provide the salt, vinegar, and the liquor ration required by the Quartering Act.

When Governor Sir Henry Moore reminded the Assembly of their duty to obey the laws of Parliament, that body replied that compliance would be inconsistent "with our obligations to our constituents." Anti-American feelings in Britain rose sharply. Even Pitt himself—now raised to the peerage as Lord Chatham— was outraged. At a meeting on March 12, 1767, the cabinet decided to have Parliament suspend the New York Assembly until that body made suitable provision for the troops under the Quartering Act.

By the time the bill passed, however, the Assembly had backed down and voted sufficient money to cover all the quartering expenses—including the liquor ration. Even so, Governor Moore reported, the Assembly still balked at the principle involved. The bill, he wrote Shelburne, "only made an appropriation of such a sum as was thought necessary to furnish all the articles, but no particular mention was made of them, nor of the money being raised in consequence of the Act of Parliament. . . . This was an evasive Proceeding, and . . . it was intended the money should appear to have been granted only upon a Requisition made by me as Governor of the Province and not in obedience to what was prescribed by the Act of Parliament."

Nonetheless, the ministry, wishing an end to the controversy, decided that the Assembly had made satisfactory provision for the troops. Thus the New York Restraining Act was never enforced—but the precedent was an ominous one for the colonies. Richard Henry Lee of Virginia declared that the act *"hangs, like a flaming sword,* over our heads"; John Dickinson would assail the measure in his *Letters from a Farmer* as "as injurious in its principle to the liberties of these colonies, as the *Stamp Act* was"; and the Declaration of Independence would list "suspending our own legislatures" among the grievances justifying rebellion.

More excitement was not aroused by the New York Restraining Act because almost simultaneously Parliament passed two other acts of even graver portent for the colonists—the Townshend Act and the act creating the American Board of Customs Commissioners. These two measures were the handiwork of Charles Townshend, the Chancellor of the Exchequer in the Pitt ministry. When Pitt took office in July, 1766, he was a sick man. With the passage of time, his gout made him increasingly unstable and remote. Pitt's illness left Townshend the strong man of the cabinet. An extremely able though unstable and widely distrusted man, Townshend was a staunch defender of the supremacy of the mother country over the colonies. To uphold this supremacy, he had for many years past advocated making the royal officials in America financially independent of the colonial assemblies—a plan that had as its corollary the raising of a colonial revenue by act of Parliament.

On January 26, 1767, when the House was considering the military estimates, Grenville moved that the expense of the troops in America should be met by the colonies themselves. His motion was handily defeated, but Townshend took the opportunity to "assert his own opinions" without prior consultation with the cabinet. Townshend said he agreed with the idea behind the Stamp Act, noting simply that the time was not suitable for its reintroduction; ridiculed the distinction between internal and external taxes; and pledged himself to find a colonial revenue to meet the expense of maintaining the troops in America.

He was encouraged in this design by the quiet American acceptance of the Revenue Act of 1766. Although reducing the duty on molasses to one penny a gallon, the act imposed the duty on British as well as foreign molasses—and thus was a clear-cut revenue measure rather than a regulation of trade, with the revenue earmarked for "defraying the necessary expenses of defending, protecting, and securing the British colonies in America." The failure of the colonists to protest appeared to confirm the widely held belief in Britain that the Americans objected only to internal taxes. Speaking with the colonies' London agents, Townshend declared, reported one, "that, although he did not in the least doubt the right of Parliament to tax the Colonies internally, and that he knew no difference between internal and external taxes, (which, by the way, is a doctrine very generally adopted here,) yet since the Americans were pleased to make that distinction he was willing to indulge them, and chose for that reason to confine himself to regulations of trade, by which a sufficient revenue might be raised in America."

Townshend soon had his opportunity. A revolt by the backbenchers in the House of Commons forced a reduction in the land tax. This was followed by the defeat of Chatham's plan to tap the territorial revenues of the East India Company. The resulting financial squeeze enabled Townshend to overbear his more reluctant colleagues. On May 13, 1767, he outlined before the House his "Plan for improving the system of Government in the Colonies in order that the Authority of the executive Power might carry with it in the several Departments the Weight and Respect essentially necessary to answer the Ends of its Institution." As Charles Garth reported to the committee of correspondence of the South Carolina Commons House, May 17, 1767:

Printed: *South Carolina Historical and Genealogical Magazine*, XXIX, No. 3 (July, 1928), 223-230.

. . . [He proposed] that, out of the Fund arising from the American Duties now, or to be imposed, His Majesty should be enabled to establish Salaries that might be better suited to support the Dignity of the respective Officers, and for which to be no longer dependent upon the pleasure of any Assembly: Was this System intended to be confined to those Officers only who are intrusted with the Administration of Justice, I think I should have no objection, as such ought to be totally independent, but to take from the people the Power of distinguishing by their Favours the different Behaviour of other Officers, I shall not for one give my Assent to; more need not be said at present, as the proposition has only been stated, and not offered to the House.—

The remainder of M^r. Townsend's Speech was upon the Subject of the American Revenue with a View to secure the Collection of such Custom and Duties as already are and may hereafter be imposed by Parliament, and also to improve the Fund by an Additional Number of Articles, which he intended to propose in the Committee of Supply; to Compass the first of these Objects, he was of Opinion the Establishment of a Custom House upon the Continent of America was absolutely necessary, the Officers there would then be obliged to Discharge their Duty, without enriching themselves at the Expence of the Public by Conniving; the people likewise with Facility and without great Expence to themselves be furnished with an Opportunity of preferring their Complaints against the Misbehavior of subordinate Officers; in this opinion he should offer a Proposition of this sort to the Consideration of the House upon a future day.—He then stated the Articles by which to improve the American Revenue, and in his purpose to offer in the Committee of Supply, and they were a Duty upon Raisons of the Sun, and other Raisons, a Duty upon Oranges Lemons and Oil, and a Duty upon Port Wine, for these purposes to allow to America the Importation thereof direct from Portugal and from any part of Spain, upon such direct Importation to pay the respective Duties to be laid thereon; there being likewise several Articles which went from hence Duty free owing to a Drawback on Exportation of the whole Duty payable by the Subjects here, in particular upon China, Glass, Paper, Red and white Lead for Painting, and coloured Papers for Furniture, a considerable sum might be got, if a Drawback only of part of the Duties thereon was allowed. and lastly as America was desirous of a Paper Currency for the several Colonies, the Act of Prohibition should be repealed, and a permission to Establish a Loan Office in the respective provinces with a power of issuing paper Currency carrying an Interest, for which paper good Security to be given according to the Quantity wanted by Individuals, and the Money arising by the interest thereon to be appropriated to the King's Service, but whether this Appropriation was to be by Act of Parliament, or by Act of Assembly and whether for the King's Service in general upon the Continent of America, or within the respective Colonies, was not sufficiently explained: At present I believe these are points not yet settled, I was with a part of Administration but two days before on this very Subject, (as indeed there has scarce been any Matter in which America has been interested that I have had more trouble about,) and I came away understanding that we should be indulged with an Act of Repeal only without any thing more, leaving it to the Crown as formerly to allow or withhold its Assent to Acts of this sort to be passed in any Legislature in America; and therefore if any Plan seemed here to be better and more proper to be adopted than another, that the King's Ministers might aprise the Colonies thereof, who upon its Communication and not approving would with all deference point out their objections thereto fully and at large for the Ministry to Deliberate and advise His Majesty upon.

There were two other Articles which the Chancellor of the Exchequer informed the Committee had been in Contemplation, And these were Tea and Salt, the first as matters were in away of Accommodation with the East India Company, could not then with Propriety be offered to Consideration; The Revenue receives upon Tea by the old and new Subidies and Additional Customs 24 and a Fraction per Cent, and by certain inland Duties of 25 [per] Cent ad Valorem and 1. per pound, these inland Duties of 25 [per] C^t. ad Valorem, and one shilling per pound, are drawn back upon Exportation, but no part of the 24 and a Fraction,—I—understand the Plan is to allow a Drawback of this also upon Tea exported to America, and in lieu thereof to impose a Duty of Six pence per pound on all Tea imported lawfully into the Colonies. with respect to Salt, it was given up from the Difficulty of adjusting the Drawback to be allowed on the Exports of cured Fish and Provision, and of Salt to cure the same at the Fisheries.—I have now gone thro' the sundry Matters propounded and I believe I have omitted nothing material for your Information, as far as my memory serves me I think I am accurate in the above Account; I have troubled you with as few Observations as possible, that I might neither mislead nor Misrepresent a Circumstance I think that should be duly attended to in Correspondence with the Colonies at this particular Juncture more especially: and therefore I should observe to you that the House would not Admit any Stranger to be present at their Debates upon that Principle. . . .

The new taxes passed Parliament with scant opposition. The Revenue Act of June 29, 1767—popularly known as the Townshend Act—imposed duties upon glass, lead, paint, paper, and tea imported into the colonies. The most important duty was that of three pence a pound on tea, and to make the price of such tea competitive with illegally imported tea, an accompanying act provided for a drawback of the entire duty paid on tea imported into Britain when that tea was re-exported to the colonies. The act further provided that the estimated £35,000-40,000 a year that would be raised should be used to pay the salaries of royal officials and judges in the colonies "where it shall be found necessary." More stringent rules were laid down for the reporting of vessels and their cargoes to prevent smuggling, while another provision specifically authorized the issuance of general writs of assistance by the supreme or superior courts of the colonies:

Printed: 7 George III, c. 46, Pickering, *Statutes at Large*, XXVII, pp. 505-512.

An act for granting certain duties in the British colonies and plantations in America; . . . and for more effectually preventing the clandestine running of goods in the said colonies and plantations.

Whereas it is expedient that a revenue should be raised, in your Majesty's dominions in America, for making a more certain and adequate provision for defraying the charge of the administration of justice, and the support of civil government, in such provinces where it shall be found necessary; and towards further defraying the expenses of defending, protecting, and securing, the said dominions; we, your Majesty's most dutiful and loyal subjects, the commons of Great Britain, *in parliament assembled, have therefore resolved to give and grant unto your Majesty the several rates and duties hereinafter mentioned;* and do most humbly beseech your Majesty that it may be enacted, and be it enacted by the King's most excellent majesty, by and with the advice and consent of the lords spiritual and temporal, and commons, in this present parliament assembled, and by the authority of the same, That from and after the twentieth day of *November,* one thousand seven hundred and sixty seven, there shall be raised, levied, collected, and paid, unto his Majesty, his heirs, and successors, for and upon the respective goods herein after mentioned, which shall be imported from *Great Britain* into any colony or plantation in *America* which now is, or hereafter may be, under the dominion of his Majesty, his heirs, or successors, the several rates and duties following; that is to say,

For every hundred weight avoirdupois of crown, plate, flint, and white glass, four shillings and eight pence.

For every hundred weight avoirdupois of green glass, one shilling and two pence.

For every hundred weight avoirdupois of red lead, two shillings.

For every hundred weight avoirdupois of white lead, two shillings.

For every hundred weight avoirdupois of painters colours, two shillings.

For every pound weight avoirdupois of tea, three pence.

For every ream of paper, usually called or known by the name of Atlas Fine, twelve shillings. . . . [There follows a list of duties on other types of paper]

IV. And it is hereby further enacted by the authority aforesaid, that . . . all the monies that shall arise by the said duties (except the necessary charges of raising, collecting, levying, recovering, answering, paying, and accounting for the same) shall be applied, in the first place, in such manner as is herein after mentioned, in making a more certain and adequate provision for the charge of the administration of justice, and the support of civil government, in such of the said colonies and plantations where it shall be found necessary; and that the residue of such duties shall be paid into the receipt of his Majesty's exchequer, and shall be entered separate and apart from all other monies paid or payable to his Majesty, his heirs, or successors; and shall be there reserved, to be from time to time disposed of by parliament towards defraying the necessary expences of defending, protecting, and securing, the *British* colonies and plantations in *America.*

V. And be it further enacted by the authority aforesaid, That his Majesty and his successors shall be, and are hereby, impowered, from time to time, by any warrant or warrants under his or their royal sign manual or sign manuals, countersigned by the high treasurer, or any three or more of the commissioners of the treasury for the time being, to cause such monies to be applied, out of the produce of the duties granted by this act, as his Majesty, or his successors, shall think proper or necessary, for defraying the charges of the administration of justice, and the support of the civil government, within all or any of the said colonies or plantations. . . .

X. *And whereas by an act of parliament made in the fourteenth year of the reign of King* Charles *the Second, intituled,* An Act for preventing frauds, and regulating abuses, in his Majesty's customs, *and several other acts now in force, it is lawful for any officer of his Majesty's customs, authorized by writ of assistance under the seal of his Majesty's court of exchequer, to take a constable, headborough, or other public officer inhabiting near unto the place, and in the day-time to enter and go into any house, shop, cellar, warehouse, or room or other place, and, in case of resistance, to break open doors, chests, trunks, and other package there, to seize, and from thence to bring, any kind of goods or merchandize whatsoever prohibited or un-customed, and to put and secure the same in his Majesty's store-house next to the place where such seizure shall be made: and whereas by an act made in the seventh and eighth years of the reign of King* William *the Third, intituled,* An act for preventing frauds, and regulating abuses, in the plantation trade, *it is, amongst other things, enacted, that the officers for collecting and managing his Majesty's revenue, and inspecting the plantation trade, in* America, *shall have the same powers and authorities to enter houses or ware-houses, to search for and seize goods prohibited to be imported or*

exported into or out of any of the said plantations, or for which any
duties are payable, or ought to have been paid; and that like assist-
ance shall be given to the said officers in the execution of their office,
as by the said recited act of the fourteenth year of King Charles *the*
Second, is provided for the officers in England; *but, no authority*
being expressly given by the said act . . . to any particular court to
grant such writs of assistance for the officers of the customs in the
said plantations, it is doubted whether such officers can legally enter
houses or other places on land, to search for and seize goods, in the
manner directed by said recited acts: To obviate which doubts for the
future, and in order to carry the intention of the said recited acts into
effectual execution, be it enacted, and it is hereby enacted by the
authority aforesaid, That from and after the said twentieth day of
November, one thousand seven hundred and sixty seven, such writs
of assistance, to authorize and impower the officers of his Majesty's
customs to enter into and go into any house, warehouse, shop, cellar,
or other place, in the *British* colonies or plantations in *America,* to
search for and seize prohibited or uncustomed goods, in the manner
directed by the said recited acts, shall or may be granted by the
superior or supreme court of justice having jurisdiction within such
colony or plantation respectively. . . .

To collect these new duties, an accompanying measure established in America a five man board of Commissioners of the
Customs for America to superintend the enforcement of the
customs laws. Previously American customs officials had taken
their orders from the Commissioners of the Customs in London;
henceforth the new board would direct their activities from
Boston. A third measure, contemplated by Townshend but not
carried out until after his death in September, 1768, set up
four regional vice-admiralty courts. Local opposition had been
so great that few cases had been taken before the Halifax court
established under the Sugar Act of 1764; to remedy the situation, Parliament passed toward the end of 1766 an act authorizing several superior courts of vice-admiralty in place of the Halifax court. An order-in-council, in July, 1768, implemented this
legislation by establishing four regional vice-admiralty courts,
to be located at Halifax, Boston, Philadelphia, and Charleston,

each having original as well as appellate jurisdiction in its district. The machinery of enforcement was thus completed.

The American reaction was not long in coming. The Townshend duties were not unduly burdensome economically. Of the goods taxed, only tea was an important article of trade, and the drawback allowed on the re-exportation of tea to the colonies made legally imported tea cheaper than before—indeed, even cheaper than smuggled tea. But the acts came at a time of widespread colonial economic distress—a slump due in no small part to the lack of a sufficient circulating medium in the colonies. The colonies' unfavorable balance of trade with the mother country led to a continuing drain of specie, and the Currency Act of 1764 had prohibited the colonies from making paper money legal tender. The ministry had failed to carry through the promised repeal, and the already currency stringency was aggravated when the Customs Commissioners insisted upon payment of the new duties in specie. The Townshend Act was thus a further blow to colonial prosperity—and the colonists were in no mood to stand idly by.

As in the Stamp Act crisis, these economic grievances added fuel to the colonists' alarm over the political implications of the legislation. The provision that the money raised should be used to pay the salaries of royal officials and judges in those colonies "where it shall be found necessary" struck at the very basis of colonial self-government—the assemblies' power of the purse.

The news of the passage of the acts reached the colonies in September, and copies appeared in the newspapers the following month. Again Boston took the lead. Making bitter complaint about "the present distressed state of this Town, . . . which Misfortune is like to be increased by means of the late additional burthen and impositions on the Trade of this Province which threaten the Country with poverty and ruin," the Boston town meeting voted, on October 28, 1767, to take "all prudent and legal Measures" to discourage the consumption of "Foreign Superfluities" and encourage domestic manufacturers.

Although similar non-consumption agreements were adopted by town after town in New England, the movement failed to make much headway in the rest of the colonies. Switching from non-consumption to non-importation, the Boston merchants took the lead in pushing for a continent-wide non-importation agreement to force repeal of the Townshend duties. A meeting of the Boston merchants on March 4, 1768, unanimously agreed to halt importation of all goods from Britain (except those required for the fisheries) provided similar resolves "be adopted by most of the principal trading Towns in this and the neighboring colonies." The Providence merchants adopted a similar agreement on March 17, and early in April the New York merchants followed suit. But the wealthy Quaker merchants of Philadelphia balked. Rather than give in, the Boston merchants resolved to act boldly regardless of Philadelphia's inaction, and, on August 1, 1768, adopted the following resolutions:

Printed: Charles M. Andrews, "Boston Merchants and the Non-Importation Movement," Colonial Society of Massachusetts *Publications*, XIX (Boston, 1918), p. 201.

The Merchants and Traders in the Town of Boston, having taken into consideration the deplorable situation of the Trade and the many difficulties it at present labours under on account of the scarcity of money, which is daily decreasing for want of other remittances to discharge our debts in Great Britain and the large sums collected by the officers of the Customs for duties on goods imported—the heavy taxes levied to discharge the debts contracted by the governments in the late warr—the embarrassments and restrictions laid on the Trade by the several late acts of parliament, together with the bad success of our Cod Fishery this season and the discouraging prospect of the Whale Fishery by which our principal sources of Remittances are like to be greatly diminished, and we thereby rendered unable to pay the debts we owe the Merchants in Great Britain and to continue the importation of goods from thence,

We, the subscribers, in order to relieve the Trade under those discouragements, to promote industry, frugality and oeconomy and to discourage luxury and every kind of extravegance, do promise and engage to and with each other as follows.

That we will not send for or import from Great Britain this Fall, either on our own account or on commission, any other goods than what are already ordered for the Fall supply.

That we will not send for or import any kind of goods or merchandize from Great Britain, either on our own account or on commission or any otherwise, from January 1, 1769, to January 1, 1770, except salt, coals, fishhooks and lines, hemp, duck, bar-lead and shot, wool-cards and card-wire.

That we will not purchase of any factors or others any kind of goods imported from Great Britain, from January 1, 1769, to January 1, 1770.

That we will not import on our own account or on commission or purchase from any who shall import from any other colony in America from January 1, 1769, to January 1, 1770, any tea, glass, paper, or other goods commonly imported from Great Britain.

That we will not from and after January 1, 1769, import into the province any tea, paper, glass, or painters' colours until the acts imposing duties on these articles have been repealed.

On August 27, 1768, the New York merchants adopted an even more stringent agreement, which stigmatized violators as "enemies to this country." The great Quaker merchants of Philadelphia continued to delay, hoping for redress from Parliament without such drastic action. But finally on March 10, 1769, they agreed to import no goods shipped from Britain after April 1, until the Townshend duties were repealed.

The southern colonies joined in. As in the northern colonies, economic grievances spurred action. Virginia's staple crop was tobacco—an "enumerated" article that could be shipped only to Britain itself—and the planters loudly protested that the British merchants exploited their monopoly position to depress the prices paid for tobacco while overcharging for the goods bought by the planters. The governor had dissolved the House of Burgesses for resolving that "the sole right of imposing taxes on the inhabitants of his Majesty's Colony and Dominion of *Virginia*, is now, and ever hath been, legally and constitutionally vested in the House

of Burgesses"; but the members of the House still in Williamsburg met on May 18, 1769, with some merchants and pledged
not to import an extensive list of goods—including slaves—
"until the late Acts of Parliament imposing duties on Tea, Paper,
Glass, &c. for the Purpose of Raising a Revenue in *America* are
repealed."

The Charlestown, South Carolina, merchants were reluctant to
join. They, in general, were more benefited than hurt by the
laws of trade. Smuggling was unimportant, while the Townshend
duties could be passed on to their customers in the form of higher
prices. But the planters and mechanics, led by Christopher
Gadsden and his lieutenant Peter Timothy, printer of the *South
Carolina Gazette,* carried the day. Going farther than any other
colony, the South Carolinians pledged to continue their boycott
until not merely the Townshend duties, but the acts establishing
the American Board of Customs Commissioners and extending
the jurisdiction of the vice-admiralty courts were repealed.

By the autumn of 1769, non-importation agreements were in
effect in all the colonies except New Hampshire. In each, local
committees were appointed to enforce compliance, and non-
cooperating merchants were publicly blacklisted. Not merely
were the recalcitrant blacklisted; the committees did not hesitate
to use violence to enforce their will.

While pursuing these measures to force repeal of the duties, the
colonists challenged the constitutionality of Parliament's action.
The most influential attack was written by John Dickinson of
Pennsylvania. The first of Dickinson's *Letters from a Farmer in
Pennsylvania to the Inhabitants of the British Colonies* appeared
in the December 2, 1767, issue of the *Pennsylvania Chronicle
and Universal Advertiser,* and subsequent letters appeared weekly
through February 15. They were reprinted in nearly every newspaper in the colonies, and in March, 1768, were issued in pamphlet form. In rapid order, seven more editions followed in the
colonies, plus one each in London, Dublin, and France.

Dickinson started with a blunt and unequivocal "total denial of the power of Parliament to lay upon these colonies any 'tax' whatever." But he accepted for the well-being of the empire as a whole Parliament's authority to regulate trade. This raised the difficulty: what if the trade regulation produced a revenue? The crucial question, answered Dickinson, was the intention of the legislation: was the intention primarily to raise a revenue, or to regulate trade? There was no doubt that the Townshend Act belonged to the first category. What was his remedy? No revolutionist, Dickinson shrunk from "turbulence and tumult." Let the colonies first petition for redress; if that failed, "let us THEN take *Another Step,* by withholding from *Great-Britain* all the advantages she has been used to receive from us":

Printed: Paul L. Ford, ed., *The Writings of John Dickinson* [*Memoirs* of the Historical Society of Pennsylvania, XIV] (Philadelphia, 1895), pp. 277-406.

. . . The parliament unquestionably possesses a legal authority to *regulate* the trade of *Great-Britain*, and all her colonies. Such an authority is essential to the relation between a mother country and her colonies; and necessary for the common good of all. He, who considers these provinces as states distinct from the *British Empire*, has very slender notions of *justice*, or of their *interests*. We are but parts of a *whole*; and therefore there must exist a power sowewhere to preside, and preserve the connection in due order. This power is lodged in the parliament; and we are as much dependent on *Great-Britain*, as a perfectly free people can be on another.

I have looked over *every statute* relating to these colonies, from their first settlement to this time; and I find every one of them founded on this principle, till the *Stamp-Act* administration. *All before,* are calculated to regulate trade, and preserve or promote a mutually beneficial intercourse between the several constituent parts of the empire; and though many of them imposed duties on trade, yet those duties were always imposed *with design* to restrain the commerce of one part, that was injurious to another, and thus to promote the general welfare. The raising a revenue thereby was never intended.

. . . Never did the *British* parliament, till the period above mentioned, think of imposing duties in *America*, FOR THE PURPOSE OF RAISING A REVENUE. Mr. *Grenville* first introduced this language, in the preamble to the 4th of *Geo.* III., Chap. 15 [the Sugar Act]. . . . A few months after came the *Stamp-Act.* . . . The last act, granting duties upon paper, *&c.* carefully pursues these modern precedents. . . .

Here we may observe an authority *expressly* claimed and exerted to impose duties on these colonies; not for the regulation of trade; not for the preservation or promotion of a mutually beneficial intercourse between the several constituent parts of the empire, heretofore the *sole objects* of parliamentary institutions; *but for the single purpose of levying money upon us.*

This I call an innovation; and a most dangerous innovation. It may perhaps be objected, that *Great-Britain* has a right to lay what duties she pleases upon her exports, and it makes no difference to us, whether they are paid here or there.

To this I answer. These colonies require many things for their use, which the laws of *Great-Britain* prohibit them from getting any where but from her. Such are paper and glass.

That we may legally be bound to pay any *general* duties on these commodities relative to the regulation of trade, is granted; but we being *obliged by the laws* to take from *Great-Britain,* any *special* duties imposed on their exportation *to us only, with intention to raise a revenue from us only,* are as much *taxes,* upon us, as those imposed by the *Stamp-Act.*

What is the difference in *substance* and *right* whether the same sum is raised upon us by the rates mentioned in the *Stamp-Act*, on the *use* of paper, or by these duties, on the *importation* of it. It is only the edition of a former book, shifting a sentence from the *end* to the *beginning.* . . .

Here then, my dear countrymen, ROUSE yourselves, and behold the ruin hanging over your heads. If you ONCE admit, that *Great-Britain* may lay duties upon her exportations to us, *for the purpose of levying money on us only,* she then will have nothing to do, but to lay those duties on the articles which she prohibits us to manufacture—and the tragedy of *American* liberty is finished. We have been prohibited from procuring manufactures, in all cases, any where but from *Great-Britain* (excepting linens, which we are permitted to import directly from *Ireland*). We have been prohibited, in some cases, from manufacturing for ourselves; and may be prohibited in others. We are therefore exactly in the situation of a city besieged, which is surrounded by the works of the besiegers in every part *but one*. If *that* is closed up, no step can be taken, *but to surrender at discretion*. If *Great-Britain* can order us to come to her for necessaries we want, and can order us to pay what taxes she pleases before we take them away, or when we land them here, we are as abject slaves as *France* and *Poland* can shew in wooden shoes, and with uncombed hair. . . .

Sorry I am to learn, that there are some few persons, who shake their heads with solemn motion, and pretend to wonder, what can be the meaning of these letters. . . . I will now tell the gentlemen, what is, "the meaning of these letters." The meaning of them is, to convince the people of these colonies, that they are at this moment exposed to the most imminent dangers; and to persuade them immediately, vigorously, and unanimously, to exert themselves, in the most firm, but most peaceable manner, for obtaining relief.

The cause of *liberty* is a cause of too much dignity to be sullied by turbulence and tumult. It ought to be maintained in a manner suitable to her nature. Those who engage in it, should breathe a sedate, yet fervent spirit, animating them to actions of prudence, justice, modesty, bravery, humanity and magnanimity. . . .

I hope, my dear countrymen, that you will, in every colony, be upon your guard against those, who may at any time endeavour to stir you up, under pretences of patriotism, to any measures disrespectful to our Sovereign and our mother country. Hot, rash, disorderly proceedings, injure the reputation of a people, as to wisdom, valor and virtue, without procuring them the least benefit. . . .

The constitutional modes of obtaining relief, are those which I wish to see pursued on the present occasion; that is, by petitions of our assemblies, or where they are not permitted to meet, of the people, to the powers that can afford us relief.

We have an excellent prince, in whose good dispositions towards us we may confide. We have a generous, sensible and humane nation, to whom we may apply. They may be deceived. They may, by artful men, be provoked to anger against us. I cannot believe they will be cruel or unjust; or that their anger will be implacable. Let us behave like dutiful children, who have received unmerited blows from a beloved parent. Let us complain to our parent; but let our complaints speak at the same time the language of affliction and veneration.

If, however, it shall happen, by an unfortunte course of affairs, that our applications to his Majesty and the parliament for redress, prove ineffectual, let us THEN take *another step*, by withholding from *Great-Britain* all the advantages she has been used to receive from us. THEN let us try, if our ingenuity, industry, and frugality, will not give weight to our remonstrances. Let us all be united with one spirit, in one cause. . . .

An objection, I hear, has been made against my second letter, which I would willingly clear up before I proceed. "There is," say these objectors, "a material difference between the *Stamp-Act* and the *late Act* for laying a duty on paper, &c. that justifies the conduct of those who opposed the former, and yet are willing to submit to the latter. The duties imposed by the *Stamp-Act* were *internal* taxes; but the present are *external*, and therefore the parliament may have a right to impose them."

To this I answer, with a total denial of the power of parliament to lay upon these colonies any "tax" whatever.

This point, being so important to this, and to succeeding generations, I wish to be clearly understood.

To the word "*tax*," I annex that meaning which the constitution and history of *England* require to be annexed to it; that is—that it is *an imposition on the subject, for the sole purpose of levying money.* . . .

In the national, parliamentary sense insisted on, the word "tax" was certainly understood by the congress at *New-York*, whose resolves may be said to form the *American* "bill of rights."

The third, fourth, fifth, and sixth resolves, are thus expressed.

III. "That it is *inseparably essential to the freedom of a people*, and the *undoubted right* of *Englishmen*, that NO TAX be imposed on them, *but with their own consent,* given personally, or by their representatives."

IV. "That the people of the colonies are not, and from their local circumstances, cannot be represented in the house of commons in *Great-Britain*."

V. "That the only representatives of the people of the colonies, are the persons chosen therein by themselves; and that NO TAXES ever have been, or can be constitutionally imposed on them, but by their respective legislatures."

VI. "That all *supplies to the crown*, being free gifts of the people, it is *unreasonable, and inconsistent with the principles and spirit of the* British *constitution*, for the people of *Great-Britain to* grant to his Majesty *the property of the colonies.*"

Here is no distinction made between *internal* and *external* taxes. It is evident from the short reasoning thrown into these resolves, that every imposition "to grant to his Majesty *the property of the colonies*," was thought a "tax;" and that every such imposition, if laid any other way than "with their consent, given personally, or by their representatives," was not only "unreasonable, and inconsistent with the principles and spirit of the *British* constitution," but destructive "to the freedom of a people."

This language is clear and important. A "TAX" means an imposition to raise money. Such persons therefore as speak of *internal* and *external* "TAXES," I pray may pardon me, if I object to that expression, as applied to the privileges and interests of these colonies. There may be *internal* and *external* IMPOSITIONS, founded on *different principles,* and having *different tendencies,* every "tax" being an imposition, tho' every imposition is not a "tax." But *all taxes* are founded on the *same principles*; and have the *same tendency.*

External impositions, for the regulation of our trade, do not "grant to his Majesty *the property of the colonies.*" They only *prevent the colonies acquiring property,* in things not necessary, in a manner judged to be injurious to the welfare of the whole empire. But the last statute respecting us, "grants to his Majesty *the property of the colonies*," by laying duties on the manufactures of *Great-Britain* which they MUST take, and which she settled on them, on purpose that they SHOULD take.

What *tax* can be more *internal* than this? Here is money drawn, *without their consent,* from a society, who have constantly enjoyed a constitutional mode of raising all money among themselves. The payment of their *tax* they have no possible method of avoiding; as they cannot do without the commodities on which it is laid, and they cannot manufacture these commodities themselves. Besides, if this unhappy country should be so lucky as to elude this act, by getting parchment enough, in the place of paper, or by reviving the antient method of writing on wax and bark, and by inventing something to serve instead of glass, her ingenuity would stand her in little stead; for then the parliament would have nothing to do but to prohibit such manufactures, or to lay a tax on *hats* and *woollen cloths,* which they have already prohibited the colonies *from supplying each other with*; or on instruments, and tools of *steel* and *iron*, which they have prohibited the provincials *from manufacturing at all:* And then, what little gold and silver they have, must be torn from their hands, or they will not be able, in a short time, to get an ax, for cutting their firewood, nor a plough, for raising their food. In what respect, therefore, I beg leave to ask, is the late act preferable to the *Stamp-Act*, or more consistent with the liberties of the colonies? For my own part, I regard them both with equal apprehensions; and think they ought to be in the same manner opposed. . . .

It may be perhaps further objected, "that it being granted that statutes made for regulating trade, are binding upon us, it will be difficult for any person, but the makers of the laws, to determine, which of them are made for the regulating of trade, and which for raising a revenue; and that from hence may arise confusion."

To this I answer, that the objection is of no force in the present case, or such as resemble it; because the act now in question, is formed *expressly* FOR THE SOLE PURPOSE OF RAISING A REVENUE.

However, supposing the design of parliament had not been *expressed*, the objection seems to me of no weight, with regard to the influence which those who may make it, might expect it ought to have on the conduct of these colonies.

It is true, that *impositions for raising a revenue*, may be hereafter called *regulations of trade:* But names will not change the nature of things. Indeed we ought firmly to believe, what is an undoubted truth, confirmed by the unhappy experience of many states heretofore free, that UNLESS THE MOST WATCHFUL ATTENTION BE EXERTED, A NEW SERVITUDE MAY BE SLIPPED UPON US, UNDER THE SANCTION OF USUAL AND RESPECTFUL TERMS. . . .

The *nature* of any impositions laid by parliament on these colonies, must determine the *design* in laying them. It may not be easy in every instance to discover that design. Wherever it is doubtful, I think submission cannot be dangerous; nay, it must be right; for, in my opinion, there is no privilege these colonies claim, which they ought in *duty* and *prudence* more earnestly to maintain and defend, than the authority of the *British* parliament to regulate the trade of all her dominions. Without this authority, the benefits she enjoys from our commerce, must be lost to her: The blessings we enjoy from our dependence upon her, must be lost to us. Her strength must decay;

her glory vanish; and she cannot suffer without our partaking in her misfortune. *Let us therefore cherish her interests as our own, and give her every thing, that it becomes* FREEMEN *to give or to receive.*

The *nature* of any impositions she may lay upon us may, in general, be known, by considering how far they relate to the preserving, in due order, the connection between the several parts of the *British* empire. One thing we may be assured of, which is this—Whenever she imposes duties on commodities, to be paid only upon their exportation from *Great-Britain* to these colonies, it is not a regulation of trade, but a design to raise a revenue upon us. Other instances may happen, which it may not be necessary at present to dwell on. I hope these colonies will never, to their latest existence, want understanding sufficient to discover the intentions of those who rule over them, nor the resolution necessary for asserting their interests. They will always have the same rights, that all free states have, of judging when their privileges are invaded, and of using all prudent measures for preserving them. . . .

Some persons may think this act of no consequence, because the duties are so *small.* A fatal error. *That* is the very circumstance most alarming to me. For I am convinced, that the authors of this law would never have obtained an act to raise so trifling a sum as it must do, had they not intended by *it* to establish a *precedent* for future use. To console ourselves with the *smallness* of the duties, is to walk deliberately into the snare that is set for us, praising the *neatness* of the workmanship. Suppose the duties imposed by the late act could be paid by these distressed colonies with the utmost ease, and that the purposes to which they are to be applied, were the most reasonable and equitable that can be conceived, the contrary of which I hope to demonstrate before these letters are concluded; yet even in such a supposed case, these colonies ought to regard the act with abhorrence. For WHO ARE A FREE PEOPLE? Not *those*, over whom government is reasonably and equitably exercised, but *those*, who live under a government so *constitutionally checked* and *controuled*, that proper provision is made against its being otherwise exercised.

The late act is founded on the destruction of this constitutional security. If the parliament have a right to lay a duty of Four Shillings and Eight-pence on a hundred weight of glass, or a ream of paper, they have a right to lay a duty of any other sum on either. They may raise the duty . . . till it "exceeds seventeen or eighteen times the value of the commodity." In short, if they have a right *to* levy a tax of *one penny* upon us, they have a right to levy a *million* upon us: For where does their right stop? At any given number of Pence, Shillings or Pounds? To attempt to limit their right, after granting it to exist at all, is as contrary to reason—as granting it to exist at all, is contrary to justice. If *they* have any right to tax *us*—then, whether *our own money* shall continue in *our own pockets* or not, depends no longer on *us*, but on *them*. "There is nothing which" we can call our own; or, to use the words of Mr. *Locke*—"WHAT PROPERTY HAVE WE IN THAT, WHICH ANOTHER MAY, BY RIGHT, TAKE, WHEN HE PLEASES, TO HIMSELF?"

These duties, which will inevitably be levied upon us—which are now levying upon us—are *expressly* laid FOR THE SOLE PURPOSES OF TAKING MONEY. This is the true definition of "*taxes*." They are therefore *taxes*. This money is to be taken from *us*. *We* are therefore *taxed*. *Those* who are *taxed* without their own consent, expressed by themselves or their representatives, are *slaves*. *We are taxed* without our own consent, expressed by ourselves or our representatives. *We* are therefore—SLAVES. . . .

I have made some observations on the PURPOSES for which money is to be levied upon us by the late act of parliament. I shall now offer to your consideration some further reflections on that subject: And, unless I am greatly mistaken, if these purposes are accomplished according to the *expressed* intention of the act, they will be found effectually to *supersede* that authority in our respective assemblies which is essential to liberty. The question is not, whether some branches shall be lopt off—The ax is laid to the root of the tree; and the whole body must infallibly perish, if we remain idle spectators of the work.

No free people ever existed, or can ever exist, without keeping, to use a common, but strong expression, "the purse strings," in their own hands. Where this is the case, *they* have a *constitutional check* upon the administration, which may thereby be brought into order *without violence:* But where such a power is not lodged in the *people*, oppression proceeds uncontrouled in its career, till the governed, transported into rage, seek redress in the midst of blood and confusion. . . .

The inhabitants of these colonies have, on numberless occasions, reaped the benefit of this authority lodged *in their assemblies*.

It has been for a long time, and now is, a constant instruction to all governors, *to obtain a* PERMANENT *support for the offices of government*. But as the author of "the administration of the colonies" says, "this order of the crown is generally, if not universally, rejected by the legislatures of the colonies."

They perfectly know *how much* their grievances would be regarded, if they had *no other* method of engaging attention, than by *complaining*. Those who rule, are extremely apt to think well of the constructions made by themselves in support of their own power. *These* are frequently erroneous, and pernicious to those they govern. Dry remonstrances, to shew that such constructions are wrong and oppressive, carry very little weight with them, in the opinions of persons who gratify their own inclinations in making these constructions. *They* CANNOT understand the reasoning that opposes *their* power and desires. But let it be made *their interest* to understand such reasoning —and a *wonderful light* is instantly thrown upon the matter; and then, rejected remonstrances become as clear as "proofs of holy writ."

The three most important articles that our assemblies, or any legislatures can provide for, are, First—the defence of the society: Secondly—the administration of justice: And Thirdly—the support of civil government.

Nothing can properly regulate the expence of making provision for these occasions, but the *necessities* of the society; its *abilities*; the *conveniency* of the modes of levying money in it; the *manner* in which the laws have been executed: and the conduct of the officers of governments. *All which* are circumstances, that *cannot* possibly be properly *known*, but by the society itself; or if they should be known, *will not* probably be properly *considered* but by that society.

If money be raised upon us by *others*, without our consent, for our "defence," those who are the judges in *levying* it, must also be the judges in *applying* it. Of consequence the money *said* to be taken from us for our defence, *may be employed* to our injury. . . .

As to "the administration of justice"— the judges ought, in a well regulated state, to be equally independent of the executive and legislative powers. Thus in *England*, judges hold their commissions from the crown "*during good behaviour*," and have salaries, suitable to their dignity, *settled* on them by parliament. The purity of the courts of law since this establishment, is a proof of the wisdom with which it was made.

But in these colonies, how fruitless has been every attempt to have judges appointed *"during good behaviour?"* Yet whoever considers the matter will soon perceive, that *such commissions* are beyond all comparison more necessary in these colonies, than they were in *England.*

The chief danger to the subject *there,* arose from the arbitrary *designs of the crown;* but *here,* the time may come, when we may have to contend with the *designs of the crown, and of a mighty kingdom.* What then must be our chance, when the laws of life and death are to be spoken by judges totally dependent on *that crown,* and *that kingdom*—sent over perhaps *from thence*—filled with *British prejudices*—and *backed by a* STANDING *army*—supported out of OUR OWN pockets, to "assert and maintain" OUR OWN "dependence and obedience."

But supposing that through the extreme lenity that will prevail in the government *through all future ages,* these colonies will never behold any thing like the campaign of chief justice *Jeffereys,* yet what innumerable acts of unjustice may be committed, and how fatally may the principles of liberty be sapped, by a succession of julges *utterly independent of the people?* Before such judges the supple wretches, who cheerfully join in avowing sentiments inconsistent with freedom, will always meet with smiles; while the honest and brave men, who disdain to sacrifice their native land to their own advantage, but on every occasion boldly vindicate her cause, will constantly be regarded with frowns.

There are two other considerations relating to this head, that deserve the most serious attention.

By the late act, the officers of the customs are "impowered to enter into any HOUSE, warehouse, shop, cellar, or other place, in the *British* colonies or plantations in *America,* to search for or seize prohibited or unaccustomed goods," &c., on "writs granted by the superior or supreme court of justice, having jurisdiction within such colony or plantation respectively."

If we only reflect that the judges of these courts are to be *during pleasure*—that they are to have *"adequate provision"* made for them, which is to continue *during their complaisant behaviour*—that they may be *strangers* to these colonies—what an engine of oppression may this authority be in such hands? . . .

If the commissions of judges are *during the pleasure of the crown,* yet if their salaries are *during the pleasure of the people,* there will be *some check* upon their conduct. Few men will consent to draw on themselves the hatred and contempt of those among whom they live, for the empty honor of being judges. It is sordid love of gain, that tempts men to turn their backs on virtue, and pay their homage where they ought not.

As to the third particular, "the support of civil government,"—few words will be sufficient. Every man of the least understanding must know, that the *executive* power may be exercised in a manner so disagreeable and harassing to the people, that it is absolutely requisite, that *they* should be enabled by the gentlest method which human policy has yet been ingenious enough to invent, that is, *by shutting their hands,* to "ADMONISH" (as Mr. *Hume* says) certain persons "OF THEIR DUTY."

What shall we now think when, upon looking into the late act, we find the assemblies of these provinces thereby stript of their authority *on these several heads?* The *declared* intention of the act is, "that a revenue should be raised IN HIS MAJESTY'S DOMINIONS IN AMERICA, for making a more certain and adequate provision *for defraying the charge of* THE ADMINISTRATION OF JUSTICE, and *the support of* CIVIL GOVERNMENT in such provinces where it shall be found necessary, and *towards further defraying the expenses of* DEFENDING, PROTECTING AND SECURING THE SAID DOMINIONS."

Let the reader pause here one moment—and reflect—whether the colony in which *he* lives, has not made such "certain and adequate provision" *for these purposes,* as is *by the colony judged suitable to its abilities, and all other circumstances.* Then let him reflect— whether if this act takes place, money is not to be raised on *that* colony *without its consent,* to make "provision" *for these purposes,* which *it does not judge to be suitable to its abilities, and all other circumstances.* Lastly, let him reflect—whether the people of that country are not in a state of the most abject slavery, *whose property may be taken from them* under the notion of right, *when they have refused to give it.*

For my part, I think I have good reason for vindicating the honor of the assemblies on this continent, by publicly asserting, that THEY *have made as "certain and adequate provision" for the purposes abovementioned, as they ought to have made,* and that it should not be presumed, that they will not do it hereafter. Why then should *these most important trusts* be wrested out of their hands? Why should they not now be permitted to enjoy that authority, which they have exercised from the first settlement of these colonies? Why should they be scandalized by this innovation, when their respective provinces are now, and will be, for several years, labouring under loads of debt, imposed on them for the very purpose now spoken of? Why should all the inhabitants of these colonies be, with the utmost indignity, treated as a herd of despicable stupid wretches, so utterly void of common sense, that they will not even make "adequate provision" for "the administration of justice, and the support of civil government" among them, or for their own "defence"—though without such "provision" every people must inevitably be overwhelmed with anarchy and destruction? Is it possible to form an idea of a slavery more *compleat,* more *miserable,* more *disgraceful,* than that of a people, where *justice is administered, government exercised,* and a *standing army maintained,* AT THE EXPENSE OF THE PEOPLE, and yet WITHOUT THE LEAST DEPENDENCE UPON THEM? If we can find no relief from this infamous situation, it will be fortunate for us, if Mr. *Greenville,* setting his fertile fancy again at work, can, as by one exertion of it he has stript us of our *property* and *liberty,* by another deprive us of so much of our *understanding;* that, unconscious of what we *have been* or *are,* and ungoaded by tormenting reflections, we may bow down our necks, with all the stupid serenity of servitude, to any drudgery, which our lords and masters shall please to command.

When the charges of the "administration of justice," the "support of civil government," and the expenses of "defending, protecting and securing" us, are provided for, I should be glad to know, upon *what occasions* the crown will ever call our assemblies together. Some few of them may meet of their own accord, by virtue of their charters. But what will they have to do, when they are met? To what shadows will they be reduced? The men, whose deliberations heretofore had an influence on every matter relating to the *liberty* and *happiness* of themselves and their constituents, and whose authority in domestic affairs at least, might well be compared to that of *Roman* senators, will *now* find their deliberations of no more consequence, than those of *constables.* They may *perhaps* be allowed to make laws *for the yoking of hogs,* or *the pounding of stray cattle.* Their influence will hardly be permitted to extend *so high,* as the *keeping roads in repair,* as *that business* may more properly be executed by those who receive the public cash. . . .

Some persons may imagine the sums to be raised by [these duties] are but small, and therefore may be inclined to acquiesce under it. A conduct more dangerous to freedom, as before has been observed, can never be adopted. Nothing is wanted at home but a PRECEDENT, the force of which shall be established, by the tacit submission of the colonies. . . . If the parliament succeeds in this attempt, other statutes will impose other duties. Instead of taxing ourselves, as we have been accustomed to do, from the first settlement of these provinces, all our usual taxes will be converted into parliamentry taxes on our importations; and thus the parliament will levy upon us such sums of money as they chuse to take, *without any other* LIMITATION, *than their* PLEASURE. . . .

Our *vigilance* and our *union* are *success* and *safety*. Our *negligence* and our *division* are *distress* and *death*. They are *worse*—they are *shame* and *slavery*. Let us equally shun the benumbing stillness of *overweening sloath*, and the feverish activity of that *ill informed zeal*, which busies itself in maintaining *little, mean,* and *narrow* opinions. Let us, with a truly wise *generosity* and *charity*, banish and discourage all *illiberal distinctions,* which may arise from differences in *situation,* forms of *government,* or modes of *religion*. Let us consider ourselves as MEN—FREEMEN—CHRISTIAN FREEMEN—*separate from the rest of the world,* and *firmly bound together* by the *same rights, interests* and *dangers*. Let *these* keep our attention inflexibly fixed on the GREAT OBJECTS, which we must CONTINUALLY REGARD, in order to *preserve those rights,* to *promote those interests,* and to *avert those dangers*.

Let these *truths* be indelibly impressed on our minds—*that we cannot be* HAPPY, *without being* FREE—that we cannot be free, *without being secure in our property*—that *we* cannot be secure in our property, *if, without our consent, others may, as by right, take it away*—that *taxes imposed on us by parliament,* do thus take it away—that *duties laid for the sole purpose of raising money,* are taxes—that *attempts* to lay such duties *should be instantly and firmly opposed*—that this opposition can never be effectual, *unless it is the united effort of these provinces*—that therefore BENEVOLENCE *of temper towards each other,* and UNANIMITY *of councils,* are essential to the welfare of the whole—and lastly, that for this reason, every man amongst us, who in any manner would encourage either *dissension, diffidence,* or *indifference,* between these colonies, is an enemy to *himself,* and to *his country.*

. . . We have *all the rights* requisite for our prosperity. The *legal authority* of *Great-Britain* may indeed lay hard restrictions upon us; but, like the spear of *Telephus,* it will cure as well as wound. Her unkindness will instruct and compel us, after some time, to discover, in our *industry* or *frugality,* surprising remedies—*if our rights continue unviolated:* For as long as the *products* of our *labor,* and the *rewards* of our *care,* can properly be called *our own,* so long it will be worth our while to be *industrious* and *frugal.* But if when we plow—sow—reap—gather—and thresh—we find that we plow—sow —reap—gather—and thresh *for others,* whose PLEASURE is to be the SOLE LIMITATION *how much* they shall *take,* and *how much* they shall *leave,* WHY should we repeat the unprofitable toil? *Horses* and *oxen* are content with *that portion of the fruits of their work,* which their *owners* assign them, in order to keep them strong enough to raise successive crops; but even *these beasts* will not submit to draw for their *masters,* until they are *subdued* by *whips* and *goads.*

Let us take care of our *rights,* and we *therein* take care of *our prosperity.* "SLAVERY IS EVER PRECEDED BY SLEEP." . . . To discharge this double duty to *yourselves,* and to your posterity, you have nothing to do, but to call forth into use the *good sense* and *spirit* of which you are possessed. You have nothing to do, but to conduct your affairs *peaceably—prudently—firmly—jointly.* By *these means* you will support the character of *freemen,* without losing that of *faithful subjects*—a good character in any government—one of the best under a *British* government—You will *prove,* that *Americans* have that true *magnanimity* of soul, that can resent injuries, without falling into rage; and that tho' your devotion to *Great-Britain* is the most affectionate, yet you can make PROPER DISTINCTIONS, and know what you owe *to yourselves,* as well as to her—You will, at the same time that you advance your *interests,* advance your *reputation*—You will convince the world of the *justice of your demands,* and the *purity of your intentions.*—While all mankind must, with unceasing applauses, confess, that YOU indeed DESERVE liberty, who so *well understand* it, so *passionately love* it, so *temperately enjoy it,* and so *wisely, bravely,* and *virtuously assert, maintain,* and *defend* it.

"Certe ego libertatem, quæ mihi a parente meo tradita est, experiar: Verum id frustra an ob rem faciam, in vestra manu situm est, quirites."

For my part I am resolved to contend for the liberty delivered down to me by my ancestors; but whether I shall do it effectually or not, depends on you, my countrymen.

"How little soever one is able to write, yet when the liberties of one's country are threatened, it is still more difficult to be silent."

A FARMER.

Is there not the strongest probability, that if the universal sense of these colonies is immediately expressed by RESOLVES of the assemblies, in support of their rights, by INSTRUCTIONS to their agents on the subject, and by PETITIONS to the crown and parliament for redress, these measures will have the same success now, that they had in the time of the *Stamp-Act.*

D.

FINIS.

Continuing to set the pace, the Massachusetts radicals took an even bolder stand. The revival late in 1767 of the threat of an Anglican bishop for the colonies made tempers the sharper in the Bay Colony. After an initial defeat, Sam Adams and James Otis pushed through the House of Representatives passage of the following circular letter of February 11, 1768, to the other colonial assemblies:

Printed: Cushing, *The Writings of Samuel Adams,* I, pp. 184-188.

Pro of Massachusetts Bay,
Feb 11 1768

SIR,

The House of Representatives of this Province have taken into their serious Consideration, the great difficultys that must accrue to themselves & their Constituents, by the operation of several acts of Parliament imposing Duties & Taxes on the American Colonys.

As it is a Subject in which every Colony is deeply interested they have no reason to doubt but your Assembly is deeply impressed with its Importance & that such constitutional measures will be come into as are proper. It seems to be necessary, that all possible Care should be taken, that the Representations of the several Assembly upon so delicate a point, should harmonize with each other: The House therefore hope that this letter will be candidly considered in no other Light, than as expressing a Disposition freely to communicate their mind to a Sister Colony, upon a common Concern in the same manner as they would be glad to receive the Sentiments of your or any other House of Assembly on the Continent.

The House have humbly represented to the ministry, their own Sentiments that His Majesty's high Court of Parliament is the supreme legislative Power over the whole Empire: That in all free States the Constitution is fixd; & as the supreme Legislative derives its Power & Authority from the Constitution, it cannot overleap the Bounds of it without destroying its own foundation: That the Constitution ascertains & limits both Sovereignty & allegiance, & therefore, his Majestys American Subjects who acknowledge themselves bound by the Ties of Allegiance, have an equitable Claim to the full enjoymᵗ of the fundamental Rules of the British Constitution. That it is an essential unalterable Right in nature, ingrafted into the British Constitution, as a fundamental Law & ever held sacred & irrevocable by the Subjects within the Realm, that what a man has honestly acquired is absolutely his own, which he may freely give, but cannot be taken from him without his consent: That the American Subjects may therefore exclusive of any Consideration of Charter Rights, with a decent firmness adapted to the Character of free men & Subjects assert this natural and constitutional Right.

It is moreover their humble opinion, which they express with the greatest Deferrence to the Wisdom of the Parliament that the Acts made there imposing Duties on the People of this province with the sole & express purpose of raising a Revenue, are Infringments of their natural & constitutional Rights because as they are not represented in the British Parliamᵗ His Majestys Commons in Britain by those Acts grant their Property without their consent.

This House further are of Opinion that their Constituents considering their local Circumstances cannot by any possibility be represented in the Parliament, & that it will forever be impracticable that they should be equally represented there & consequently not at all; being seperated by an Ocean of a thousand leagues: and that his Majestys Royal Predecessors for this reason were graciously pleasd to form a subordinate legislature here that their subjects might enjoy the unalienable Right of a Representation. Also that considering the utter Impracticability of their ever being fully & equally represented in parliam^t, & the great Expence that must unavoidably attend even a partial representation there, this House think that a taxation of their Constituents, even without their Consent, grievous as it is, would be preferable to any Representation that could be admitted for them there.

Upon these principles, & also considering that were the right in Parliament ever so clear, yet, for obvious reasons it w^d be beyond the rules of Equity that their Constituents should be taxed on the manufactures of Great Britain here, in Addition to the dutys they pay for them in England, & other Advantages arising to G Britain from the Acts of trade, this House have preferrd a humble dutifull & loyal Petition to our most gracious Sovereign, & made such Representations to his Majestys Ministers. as they apprehended w^d tend to obtain redress.

They have also submitted to Consideration whether any People can be said to enjoy any degree of Freedom if the Crown in addition to its undoubted Authority of constituting a Govr, should also appoint him such a Stipend as it may judge proper without the Consent of the people & at their Expence; and whether while the Judges of the Land & other Civil officers hold not their Commission during good Behavior, their having salarys appointed for them by the Crown independent of the people hath not a tendency to subvert the principles of Equity & endanger the Happiness & Security of the Subject. . . .

These are the Sentiments & proceedings of this House; & as they have too much reason to believe that the Enemys of the Colonys have represented them to his Majestys Ministers & the parl^t as factious disloyal & having a disposition to make themselves independent of the Mother Country, they have taken occasion in the most humble terms to assure his Majesty & his ministers that with regard to the People of this province & as they doubt not of all the colonies the charge is unjust.

The house is fully satisfyd that your Assembly is too generous and enlargd in sentiment, to believe, that this Letter proceeds from an Ambition of taking the Lead or dictating to the other Assemblys: They freely submit their opinions to the Judgment of others, & shall take it kind in your house to point out to them any thing further which may be thought necessary.

This House cannot conclude without expressing their firm Confidence in the King our common head & Father, that the united & dutifull Supplications of his distressed American Subjects will meet with his royal & favorable Acceptance.

The circular letter brought a prompt reaction in Britain. Townshend had died in September, 1767. Chatham remained incapacitated, and the titular head of the ministry, the Duke of Grafton, was weak and indecisive. A cabinet reshuffle that December had strengthened the hand of those favoring stronger action against the colonies, and the administration of American affairs was taken from the more sympathetic Earl of Shelburne and turned over to the Earl of Hillsborough, who was appointed to the newly created post of Secretary of State for the Colonies. Hillsborough was no friend of the colonies; Connecticut agent William Samuel Johnson found him "too fond of his own opinions and systems, and too apt to be inflexibly attached to them; by no means so gentle and easy to be entreated as his predecessor in that branch of business."

Learning of the Massachusetts circular letter, Hillsborough ordered royal governors to exert their "utmost influence"— including even "immediate Prorogation or Dissolution"—to prevent their assemblies from giving "any Countenance to this Seditious Paper." As for Massachusetts itself, he instructed Governor Francis Bernard to demand that the House of Representatives rescind the letter on pain of immediate dissolution. Hillsborough's warning to the governors came too late; seven colonies gave their endorsement. Even less successful was his demand that the Massachusetts House rescind the circular letter. On June 30, 1768, the House refused by a vote of 92 to 17. "In all this," its reply declared, "we have been actuated by a conscientious, and, finally, a clear and determined sense of duty to God, to our King, our country, and our latest posterity."

Massachusetts' defiance was not limited to the passage of resolutions. The arrival of the American Board of Customs Commissioners in Boston in November, 1767, gave rise to friction between the townspeople and the customs officials. Professor Oliver Dickerson has ascribed the ill-feeling to "customs racketeering" by these officials; but even if the authorities had pursued their activities with the most scrupulous honesty, their efforts to halt illicit trade would have aroused stiff opposition. Open warfare raged on the waterfront; seized vessels were recaptured; and informers suffered the "effectual Operation" described by embittered Tory Peter Oliver:

> Printed: Douglass Adair and John A. Schutz, *Peter Oliver's Origin and Progress of the American Rebellion: A Tory View* (San Marino, Calif., 1961), p. 94.

The following is the Recipe for an effectual Operation. "First, strip a Person naked, then heat the Tar until it is thin, & pour it upon the naked Flesh, or rub it over with a Tar Brush, *quantum sufficit.* After which, sprinkle decently upon the Tar, whilst it is yet warm, as many Feathers as will stick to it. Then hold a lighted Candle to the Feathers, & try to set it all on Fire; if it will burn so much the better. But as the Experiment is often made in cold Weather; it will not then succeed—take also an Halter, & put it round the Person's Neck, & then cart him the Rounds." This is the Method, according to the first Invention. And I knew an honest man, of 60 Years of Age, who was thus disciplined in the cold Month of *March,* from nine o'clock at Night until one o'clock the next Morning, until Life was near expiring. And after a Prosecution for ye. Torture, a *Boston* Jury would not give £20 Damages.

The Commissioners themselves could not rest assured of their personal safety. A riotous demonstration by the Boston mob on the anniversary of the repeal of the Stamp Act exposed the precariousness of their situation. In response to the Commissioners' appeal for assistance, Commodore Samuel Hood, commander-in-chief of the Royal Navy in North America, sent the man-of-war *Romney* to Boston to aid in the execution of the customs laws. The *Romney* arrived in Boston on May 17; eight days earlier John Hancock's sloop *Liberty* had come into port. Emboldened by the presence of the *Romney*, the Commissioners resolved to move against the obnoxious Mr. Hancock. Hancock was one of the wealthiest merchants in the colonies, a supporter of the radical party in Massachusetts, and a man who had done much to make life unpleasant for the customs officials. On June 10, customs officials seized the vessel for loading without a permit and towed her out into the harbor under the protection of the *Romney*. Although the *Liberty* was following normal practice in loading without a permit, the customs officials took advantage of a legal technicality to make an example of Hancock. The violent reaction to the seizure, Lt. Governor Thomas Hutchinson reported to Richard Jackson, June 16, 1768, frightened the Commissioners into flight, first to the *Romney*, then behind the walls of Castle William:

Printed: George G. Wolkins, "The Seizure of John Hancock's Sloop *Liberty*," Massachusetts Historical Society *Proceedings*, LV (Boston, 1923), pp. 281-284.

June 16, 1768

I rec'd today your very kind Letter by the [torn] Pacquet designed a month sooner but by a blunder in the Post Office was sent I suppose to Boston in Lincolnshire and returned. You will be amazed at the proceedings of our people since my last. The 9 [sic] in the evening the Cust. h. Officers seizd a Sloop belong. to M^r. H. one of the Boston Rep. for making a false entry. It is said a Cargo of Mad. Wine was landed in the night and the next morn. the master entred 4 or 5 pps and swore it was the whole of her Cargo. This was the town talk for several weeks but it was supposed nobody would dare make a seizure. The Offics differd in Opinion the Collect [or] thinking she might lay at the wharffe after she had the broad arrow but the

Comptroller thot it best to move her under the Guns of the *Romney* which lay a quarter of a mile from the Shoar and made a signal for the man of war boats to come ashoar. The people upon the wharffe said there was no occasion she would ly safe and no Officer had a right to move her but the master of the Man of War cut her Moorings and carried her off. A Mob presently gathered and insulted the Custom H Offic^s and carried them in triumph as trespassers up the Wharffe tore their cloaths and bruised and otherways hurt them until one after another they escaped. The mob increased to 2 or 3000 chiefly sturdy boys and negroes and broke the windows of the Comptrollers house and then the Inspector's Williams and then went in search of the M of War's boats wch. not finding they took a boat belong^g to M^r. H. the Collector dragged her into the Common and burnt her and about one o'Clock dispersed. This was friday. Saturday and Sunday evenings are sacred. Monday it was supposed would produce something more important but in the aftern. printed tickets were put up in diff't quarters notifying the Sons of Lib. to meet the next day at 10 o'Clock at Liberty Hall or Lib. Tree which is all one to consult what was proper to be done in these times of Oppression and Distraction to preserve peace and order and maintain their Rights etc. This diverted the Evenings work but at the appointed time some thousands of the Rabble met but it being a rainy day they adjourned to Fan. Hall where a proposal was made to send the Constables to notify a legal Town meet. for the aftern. at [the] South Ch[urch] the Hall not being large eno accord. the same Convention met in the aft. under a new name and chose Otis their Moderator who after haranguing them some time from the Pulpit suffered them to harangue one another until they had agreed upon an Address to the G. the most extrad. thing that has yet appeared and appointed 21 of their number to wait on him with it and then adjourned to the next day for an Answer. The G. let them know he could not comply with what they princip[ally] desired which was to order the *Romney* out of the Harb. but should be glad to do every thing for the good of the Town, and Prov. consist. with his Duty to the Crown etc. Upon receiving this Answer they adjourned until tomorrow evn'g to consider what further measures are proper. The Commis. Hulton Burch Paxton & Robi[nson] remained pretty easy Saturday and Sunday but Mond. morning early they sent a card to the G. to let him know they were going abroad the *Romney* and desired his orders for their Recept at the Castle which he readily gave. The Collect and Comptroller and most of the other Officers of the Cust[oms] are also withdrawn and it is by no means advisable at present for any of them to return.

I have been with my family several weeks in the Country. The G. is at his house in the Country but goes to Council every day or two. Tuesday morning he sent one of his sons to me to desire me to come to him being in expect. of very import. news from Town. I went immed. when he acquainted me that he had been endeavouring all Saturday and Monday to prevail upon the C. to come into some spirited measures but all to no purpose, that when he sent his son away he was apprehensive he should receive such advices of the proceed. of the Sons of Lib. at Boston as that it would be necessary for him to withdraw but happily before my arrival he had more favorable accounts. It is now the talk among the Populace that neither the Commiss'rs nor the Comptroller shall be suffered to return to Town and just before noon today I saw a printed notification upon the Change requiring a full meet tomorrow as the fate of the Prov. and of America depended upon the measures to be then taken.

It is very natural to ask where the Justices and Sheriffs are upon these occasions. The persons who are to assist the Sheriff in the execution of his Office are Sons of Liberty and determined to oppose him in every thing which shall be contrary to their Schemes. Some of the Justices are great favourers of them and those who are not are afraid of being sacrificed by them and will issue out no warrant to apprehend them. Let an Officer behave ever so ill even if he was to abet the Disorders he ought to suppress I do not think it would be practicable to remove him seeing it cannot be done without the advice of C. and they would be afraid to give the advice. . . .

The ship was condemned in vice-admiralty court for loading without a permit on August 1. But that did not end the story. There had been rumors that the *Liberty* had carried an illicit cargo of Madeira wine, and on June 10, one of the customs officers who had supervised the unloading charged that Hancock's men had held him captive while secretly unloading the wine without paying the duty of seven pounds a tun imposed by the Sugar Act. On the basis of this testimony, the authorities filed suit in vice-admiralty court against Hancock himself for treble damages. Although the Commissioners exerted the utmost efforts to gain a conviction in disregard of all regular legal procedures and safeguards, Hancock's attorney, John Adams, so successfully refuted the prosecution that the case was finally dropped. The case made the name John Hancock famous throughout the colonies, and John Adams' eloquent attack upon admiralty court jurisdiction, and the legislative authority of Parliament in general, was widely reported in newspapers. Adams' argument for the defense was a landmark in the broadening of the colonists' attack upon parliamentary authority to include not simply taxation, but legislation adopted without their consent:

Printed: Josiah Quincy, Jr., *Reports of Cases Argued and Adjudged in the Superior Court of Judicature of the Province of Massachusetts Bay, between 1761 and 1772* (Boston, 1865), pp. 459-461.

. . . Among the Groupe of Hardships which attend this Statute [the Sugar Act], the first that ought always to be mentioned, and that ought never to be forgotten is

That it was made without our Consent. My Clyent Mr Hancock never consented to it. He never voted for it himself, and he never voted for any Man to make such a Law for him. In this Respect therefore the greatest consolation of an Englishman, suffering under any Law, is torn from him, I mean the Reflection, that it is a Law of his own Making, a Law that he sees the Necessity of for the Public. Indeed the Consent of the subject to all Laws, is so clearly necessary that no Man has yet been found hardy enough to deny it. The Patrons of these Acts allow that Consent is necessary, they only contend for a Consent by Construction, by Interpretation, a virtual Consent. But this is deluding Men with Shadows instead of Substances. Construction, has made Treason where the law has made none. Constructions . . . have always been the Instruments of arbitrary Power, the means of lulling and ensnaring Men into their own Servitude, for whenever we leave Principles and clear positive Laws, and wander after Constructions, one Construction or Consequence

is piled upon another untill we get at an immense distance from
Fact and Truth and Nature, lost in the wild Regions of Imagination
and Possibility, where arbitrary Power sitts upon her brazen Throne
and governs with an iron Scepter. It is an Hardship therefore, scarcely
to be endured that such a penal Statute, should be made to govern
a Man and his Property, without his actual Consent and only upon
such a wild Chimæra as a virtual and constructive Consent.

But there are greater Proofs of the Severity of this Statute, yet
behind. The Legislative Authority by which it was made is not only
grievous, but the Executive Courts by which it is to be carried into
Effect, is another. In the 41ˢᵗ § of this act 4 G. 3, c.15 [the Sugar
Act], we find that all forfeitures and Penalties inflicted by this or any
other Act of Parliament, relating to the Trade and Revenues of the
said British Colonies or Plantations in America, which shall be incurred there, shall and may be prosecuted, sued for, and recovered,
in any Court of Record, or *in any Court of Admiralty.* . . . Thus,
these extraordinary Penalties and Forfeitures are to be heard and
try'd,—how? Not by a Jury, not by the Law of the Land, but by
the civil Law and a Single Judge. Unlike the ancient Barons who
unâ Voce responderunt, Nolumus Leges Angliæ mutāri—The Barons
of modern Times, have answered, that they are willing, that the Laws
of England should be changed, at least with Regard to all America,
in the most tender Point, the most fundamental Principle. And this
Hardship is the more severe as we see in the same Page of the
Statute and the very preceeding §, 40, That all Penalties and Forfeitures, herein before mentioned, which shall be incurred in Great
Britain, shall be prosecuted, sued for and recovered in any of his
Majesty's Courts of Record in Westminster or in the Court of
Exchequer in Scotland respectively. Here is the Contrast that stares
us in the Face! The Parliament in one Clause guarding the People
of the Realm, and securing to them the benefit of a Tryal by the
Law of the Land, and by the next Clause, depriving all Americans
of that Privilege. What shall we say to this Distinction? Is there not
in this Clause, a Brand of Infamy, of Degradation, and Disgrace,
fixed upon every American? Is he not degraded below the Rank of
an Englishman? Is it not directly, a Repeal of the Magna Charta, as
far as America is concerned. . . .

But if the American position was hardening, so was the British.

Even before hearing the news of the rioting in Boston, Hillsborough had responded to the Commissioners' appeals for assistance by sending on June 8, a "Secret and Confidential" dispatch instructing General Gage to send "one Regiment, or such Force as you shall think necessary, to Boston, to be Quartered in that Town, and to give every legal assistance to the Civil Magistrate in the Preservation of the Public Peace; and to the Officers of the Revenue in the Execution of the laws of Trade and Revenue." On July 30, after learning of the riot, he ordered two additional regiments sent to Boston "for inducing a due Obedience to the Laws of this Kingdom."

The June 8 dispatch reached General Gage late in August, and he immediately ordered two regiments from Halifax to Boston. The news of the impending arrival of the regulars stirred a violent reaction. When Governor Bernard refused to summon the assembly, the Boston town meeting acted, and, on September 12, 1768, resolved "that no law in the Society can be binding on any Individuals, without his Consent, given by himself in Person or by his Representative of his own free Election." All the towns of the colony were urged to send delegates to a convention to decide what action to take. Adopting the subterfuge that "there is at this Time a prevailing apprehension, in the Minds of many, of an approaching War with France," the meeting closed by calling upon all citizens to provide themselves with arms:

Printed: *Boston Town Records, 1758–1769,* pp. 261-264.

The Committee appointed to take the state of our public Affairs into Consideration, Reported the following Declaration and Resolves—

Whereas it is the first Principle in Civil Society, founded in Nature and Reason, that no Law of the Society can be binding on any Individuals, without his Consent, given by himself in Person, or by his Representative of his own free Election: And whereas in and by an Act of the British Parliament passed in the First Year of the Reign of King William and Queen Mary, of glorious and blessed Memory, entitled an Act declaring the Rights and Liberties of the Subject, and Settling the Succession of the Crown. . . . It is expressly among other Things declared, That the levying Money for the use of the Crown, by Pretence of Prerogative, without Grant of Parliament for a longer Time or in other manner than the same is granted, is illegal. *And whereas* in the Third Year of the Reign of the same King William & Queen Mary, their Majestys were graciously pleased, by their Royal Charter to give and grant to the Inhabitants of His Majestys Province, all the Territory therein discribed, to be holden in free and common Soccage: And also to Ordain & Grant to the said Inhabitants certain Rights, Liberties and Privileges therein expressly mentioned; among which it is Granted established and Ordained, that all and every the Subjects of them their Heirs & Successors, which shall go to Inhabit within said Province and Territory, and every of their Children which shall happen to be born there, or on the Seas in going thither, or returning from thence, shall have & enjoy all Libertes and Immunities of free and natural Subjects, within any of the Dominions of them, their Heirs and Successors, to all intents Purposes and Constructions whatever, as if they and every of them, were born within the Realm of England. . . .

And whereas by the said Royal Charter it is specially granted to the Great & General Court or Assembly therein constituted, to impose and levy proportionable and reasonable Assessments, Rates & Taxes upon the Estates and Persons of all and every the Proprietors & Inhabitants of said Province or Territory, for the Service of the King in the necessary defence and support of his Government of this Province, & the protection and preservation of his Subjects therein, therefore

Voted, as the Opinion of this Town; that the levying Money within this Province for the use and service of the Crown, in other manner than the same is granted by the Great & General Court or Assembly of this Province is in violation of the said Royal Charter; and the same is also in violation of the undoubted natural Rights of Subjects, declared in the aforesaid Act of Parliament, freely to give and grant their own Money for the service of the Crown, with their own consent, in Person, or by Representatives of their own free Election—

And whereas in the aforesaid Act of Parliament it is declared That the raising or keeping a standing Army, within the Kingdom in time of peace, unless it be with the consent of Parliament, is against Law; It is the Opinion of this Town; that the said Declaration is founded in the indefeaseble Right of the Subjects to be *consulted;* and to give their *free Consent in Person,* or by Representatives of their own free Election to the raising & keeping a standing Army among them; and the Inhabitants of this Town being free Subjects, have the same Right derived from Nature & confermed by the British Constitution, as well as the said Royal Charter; and therefore the raising or keeping a standing Army, without their consent in Person or by Representatives of their own free Election, would be an infringement of their natural, constitutional and Charter Rights; and the employing such Army for the enforcing of Laws made without the consent of the People, in Person, or by their Representatives would be a Grievance.—

The aforegoing Report being diverse Times distinctly Read, & considered by the Town—The Question was put—Whether the same shall be accepted & recorded;—and passed unanimously in the Affermative—

Upon a Motion made and seconded, the following Votes was unanimously passed—Viz^t.—

Whereas by an Act of Parliament of the First of King William and Queen Mary, it is declared; that for the Redress of all Grieveances, and for Amending Strengthning, and preserving the Laws, Parliaments ought to be held frequently, and in as much as it is the Opinion of this Town, that the People labour under many intollerable Grievances, which unless speedily Redressed; threaten the total distruction of our invaluable natural, constitutional and Charter Rights.

And furthermore As his Excellency the Governor has declared himself unable at the Request of this Town to call a General Court, which is the Assembly of the States of this Province, for the Redress of such Grieveances;

Voted, that this Town will now make choice of a suitable number of Persons to Act for them as a Committee in Convention, with such as may be sent to Join them from the several Towns in this Province, in order that such Measures may be consulted and Advised as his Majestys service, and the peace and safety of his Subjects in this Province may require—whereupon

The Honble. James Otis Esq.

The Honble. Thomas Cushing Esq.

M^r. Samuel Adams—&

John Hancock Esq.

were appointed a Committee for the said purpose—The Town hereafter to take into Consideration what recompence shall be made
them for the service they may perform—

Voted, that the Selectmen be directed to write to the Selectmen
of the several Towns within this Province informing them of the
aforegoing Vote, and to propose that a Convention be held, if they
shall think proper at Faneuil Hall, in this Town, on Tuesday the
22^d. Day of September Instant, at 10. O'Clock Before Noon.

Upon a Motion made and seconded, the following Vote was passed
by a very great Majority—Viz^t.—

Whereas, by an Act of Parliament of the First of King William
and Queen Mary it is declared that the Subjects being Protestants,
may have Arms for their Defence; It is the Opinion of this Town,
that the said Declaration is founded in Nature Reason and sound
Policy, and is well adapted for the necessary defence of the Community—

And for as much as by a good and wholesome Law of this
Province, every listed Soldier, and other Householder (except
Troopers who by Law are to be otherwise provided) shall be always
provided with a well fixed Fire Lock Musket Accoutrement and
Ammunition as in said Law particularly mentioned, to the satisfaction of the Commission Officers of the Company; and as there is at this
Time a prevailing apprehension, in the Minds of many, of an approaching War with France: In order that the Inhabitants of this
Town may be prepared in case of sudden danger; Voted, that those of
the said Inhabitants who may at present be unprovided, be and
hereby are requested duly to observe the said Law at this Time—

Alarmed by these "Treasonable and desperate resolves," British commander-in-chief Thomas Gage prepared for open warfare. When the convention met on September 22, hotheads led
by Samuel Adams favored armed rebellion, but cooler heads
prevailed and the British troops landed on October 1, without
any resistance.

Even though the threat of armed rebellion had passed, Parliament when it met in November, 1768, was, South Carolina's

London agent reported, in the mood for strong action to vindicate its authority. Chatham had formally resigned in October,
followed by Shelburne. No longer shackled by their moderating
influence, Hillsborough was resolved, Connecticut Agent William Samuel Johnson informed Governor William Pitkin, January 3, 1769, to uphold "the supremacy and legislative authority
of Parliament":

Printed: *Trumbull Papers,* Massachusetts Historical Society
Collections, 5th Series, IX (Boston, 1885), pp. 304-312.

London, January 3, 1769.

SIR,—Parliament having now taken the usual recess for the holi-
days, and adjourned to the 19th of January, I am to acquaint you
with what has hitherto occurred relating to the Colonies. The Agents
having had various meetings, and concerted the best measures they
could devise for effecting the good purposes aimed at by their constituents, in pursuance of the plan agreed upon, among other steps
repeatedly, but separately, waited upon Lord Hilsborough to solicit
this important business. His Lordship, for some time, only entered
into general discussions upon the subject, but gave no determinate
answers, till at length he acquainted us that, it being necessary that
the matter should soon come before Parliament, a Cabinet Council
would be held to determine the measures which government would
take upon this occasion; after which, to save him the trouble of a
particular explanation with each individual, he wished us to attend
him together, which we accordingly did. He then acquainted us, that
Administration had taken the matter into consideration, and concluded to enforce the authority of the Legislature of Great Britain
over the Colonies in the most effectual manner, but to proceed therein
with all the moderation and lenity that the nature of the thing would
admit of; that all the petitions they had received were very offensive,
as containing a denial of the authority of Parliament to bind the
Colonies by their laws, though some of them were expressed in more
decent terms than others; that as to the acts complained of, they had
no particular fondness for them, and particularly the late Duty Act
was so anti-commercial that he wished it had never existed, and
it would certainly have been repealed had the Colonies said nothing

about it, or petitioned only upon the ground of its inexpediency; but that the principle they went upon equally extended to all laws whatsoever, and they could not therefore think of repealing it, at least this session of Parliament, or until the Colonies had properly submitted to the authority of Parliament and dropped the point of right; that the conduct of the people of Boston, in particular, had been such as rendered it impossible for government to recede in the least degree, or even let their proceedings pass without a severe censure, and that the matter would in a few days come before Parliament, when he hoped we should see that the sense of the Legislature was conformable to that of Administration. To this general declaration he added his usual observations in support of his general principles and the necessity of obedience on the part of the Colonies; which were again answered, and the various arguments in favor of the Colonies fully urged, by the Agents, in the course of a lengthy discussion; but he remained inflexible, and left it to the decision of Parliament. . . .

. . . The matter was first taken up in the House of Lords, when Lord Hilsborough opened the subject with a very long speech, in which he expatiated upon his affection for the Colonies and attention to their interests, the views he had in coming into that branch of administration, and his real intention to serve them to the best of his abilities; gave a history of the proceedings relative to the Stamp Act, and his own opinions with respect to it; said it had been always his opinion that nothing was more clear than the right of Parliament to tax the Colonies; but that he thought the Stamp Act was inexpedient, had advised against it when first proposed, and voted for its repeal upon that principle, as he believed almost everybody else had done; —that he hoped the repeal of that act, together with the Declaratory Act, would have established the right, at the same time that it gave peace to both countries; but was very sorry to find it had not produced that good effect;—that the Colonies, and especially the Massachusetts Bay, had gone on ever since to deny the right, and to call in question the authority of Parliament upon every occasion, and, instigated by flagitious and designing men, had carried their opinions into practice, and broke out into the most violent resistance to the laws and abuse of the King's officers, into riots and tumults destructive to all good order and legal government. And having dwelt long and largely upon this subject, and mentioned minutely the occurrences at Boston, and given a comment upon them showing their nature and tendency, he said the matter was now brought to a point; that Parliament must now give up its authority over the Colonies, or they be brought to effectual submission to its laws; that he thought their Lordships would see it absolutely necessary to stand firm, and not recede an ace; that for his part he could not entertain a thought of repealing the late acts, and hoped nobody would even move it, or so much as wish for it; that it was not the amount of the duties (which he believed would not be more than £ 8,000 or £ 10,000 per annum in all North America) that was complained of, but the principle upon which the laws were founded, the supremacy and legislative authority of Parliament,—a principle essential to the existence of the empire; that legislation and taxation were essentially connected, and would stand and fall together; that the notions the Americans entertained (which he called a polytheism in politics) were the most absurd that could be imagined, fatal to the constitution, and must never be admitted here; that, however, he wished them to proceed with moderation and temper; that he considered the North Americans in general as a very good set of people, and only misled by their leaders,—a *few* wicked, factious, and designing men (upon whom he was most severe), but who he hoped might by prudent and moderate measures be brought to a sense of their duty, and a submission to Parliamentary authority; that therefore he would, for the present, only propose to them to come to several resolutions which might show America the sense of the legislature upon this subject, and convince them of the firm purpose of this country to maintain its authority over its Colonies, by means of which he hoped they would see their error and quietly submit, in which case it would be right to give them every relief and encouragement that they could reasonably desire; that this he hoped would be sufficient, but if it was not, that the hand of power must be so lifted up, and the whole force of this country exerted to enforce its laws, and bring the Colonies into due subjection. Having largely canvassed all these topics, he finally concluded with reading his resolutions. . . .

The resolutions presented by Hillsborough condemned the resolves adopted by the Massachusetts House denying Parliament's right to tax the colonies as "proceedings of a most unwarrantable and dangerous nature, calculated to inflame the minds of his Majesty's subjects in the other colonies, tending to create unlawful combinations, repugnant to the laws of Great Britain, and subversive of the constitution." An accompanying address to the king, moved by the Duke of Bedford, head of the strongly anti-American Bedfordite faction, demanded punishment of "the chief authors and instigators of the late disorders" under a treason law dating from Henry VIII. Both the Lords and Commons approved the resolutions and the address by overwhelming margins. Thus emboldened, Hillsborough proposed even more stringent measures—the most important of which provided for automatic cancellation of the Massachusetts Charter should the assembly deny or question Parliament's authority "to bind the said Province in all Cases whatsoever."

At this juncture, however, George III, interceded to block adoption of the plan. As Sir Lewis Namier has shown, "of the measures which brought on the American conflict none was of the King's making: neither George Grenville's Stamp Act, nor the Declaratory Act of the Rockinghams, nor the Townshend Duties." But once the conflict started, George III threw himself wholeheartedly behind the cause of parliamentary supremacy. He never wavered in his belief, as he wrote the Duke of Grafton in October, 1768, that "the superiority of the mother country over her colonies must be supported." Nevertheless, he demurred at Hillsborough's drastic proposals. That program, he complained, "is of so strong a nature that it rather seems calculated to increase the unhappy feudes that subsist than to assuage them."

Other influences helped make for moderation. There were rumors of an impending war with France and Spain. The colonial non-importation agreements were having their effect. The value of exports to North America had dropped from nearly £2,500,000 in 1768 to £1,635,000 in 1769. The continuing furor over the Wilkes affair at home gave the ministers pause about "the internal state of the country." At a meeting of the cabinet on May 1, 1769, four of the nine ministers favored repeal of all the Townshend duties; but the new strong man of the cabinet, Lord North, Townshend's successor as Chancellor of the

Exchequer, cast the deciding vote for retaining the duties on tea to vindicate Parliament's authority.

Sufficient pressure at this time from British merchants and manufacturers might have swung the balance in favor of total repeal. But such pressure failed to materialize. The opening of new markets had eased the pinch of the colonial boycott, while many merchants had begun to fear that further concessions to the Americans would end in the complete overthrow of the laws of trade. Thus the ministry, William Samuel Johnson wrote Connecticut's new governor, Jonathan Trumbull, December 5, 1769, remained adamant on the constitutional question:

Printed: *Trumbull Papers,* Massachusetts Historical Society *Collections,* 5th Series, IX, pp. 382-388.

. . . Parliament having been postponed beyond its usual time of meeting, neither American affairs nor any other political matters can, you are sensible, have come to any decisive crisis. The King's Ministers, amongst the variety of schemes which have been proposed relative to that country, seem of late to have resumed and adhered to their first design of repealing the late revenue acts, so far only as they were anti-commercial, and to try the effect that would have before they proceeded farther. The apprehension of endangering the supremacy of Parliament, of which they have formed the most exalted ideas, seems to have absorbed all other considerations. They affect to imagine, that, by giving way in any measure to the claims of the Colonies, they should hazard the loss of all their hold of them; that one indulgence would require another, and one relaxation induce still farther concessions, until the Colonies would become totally independent of this country. On this idea they determined to retain such parts of the late revenue acts as were necessary to mark the subordination of the Colonies, and to rescind only so much of them as appeared to be evidently contradictory to the immediate interests of this country. The Americans, said they, claim too much; we can therefore grant them nothing upon the ground of those claims, but we will remove every impediment to the commerce of Britain, by which means we shall acquire the affections of this country, and engage their support in establishing the subordination of the Colo-

nies. Two circumstances have, more especially, encouraged them to
adhere to these ideas. The one is, that the Opposition have of late
rather lost ground. Their efforts have, in several late instances, been
unsuccessful, and of consequence the Administration found themselves strengthened, and more at liberty, and more able, to pursue
their own system of inflexibility. The other and more important consideration is this: that they found the American resolutions of non-
importation of goods had hitherto made little or no impression upon
the manufacturing and commercial part of the kingdom. That they
have not is, unfortunately, fact. This we imputed at first to the failures
of the Americans themselves in adhering to those agreements; but,
upon a more minute examination of the subject, it appears that,
though those breaches of the agreements have contributed their share,
yet a surprising and unexpected coincidence of commercial causes has
more especially prevented those resolutions from having the effects
that were expected from them. The northern war between the Turks
and Russians has occasioned a vast demand for British manufactures
in that quarter. The East India Company have exported prodigious
quantities to supply an extraordinary demand in that part of the
world. New sources of trade have arisen in Germany, and avenues for
exportation have been opened into France itself, while at home all
the supernumerary hands in the kingdom have, during the summer
past, found full employment in the vast works which are carrying on
in divers parts of the kingdom, to extend and enlarge its inland
navigation by cutting amazing canals, and, with immense labor, opening convenient communications between the principal trading towns.
These, and some other lesser causes, have for the present prevented
their feeling the decrease of the American trade; insomuch that the
manufacturers, upon application to them upon the subject of peti-
tioning, have declared that they have no cause to complain, but, in
fact, have hitherto had greater demands for goods than it was possible
for them to supply. Most of these causes are indeed temporary, but
for the present the Ministers have found themselves under no necessity to depart from their plans, or vary their measures, by any apprehensions from the manufacturers or merchants. In this situation of
things a new scene, all of a sudden, opened to us, by which the whole
face of affairs may perhaps very soon be changed. . . .

Grafton resigned as First Lord of the Treasury in January,

1770, and was succeeded by Lord North. The King had at last found the man who could manage the House of Commons while he regained his rightful place in British politics, and North would continue to head the ministry for the next ten years. On March 5, 1770, the new chief minister formally asked Parliament to repeal all the Townshend duties except that on tea, which should be retained "as a mark of the supremacy of Parliament, and an efficient declaration of their right to govern the Colonies."

But on the very same day the rising tension in the colonies broke out into bloody violence in Boston. Although the British troops had landed peacefully, friction steadily increased between the regulars and townspeople. The troops were cursed, stoned, and even spat upon. To add insult to injury, Sam Adams and his radical friends published inflammatory accounts of the troops' ill-behavior that were circulated throughout the colonies. Many of these accounts were based substantially upon fact; others were outright fabrications—but all were calculated to heighten the townspeople's antipathy toward the soldiers. The climax came on March 5, 1770, when British troops under the command of Captain Thomas Preston fired upon an abusive mob killing five persons. This incident—known to history as the Boston Massacre—threatened to ignite open hostilities between the troops and the citizenry. Governor Bernard had returned to England, leaving Lieutenant-Governor Hutchinson in charge. Acting swiftly, Hutchinson succeeded in dispersing the mob that had gathered after the shooting without more bloodshed. To prevent further clashes, Hutchinson and the British commander in town, Lieutenant Colonel Dalrymple, reluctantly acceded to the demand that the troops be withdrawn from the town and transferred to Castle Island. Captain Preston and his men were arrested and charged with murder. The Boston radicals demanded an immediate trial to take advantage of the popular excitement; but Hutchinson succeeded in postponing the trial until the fall. The arrival late in April, 1770, of the news of the repeal of the Townshend duties relieved the tension. When the trial took place, John Adams and Josiah Quincy, Jr., acted as counsel for Preston, and secured his acquittal.

The acquittal of Preston reflected the slackening of colonial excitement with the news of the repeal of the Townshend duties. The violence that had accompanied resistance to the Townshend duties had opened a cleavage between the more conservatively inclined merchants and the more radical leadership of the Sons of Liberty in the different colonies. Increasingly the Sons of Liberty drew their support from the poorer classes—the shopkeepers, mechanics, and artisans of the towns who felt the pinch of non-importation slightly or not at all. Not so the merchants: except for those profiting by smuggling, the merchants suffered heavy losses, while the riotous behavior of the more boisterous Sons of Liberty alarmed men of property everywhere.

Under the prodding of Sam Adams, the Boston merchants resolved to stand by the agreement and not "send for any goods from Great Britain until the act imposing the duty on tea" was repealed. But the New York merchants broke the solid front. Mob violence by the Sons of Liberty had led to a conservative reaction there. The reluctance of the New York merchants to continue non-importation was heightened by their not unfounded suspicions that their rivals in Boston and Philadelphia were secretly breaking the agreement. Undeterred by the "Riots, Clamour and threats" of the Sons of Liberty, the New York merchants voted early in July to resume importation of all goods except tea. The boycott was broken, and one after another of the towns followed in New York's wake.

With the breakdown of non-importation came three years of relative calm and peace. But that quiet was illusory and precarious. The retreat of the British ministry in repealing all the duties except that on tea had not resolved the clash of constitutional principles dividing colonies and mother country; instead, the years of controversy had brought a steady hardening of position on each side of the Atlantic. Watching the growing boldness and violence of the colonists, General Thomas Gage, the British commander-in-chief for North America, bitterly lamented his government's failure to take effective action to vindicate the authority of Parliament. Writing privately to Secretary at War Barrington on July 6, 1770, he complained:

Printed: Clarence E. Carter, ed., *The Correspondence of General Thomas Gage* (2 vols., New Haven, 1931–1933), II, pp. 545-547.

. . . What Measures will, or ought to be pursued with these People, I don't pretend to judge; but I am to hope, if our Councils breathe Spirit and Vigour, that nothing will be done by halves. No common Means will reduce them now to a legal Obedience and Subordination; you have tried the temper of the Council, and of the Magistrates, and you have found upon trial, that every Part of the Civil Government is of the same Leaven with the People. You have found also that lenient Measures, and the cautious and legal Exertion of the coercive Powers of Government, have served only to render them more daring and licentious. No Laws can be put in Force; for those who shou'd execute the Laws, excite the People to break them, and defend them in it. Nothing will avail in so total an Anarchy, but a very considerable Force, and that Force empower'd to act. If that is done at once, with a determined Resolution to reduce them, Matters may still end without Bloodshed. But if you pursue another Conduct, and make a Shew only of Resistance, it is the Opinion of many you will draw them into Arms. Better therefore to do Nothing. Every Body must have observed how they have gone Step by Step to their present Degree of Licentiousness, and the same Conduct towards them continued, will carry them still higher.

Suspicions were on the rise in Britain that the colonists aimed to overthrow that due subordination to the mother country which nearly all politically conscious Britons thought indispensable. Even Chatham, now partially recovered from his illness and returned to the political arena, insisted upon that. As he explained early in 1770:

Printed: *Trumbull Papers,* Massachusetts Historical Society *Collections,* 5th Series, IX, pp. 239-242.

. . . I have been thought to be, perhaps, too much the friend of America. I own I am a friend to that country. I love the Americans because they love liberty, and I love them for the noble efforts they made in the last war. But I must own I find fault with them in many things: I think they carry matters too far; they have been wrong in many respects. I think the idea of drawing money from them by taxes was ill-judged. Trade is your object with them, and they should be encouraged; those millions who keep you, who are the industrious hive employed, should be encouraged. But (I wish every sensible American, both here and in that country, heard what I say) if they carry their notions of liberty too far, as I fear they do,—if they will not be subject to the laws of this country,—especially if they would disengage themselves from the laws of trade and navigation, of which I see too many symptoms, as much of an American as I am, they have not a more determined opposer than they will find in me. They must be subordinate. In all laws relating to trade and navigation especially, this is the mother country, they are the children; they must obey, and we prescribe. It is necessary; for in these cases, between two countries so circumstanced as these two are, there must be something more than connection, there must be subordination, there must be obedience, there must be dependence; and, if you do not make laws for them, let me tell you, my lords, they do, they will, they must, make laws for you. I say this, though rather foreign to the present question, because I may not have opportunity, my health may not permit me, to explain myself again upon this subject. . . .

At the same time, the American colonists were moving to more sweeping claims. As early as 1766, Richard Bland in his *An Enquiry into the Rights of the British Colonies* argued that the colonies were joined with the mother country simply by common allegiance to the same king and hence were not subject to the Parliament at Westminster. By 1770, Benjamin Franklin had come to this same conclusion. Writing from England to Samuel Cooper, June 8, 1770, Franklin denied the "Claim of Subjects in one Part of the King's Dominions to be Sovereign over their Fellow Subjects in another Part of his Dominion":

Printed: A. H. Smyth, ed., *The Writings of Benjamin Franklin* (10 vols., New York, 1905–1907), II, pp. 259-262.

. . . That the Colonies originally were constituted distinct States, and intended to be continued such, is clear to me from a thorough Consideration of their original Charters, and the whole Conduct of the Crown and Nation towards them until the Restoration. Since that Period, the Parliament here has usurp'd an Authority of making Laws for them, which before it had not. We have for some time submitted to that Usurpation, partly through Ignorance and Inattention, and partly from our Weakness and Inability to contend: I hope, when our Rights are better understood here, we shall, by prudent and proper Conduct, be able to obtain from the Equity of this Nation a Restoration of them. And in the mean time, I could wish, that such Expressions as *the Supreme Authority of Parliament; the Subordinacy of our Assemblies to the Parliament,* and the like, (which in Reality mean nothing, if our Assemblies, with the King, have a true Legislative Authority); I say, I could wish that such Expressions were no more seen in our publick Pieces. They are too strong for Compliment, and tend to confirm a Claim of Subjects in one Part of the King's Dominions to be Sovereigns over their Fellow Subjects in another Part of his Dominions, when in truth they have no such Right, and their Claim is founded only in Usurpation, the several States having equal Rights and Liberties, and being only connected, as England and Scotland were before the Union, by having one common Sovereign, the King.

This kind of Doctrine the Lords and Commons here would deem little less than Treason against what they think their Share of the Sovereignty over the Colonies. To me those Bodies seem to have been long encroaching on the Rights of their and our Sovereign, assuming too much of his Authority, and betraying his Interests. By our Constitution he is, with his plantation Parliaments, the sole Legislator of his American Subjects, and in that Capacity is, and ought to be, free to exercise his own Judgment, unrestrained and unlimited by his Parliament here. And our Parliaments have right to grant him Aids without the Consent of this Parliament, a Circumstance, which, by the way, begins to give it some Jealousy. Let us, therefore, hold fast our Loyalty to our King, who has the best Disposition towards us, and has a Family Interest in our Prosperity; as that steady Loyalty is the most probable means of securing us from the arbitrary Power of a corrupt Parliament, that does not like us, and conceives itself to have an Interest in keeping us down and fleecing us.

If they should urge the *inconvenience* of an empire's being divided into so many separate States, and from thence conclude, that we are not so divided, I would answer, that an Inconvenience proves nothing but itself. England and Scotland were once separate States, under the same King. The Inconvenience found in their being separate States did not prove, that the Parliament of England had a right to govern Scotland. A formal Union was thought necessary, and England was a hundred Years soliciting it, before she could bring it about. If Great Britain now think such a Union necessary with us, let her propose her Terms, and we may consider them. Were the general Sentiments of this Nation to be consulted in the Case, I should hope the Terms, whether practicable or not, would at least be equitable; for I think, that, except among those with whom the spirit of Toryism prevails, the popular Inclination here is, to wish us well, and that we may preserve our Liberties.

The Massachusetts radicals had reached a similar conclusion. On July 1, 1769, the House of Representatives resolved "that no man can be taxed, or bound in Conscience to obey any Law, to which he has not given his Consent in Person, or by his Representative." Although in the resulting uproar this resolution was modified to claim no more than the sole right of imposing taxes "for the Massachusetts House," the first draft revealed the drift of colonial sentiment.

V. Boston Holds a Tea Party

WITH the breakdown of non-importation, a temporary calm descended upon the colonies. The violence of the popular agitation had frightened conservatively minded men of property. The return of prosperity dulled the edge of lower class discontent. Even though the duty on tea continued, widespread smuggling from Holland guaranteed an ample supply of the non-taxed article. The British government showed no inclination to upset the calm by any precipitate action.

But this quiet was precarious. In Massachusetts, Samuel Adams kept up his fire. Thinking Britain moving to a "total Depravation of principles and manners," he had become since at least 1768 a secret advocate of complete independence. Taking every occasion to stir men's passions, he assailed the continued taxation of tea; he railed against the activities of the customs commissioners; he fulminated against the continued presence of British troops. When by royal instruction the meeting of the Massachusetts Assembly was moved from Boston to Cambridge, Adams pushed through the House of Representatives a resolution affirming that "this House has the same inherent Rights in this Province, as the House of Commons has in Great Britain." The appointment of his arch-foe Thomas Hutchinson as royal governor was a bitter pill, and when the British ministry acted to make Hutchinson financially independent of the legislature by paying his salary from the customs revenue, Adams again sought to raise the alarm.

Nothing, however, could shake the apathy that appeared to have settled upon the populace. Then in 1772 came the rumor that judges of the Massachusetts superior court were likewise to be paid from the customs revenue. Since judges in the colonies held their commissions at pleasure rather than during good behavior as in Britain itself, an independent salary would have placed them wholly beyond local control. Brandishing the threat of a subservient judiciary, Adams forced the more hesitant "patriot" leaders into calling together the town meeting. On November 2, he pushed through a resolution for the appointment of a standing committee of correspondence "to state the Rights of the Colonists and of this Province in particular, as Men, as Christians, and as subjects; to communicate the same to the several Towns in this Province and to the World as the sense of this Town, with the Infringements and Violations thereof that have been, or from time to time may be made."

Then, on November 20, Adams won approval of the following set of resolves. Looking back in his *History,* Governor Hutchinson described these resolutions as "calculated to strike the colonists with a sense of their just claim to independence, and to stimulate them to assert it." They outlined the "Natural Rights of the Colonists as Men," "The Rights of the Colonists as Christians," and "The Rights of Colonists as Subjects." There followed a lengthy "List of Infringements and Violations of Rights": taxation without representation, the activities of the customs commissioners; the use of writs of assistance; the presence of "standing Armies in a free County in times of peace," independent salaries for the governor and judges; the extension of vice-admiralty courts; and interference in home rule through royal instructions:

Printed: *Boston Town Records, 1770–1777* (18th Report of the Boston Record Commissioners, Boston, 1887) pp. 94-106.

1ˢᵗ.   Natural Rights of the Colonists as Men.—
Among the natural Rights of the Colonists are these First. a Right to *Life*; Secondly to *Liberty*; thirdly to *Property*; together with the

Right to support and defend them in the best manner they can— Those are evident Branches of, rather than deductions from the Duty of Self Preservation, commonly called the first Law of Nature—

All Men have a Right to remain in a State of Nature as long as they please: And in case of intollerable Oppression, Civil or Religious, to leave the Society they belong to, and enter into another.—

When Men enter into Society, it is by voluntary consent; and they have a right to demand and insist upon the performance of such conditions, And previous limitations as form an equitable *original compact.*—

Every natural Right not expressly given up or from the nature of a Social Compact necessarily ceded remains.—

All positive and civil laws, should conform as far as possible, to the Law of natural reason and equity. . . .

In the state of nature men may as the *Patriarchs* did, employ hired servants for the defence of their lives, liberty and property: and they should pay them reasonable wages. Government was instituted for the purposes of common defence; and those who hold the reins of government have an equitable natural right to an honourable support from the same principle "that the labourer is worthy of his hire" but then the same community which they serve, ought to be assessors of their pay: Governors have no right to seek what they please; by this, instead of being content with the station assigned them. that of honourable servants of the society, they would soon become Absolute masters, Despots, and Tyrants. Hence as a private man has a right to say, what wages he will give in his private affairs, so has a Community to determine what they will give and grant of their Substance, for the Administration of publick affairs. And in both cases more are ready generally to offer their Service at the proposed and stipulated price, than are able and willing to perform their duty.—

In short it is the greatest absurdity to suppose it in the power of one or any number of men at the entering into society, to renounce their essential natural rights, or the means of preserving those rights when the great end of civil government from the very nature of its institution is for the support, protection and defence of those very rights: the principal of which as is before observed, are life liberty and property. If men through fear, fraud or mistake, should *in terms* renounce & give up any essential natural right, the eternal law of reason and the great end of society, would absolutely vacate such renunciation; the right to freedom being *the gift* of God Almighty, it is not in the power of Man to alienate this gift, and voluntarily become a slave—

2^d. *The Rights of the Colonists as Christians*—

These may be best understood by reading—and carefully studying the institutes of the great Lawgiver and head of the Christian Church: which are to be found closely written and promulgated in the *New Testament*—

By the Act of the British Parliament commonly called the Toleration Act, every Subject in England except Papists &^{e} was restored to, and re-established in, his natural right to worship God according to the dictates of his own conscience. And by the Charter of this Province it is granted ordained and established that it is declared as an original right) that there shall be liberty of conscience allowed in the worship of God, to all christians except Papists, inhabiting or which shall inhabit or be resident within said Province or Teritory. . . .

3^d. *The Rights of the Colonists as Subjects*

A Common Wealth or state is a body politick or civil society of men, united together to promote their mutual safety and prosperity, by means of their union

The *absolute Rights* of Englishmen, and all freemen in or out of Civil society, are principally, *personal security personal liberty* and *private property.*

All Persons born in the British American Colonies are by the laws of God and nature, and by the Common law of England, *exclusive of all charters from the Crown,* well entitled, and by Acts of the British Parliament are declared to be entitled to all the natural essential, inherent & inseperable Rights Liberties and Privileges of Subjects born in Great Britain, or within the Realm. Among those Rights are the following; which no men or body of men, consistently with their own rights as men and citizens or members of society, can for themselves give up, or take away from others

First, "The first fundamental positive law of all Common-wealths or States, is the establishing the legislative power; as the first fundamental *natural* law also, which is to govern even the legislative power itself, is the preservation of the Society."

Secondly, The Legislative has no right to absolute arbitrary power over the lives and fortunes of the people: Nor can mortals assume a prerogative, not only too high for men, but for Angels; and therefore reserved for the exercise of the *Deity* alone.——

"The Legislative cannot Justly *assume* to itself a power to rule by extempore arbitrary decrees; but it is bound to see that Justice is dispensed, and that the rights of the subjects be decided, by promulgated, standing and known laws, and authorized *independent Judges*;" that is independent as far as possible of Prince or People. *"There shall be one rule of Justice for rich and poor; for the favorite in Court, and the Countryman at the Plough."*

Thirdly, The supreme power cannot Justly take from any man, any part of his property without his consent, in person or by his Representative.—

These are some of the first principles of natural law & Justice, and the great Barriers of all free states, and of the British Constitution in particular. It is utterly irreconcileable to these principles, and to many other fundamental maxims of the common law, common sense and reason, that a British house of commons, should have a right, at pleasure, to give and grant the property of the Colonists. . . . Now what liberty can there be, where property is taken away without consent? Can it be said with any colour of truth and Justice, that this Continent of three thousand miles in length, and of a breadth as yet unexplored, in which however, its supposed, there are five millions of people, has the least voice, vote or influence in the decisions of the British Parliament? Have they, all together, any more right or power to return a single number to that house of commons, who have not inadvertently, but deliberately assumed a power to dispose of their lives, Liberties and properties, than to choose an Emperor of China! Had the Colonists a right to return members to the british parliament, it would only be hurtful; as from their local situation and circumstances it is impossible they should be ever truly and properly represented there. The inhabitants of this country in all probability in a few years will be more numerous, than those of Great Britain and Ireland together; yet it is absurdly expected by the promoters of the present measures, that these, with their posterity to all generations, should be easy while their property, shall be disposed of by a house of commons at three thousand miles distant from them; and who cannot be supposed to have the least care or concern for their real interest: Who have not only no natural care for their interest, but must be *in effect* bribed against it; as every burden they lay on the colonists is so much saved or gained to themselves. Hitherto many of the Colonists have been free from Quit Rents; but if the breath of a british house of commons can originate an act for taking away all our money, our lands will go next or be subject to rack rents from haughty and relentless landlords who will ride at ease, while we are trodden in the dirt. The Colonists have been branded with the odious names of traitors and rebels, only for complaining of their grievances; How long such treatment will, or ought to born is submitted.

A List of Infringements & Violations of Rights

We cannot help thinking, that an enumeration of some of the most open infringments of our rights, will by every candid Person be Judged sufficient to Justify whatever measures have been already taken, or may be thought proper to be taken, in order to obtain a redress of the Grievances under which we labour. Among many others we humbly conceive, that the following will not fail to excite the attention of all who consider themselves interested in the happiness and freedom of mankind in general, and of this continent and province in particular.——

1st The British Parliament have assumed the power of legislation for the Colonists in all cases whatsoever, without obtaining the consent of the Inhabitants, which is ever essentially necessary to the right establishment of such a legislative—

2^{d} They have exerted that assumed power, in raising a Revenue in the Colonies without their consent; thereby depriving them of that right which every man has to keep his own earnings in his own hands untill he shall in person, or by his Representative, think fit to part with the whole or any portion of it. . . .

3^{d} A number of new Officers, unknown in the Charter of this Province, have been appointed to superintend this Revenue, whereas by our Charter the Great & General Court or Aseembly of this Province has the sole right of appointing all civil officers, excepting only such officers, the election and constitution of whom is in said charter expressly excepted; among whom these Officers are not included.—

4th These Officers are by their Commission invested with powers altogether unconstitutional, and entirely destructive to that security which we have a right to enjoy; and to the last degree dangerous, not only to our property; but to our lives. . . .

5th Fleets and Armies have been introduced to support these unconstitutional Officers in collecting and managing this unconstitutional Revenue; and troops have been quarter'd in this Metropolis for that purpose. Introducing and quartering standing Armies in a free Country in times of peace without the consent of the people either by themselves or by their Representatives, is, and always has been deemed a violation of their rights as freemen; and of the Charter or Compact made between the King of Great Britain, and the People of this Province, whereby all the rights of British Subjects are confirmed to us.—

6th. The Revenue arising from this tax unconstitutionally laid, and committed to the management of persons arbitrarily appointed and supported by an armed force quartered in a free city, has been in part applyed to the most destructive purposes. It is absolutely necessary in a mixt government like that of this Province, that a due proportion or balance of power should be established among the several branches of legislative. . . . As it has been untill the establishment of this Revenue, the constant practise of the General Assembly to provide for the support of Government, so it is an essential part of our constitution, as it is a necessary means of preserving an *equilibrium*, without which we cannot continue a free state.—

In particular it has always been held, that the dependence of the Governor of this Province upon the General Assembly for his support, was necessary for the preservation of this *equilibrium;* nevertheless his Majesty has been pleased to apply fifteen hundred pounds sterling annually out of the American revenue, for the support of the Governor of this Province independent of the Assembly, whereby the ancient connection between him and this people is weakened, the confidence in the Governor lessened and the equilibrium destroyed, and the constitution essentially altered.—

And we look upon it highly probable from the best intelligence we have been able to obtain, that not only our Governor and Lieuetenant Governor, but the Judges of the Superior Court of Judicature, as also the Kings Attorney and Solicitor General are to receive their support from this grievous tribute. This will if accomplished compleat our slavery. For if taxes are raised from us by the Parliament of Great Britain without our consent, and the men on whose opinions and decisions our properties liberties and lives, in a great measure depend, receive their support from the Revenues arising from these taxes, we cannot, when we think on the depravity of mankind, avoid looking with horror on the danger to which we are exposed. . . .

7th. We find ourselves greatly oppressed by Instructions sent to our Governor from the Court of Great Britain, whereby the first branch of our legislature is made merely a ministerial engine. And the Province has already felt such effects from these Instructions, as we think Justly intitle us to say that they threaten an entire destruction of our liberties, and must soon, if not checked, render every branch of our Government a useless burthen upon the people. . . .

While we are mentioning the infringement of the rights of this Colony in particular by means of Instructions, we cannot help calling to remembrance the late unexampled suspension of the legislative of a Sister Colony, *New York* by force of an Instruction, untill they should comply with an Arbitrary Act of the British Parliament for quartering troops, designed by military execution, to enforce the raising of a tribute.—

8th. The extending the power of the Courts of Vice Admirality to so enormous a degree as deprives the people in the Colonies in a great measure of their inestimable right to tryals by *Juries:* which has ever been Justly considered as the grand Bulwark and security of English property.

This alone is sufficient to rouse our jealousy: And we are again obliged to take notice of the remarkable contrast, which the British Parliament have been pleased to exhibit between the Subjects in Great Britain & the Colonies. In the same Statute, by which they give up to the decision of one dependent interested Judge of Admirality the estates and properties of the Colonists, they expressly guard the estates & properties of the people of Great Britain; for all forfeitures & penalties inflicted by the Statute of George the Third, or any other Act of Parliament relative to the trade of the Colonies, may be sued for in any Court of Admiralty in the Colonies; but all penalties and forfeitures which shall be incurred in great Britain, may be sued for in any of his Majestys Courts of Record in Westminster or in the Court of Exchequer in Scotland, respectively. Thus our Birth Rights are taken from us; and that too with every mark of indignity, insult and contempt. We may be harrassed and dragged from one part of the

Continent to the other (which some of our Brethren here and in the Country Towns already have been) and finally be deprived of our whole property, by the arbitrary determination of one biassed, capricious Judge of the Admirality.—

9th. The restraining us from erecting Stilling Mills for manufacturing our Iron the natural produce of this Country, is an infringement of that right with which God and nature have invested us, to make use of our skill and industry in procuring the necessaries and conveniences of life. And we look upon the restraint laid upon the manufacture and transportation of Hatts to be altogether unreasonable and grievous. . . .

11th. As our Ancestors came over to this Country that they might not only enjoy their civil but their religeous rights, and particularly desired to be free from the Prelates, who in those times cruilly persecuted all who differed in sentiment from the established Church; we cannot see without concern the various attempts, which have been made and are now making, to establish an American Episcopate. Our Episcopal Brethren of the Colonies do enjoy, and rightfully ought ever to enjoy, the free exercise of their religeon, we cannot help fearing that they who are so warmly contending for such an establishment, have views altogether inconsistent with the universal and peaceful enjoyment of our christian privileges: And doing or attempting to do any thing which has even the remotest tendency to endanger this enjoyment, is Justly looked upon a great grievance, and also an infringement of our Rights, which is not barely to exercise, but peaceably & securely to enjoy, that liberty wherewith CHRIST has made us free.—

And we are further of Opinion, that no power on Earth can justly give either temporal or spiritual Jurisdiction within this Province, except the Great & General Court. We think therefore that every design for establishing the Jurisdiction of a Bishop in this Province, is a design both against our Civil and Religeous rights: And we are well informed, that the more candid and Judicious of our Brethren of the Church of England in this and the other Colonies, both Clergy and Laity, conceive of the establishing an American Episcopate both unnecessary and unreasonable. . . .

Copies of these resolves were sent to all the towns in the colony with an accompanying letter warning of "a constant, un-

remitted, uniform aim to enslave us" and urging that the colonists "stand firm as one man, to recover and support" their rights.
One after another the towns voted approval and set up their own
committees of correspondence to keep in touch with the Boston
body. Adams hoped to extend the committees of correspondence
throughout the colonies, but how? The salary issue was a local
matter not likely to arouse the people of the other colonies. The
impetus came from popular excitement over another incident—
the Gaspee affair.

The revenue schooner *Gaspee* under the command of Lieutenant William Dudingston had begun in March, 1772, vigorous
enforcement of the trade laws in the Narragansett Bay area of
Rhode Island. Rhode Island had long been a smuggler's paradise,
but Dudingston's overzealous efforts won him the enmity of even
legitimate traders. On June 9, 1772, while chasing a fleeing ship
up the Providence River, the *Gaspee* ran aground. That night
a mob led by wealthy merchant John Brown boarded the ship,
wounded Dudingston, and overpowered the crew, and then set
the ship afire.

The news of the outrage brought prompt action from the
mother country. On August 20, the ministry resolved "that a
commission be issued to take proceedings for the discovery of
the perpetrators of the outrage." The commission of investigation
consisted of the governor of Rhode Island, the judge of the vice-
admiralty court in Boston, and the chief justices of New York,
New Jersey, and Massachusetts. When the culprits were identi-
fied, they were to be arrested and taken to England for trial
on the charge of high treason.

The popular reaction to the news was swift. The royal commission appeared a threat to Rhode Island's nearly complete
independence of royal control. Most alarming was that the stipulation for the removal of suspects to Britain for trial. That,
complained "Americanus" in the *Providence Gazette,* Decem-

ber 26, 1772, violated the right of Englishmen to a trial by a
jury from his locality:

Printed: John R. Bartlett, ed., *Records of the Colony of
Rhode Island and Providence Plantations in New England*
(10 vols., Providence, 1856–1865), VII, pp. 112-113.

To be, or not to be, that's the question; whether our unalienable
rights and privileges are any longer worth contending for, is now to
be determined. Permit me, my countrymen, to beseech you to attend
to your alarming situation.

The stamp act you opposed with a spirit and resolution becoming
those who were truly solicitous to transmit to posterity those blessings
which our forefathers purchased for us in the wilds of America, at an
immense expense of blood and treasure.

But behold, an evil infinitely worse, in its consequences, than all the
revenue laws which have been passed from the reign of Charles the
First, to this time, now threatens this distressed, *piratically plundered*
country.

A court of inquisition, more horrid than that of Spain or Portugal,
is established within this colony, to inquire into the circumstances of
destroying the Gaspee schooner; and the persons who are the commissioners of this new-fangled court, are vested with most exorbitant
and unconstitutional power. They are directed to summon witnesses,
apprehend persons not only impeached, but even suspected! and
them, and every of them, to deliver them to Admiral Montagu, who
is ordered to have a ship in readiness to carry them to England,
where they are to be tried.

Three of the commissioners are a quorum, who are directed to
apply to General Gage, for troops to protect them in their offices, and
preserve the colony from riots and disturbances. The royal commission for these gentlemen, together with their instructions, is transmitted
to Admiral Montagu, who, upon being notified that they are con-
vened in conformity to their appointment, is to attend them, and
then deliver their commission and instructions, and to be aiding with
his sage counsel and advice, whenever necessary.

So much has transpired, respecting this alarming star-chamber
inquisition. And who among the natives of America, can hear it

without emotion? Is there an American, in whose breast there glows the smallest spark of public virtue, but who must be fired with indignation and resentment, against a measure so replete with the ruin of our free constitution? To be tried by one's peers, is the greatest privilege a subject can wish for; and so excellent is our constitution, that no subject shall be tried, but by his peers.

This establishment is the grand barrier of our lives, liberties and estates; and whoever attempts to alter or invade this fundamental principle, by which the liberties of the people have been secured from time immemorial, is a declared enemy to the welfare and happiness of the King and state. The tools of despotism and arbitrary power, have long wished that this important bulwark might be destroyed, and now have the impudence to triumph in our faces, because such of their fellow subjects in America, as are suspected of being guilty of a crime, are ordered to be transported to Great Britain for trial, in open violation of Magna Charta.

Thus are we robbed of our birth-rights and treated with every mark of indignity, insult and contempt; and can we possibly be so supine, as not to feel ourselves firmly disposed to treat the advocates for such horrid measures with a detestation and scorn, proportionate to their perfidy and baseness?

Luxury and avarice, a more fatal and cruel scourge than war, will ere long ravage Britain and ultimately bring on the dissolution of that once happy kingdom. Ambition, and a thirst for arbitrary sway, have already banished integrity, probity and every other virtue, from those who are entrusted with the government of our mother country. Her colonies loudly complain of the violences and vexations they suffer by having their moneys taken from them, without their consent, by measures more unjustifiable than highway robbery; and applied to the basest purposes,—those of supporting *tyrants* and *debauchees.* No private house is inaccessible to the avarice of custom-house officers; no place so remote whither the injustice and extortion of these miscreant tools in power, have not penetrated.

Upon the whole, it is more than probable, it is an almost absolute certainty, that, according to the present appearances, the state of an American subject, instead of enjoying the privileges of an Englishman, will soon be infinitely worse than that of a subject of France, Spain, Portugal, or any other the most despotic power on earth; so that, my countrymen, it behoves you, it is your indispensable duty to stand forth in the glorious cause of freedom, the dearest of all your earthly enjoyments; and, with a truly Roman spirit of liberty, either prevent the fastening of the infernal chains now forging for you, and your posterity, or nobly perish in the attempt.

To live a life of rational beings, is to live free; to live a life of slaves, is to die by inches. Ten thousand deaths by the halter, or the axe, are infinitely preferable to a miserable life of slavery in chains, under a pack of worse than Egyptian tyrants, whose avarice nothing less than your whole substance and income, will satisfy; and who, if they can't extort that, will glory in making a sacrifice of you and your posterity, to gratify their master the devil, who is a tyrant, and the father of tyrants and of liars. AMERICANUS.

The investigation proved a fiasco. The commissioners held two sessions, one in January, 1763, the other in May and June, 1763, without discovering any evidence as to the identity of the guilty. But when the news of this latest British invasion of colonial rights reached Virginia, the House of Burgesses, led by Thomas Jefferson, Patrick Henry, and Richard Henry Lee, adopted on March 12, 1773, a resolution assailing the commission as a threat to the colonists' "ancient, legal and constitutional Rights" and appointing a committee of correspondence "to keep up and maintain a Correspondence and Communication with our Sister Colonies."

Copies of the resolution were sent to the speakers of the other colonial assemblies. By the end of the year, all but one of the assemblies had followed the lead of Virginia and set up their own committees of correspondence—only Pennsylvania had failed to act. This development marked a critical step in the evolution of a united revolutionary front to meet any further British encroachments. At the same time, the failure of the government to punish those guilty of burning the *Gaspee* emboldened the colonial radicals. "Here is," lamented Edward Dudley, the collector of the customs for Rhode Island, "an end to security for government servants, here is an end to collecting a revenue and enforcing the Acts of Trade."

Amid all this inflammatory tinder, the British government un-wittingly provided the spark that set off the revolutionary con-flagration. The major problem facing the ministry early in 1773 was not America but the financial plight of the East India Com-pany. The Townshend Act had provided for a drawback of all duties paid upon tea entering Britain when that tea was re-exported to America, with the East India Company reimbursing the government for the loss of revenue. A second act, passed in June, 1772, when the Company was in severe financial straits, relieved the company of this burden, while reducing the draw-back to only three-fifths of the British duties. These measures were intended to make the price of legal tea in America competi-tive with that of smuggled tea; but neither succeeded in curtailing the smuggling of foreign tea into the colonies.

Faced with the impending financial collapse of the East India Company, the British government moved in the spring of 1773 to aid the Company sell its backlog of 7,000,000 pounds of tea in the colonies. To undercut the smugglers, the Company asked for removal of the Townshend duty on tea. But Lord North refused, fearing lest such an action be regarded as a surrender of Parliament's right to tax the colonies—a right which he re-garded as essential to the maintenance of the mother country's supremacy. So North tried a different tack—and on April 27, 1773, introduced in the House of Commons a bill designed to reduce the price of legally imported tea in the colonies while retaining the Townshend duty. This measure restored the draw-back of all duties paid at the British end when the tea was re-exported to America; the strikingly new feature was the per-mission granted the Company to export its tea directly to America insead of selling it at public auction in England to wholesalers.

Since the Company could sell directly to the American retailer and thus eliminate the middleman, its tea could undersell the smuggled variety. The measure passed with scant debate, and the Company secured in August a license to export 600,000 pounds of tea to America. Instead of setting up its own branches, the Company selected American firms as consignees. News of these plans provoked a furor in America. The loudest outcry came from the smugglers, whose business would be ruined if the colonists could buy legal tea more cheaply than smuggled tea. They were joined by law-abiding merchants, who assailed the measure as giving a monopoly of the market to the company and its picked agents. And the measure again brought to the forefront the question of the colonists' political rights. Here was a ruse, patriotic leaders exclaimed, by which the ministry would tax the colonies and then use the money raised to make governors and judges independent of the assemblies.

Philadelphia took the lead. A meeting on October 16, 1773, adopted the following eight resolutions attacking the tea duty as taxation without representation and denouncing anyone supporting "this ministerial plan" as "an enemy to his country":

Printed: Jensen, *English Colonial Documents,* IX, pp. 773-774.

1. That the disposal of their own property is the inherent right of freemen; that there can be no property in that which another can, of right, take from us without our consent; that the claim of Parliament to tax America is, in other words, a claim of right to levy contributions on us at pleasure.

2. That the duty imposed by Parliament upon tea landed in America is a tax on the Americans, or levying contributions on them without their consent.

3. That the express purpose for which the tax is levied on the Americans, namely, for the support of government, administration of justice, and defence of his Majesty's dominions in America, has a direct tendency to render assemblies useless and to introduce arbitrary government and slavery.

4. That a virtuous and steady opposition to this ministerial plan of governing America is absolutely necessary to preserve even the shadow of liberty and is a duty which every freeman in America owes to his country, to himself, and to his posterity.

5. That the resolutions lately entered into by the East India Company to send out their tea to America, subject to the payment of

duties on its being landed here, is an open attempt to enforce this
ministerial plan and a violent attack upon the liberties of America.

6. That it is the duty of every American to oppose this attempt.

7. That whoever shall, directly or indirectly, countenance this attempt or in any wise aid or abet in unloading, receiving, or vending
the tea sent or to be sent out by the East India Company while it
remains subject to the payment of a duty here, is an enemy to his
country.

8. That a committee be immediately chosen to wait on those gentlemen who, it is reported, are appointed by the East India Company to
receive and sell said tea and request them, from a regard to their
own characters and the peace and good order of the city and province,
immediately to resign their appointment.

The situation there, one of the Philadelphia consignees informed London, was such that "Should the tea be sent subject
to the payment of the duty I am satisfied it will not be suffered
to be landed, and that it must be returned to London."

A similar ferment was at work in New York. But it was in
Boston that the issue would come to a decisive climax. There
Governor Thomas Hutchinson resolved to enforce the tea act—a
resolve made all the stronger inasmuch as the Boston consignees
were his sons and cousin. So the stage was set for a last ditch
struggle—for Sam Adams aimed to use the issue to push Massachusetts irrevocably into revolution and independence. From the
arrival of the first tea ship, the *Dartmouth,* on November 27,
tension steadily mounted. The Boston "patriots" were determined
that the ship return to England without unloading; Hutchinson
was as determined that the tea be landed. The showdown came
on December 16. Under the law, the Dartmouth was liable to
seizure for non-payment of duties after twenty days in port—and
December 16 was the twentieth day. The townspeople feared
that if the tea were seized and landed, its sale would follow.
When Governor Hutchinson adamantly refused to permit the
vessel to sail without paying the duties, the mob took over. The
following report of what happened was written by John Andrews
to his brother-in-law, William Barrell, December 18, 1773:

Printed: "The Letters of John Andrews," Massachusetts
Historical Society *Proceedings,* First Series, VIII (Boston,
1866), pp. 325-326.

. . . A general muster was assembled, from this and all yᵉ. neighbouring towns, to the number of five or six thousand, at 10 o'clock
Thursday morning in the Old South Meeting house, where they pass'd
a *unanimous* vote that the *Tea* should go out of the *harbour* that
afternoon, and sent a committee with Mr. Rotch [the owner of the
Dartmouth] to yᵉ. Custom house to *demand* a clearance, which the
collector told 'em was not in his power to give, without the duties
being first paid. They then sent Mr. Rotch to Milton, to ask a pass
from yᵉ. Governor, who sent for answer, that "consistent with the
rules of government and his duty to the King he could not grant one
without they produc'd a previous clearance from the office."—By
the time he return'd with this message the candles were light in [the]
house, and upon reading it, such prodigious shouts were made, that
induc'd me, while drinking tea at home, to go out and know the
cause of it. The house was so crouded I could get no farther than yᵉ
porch, when I found the moderator was just declaring the meeting to
be *dissolv'd,* which caused another general shout, out doors and in,
and three cheers. What with that, and the consequent noise of breaking
up the meeting, you'd thought that the inhabitants of the infernal
regions had broke loose. For my part, I went contentedly home and
finish'd my tea, but was soon inform'd what was going forward: but
still not crediting it without ocular demonstration, I went and was
satisfied. They muster'd, I'm told, upon Fort Hill, to the number of
about two hundred, and proceeded, two by two, to Griffin's wharf,
where Hall, Bruce, and Coffin lay, each with 114 chests of the *ill
fated* article on board; the two former with *only* that article, but yᵉ.
latter arriv'd at yᵉ. wharf only yᵉ. day before, was freighted with a
large quantity of other goods, which they took the *greatest* care not
to injure in the least, and before *nine* o'clock in yᵉ. evening, every
chest from on board the three vessels was knock'd to pieces and flung
over yᵉ. sides. They say the actors were *Indians* from *Narragansett.*
Whether they were or not, to a transient observer they appear'd as
such, being cloath'd in Blankets with the heads muffled, and copper
color'd countenances, being each arm'd with a hatchet or axe, and
pair pistols, nor was their *dialect* different from what I conceive these

geniusses to *speak,* as their jargon was unintelligible to all but themselves. Not the least insult was offer'd to any person, save one Captain
Conner, a letter of horses in this place, not many years since remov'd
from *dear Ireland,* who had ript up the lining of his coat and waist-
coat under the arms, and watching his opportunity had nearly fill'd
'em with tea, but being detected, was handled pretty roughly. They
not only stripp'd him of his cloaths, but gave him a coat of mud,
with a severe bruising into the bargain; and nothing but their utter
aversion to make *any* disturbance prevented his being tar'd and
feather'd. . . .

Perhaps the best contemporaneous newspaper account of the
destruction of the tea appeared in the *Massachusetts Gazette* of
December 23, 1773:

Printed: "Tea-Party Anniversary," Massachusetts Historical Society *Proceedings,* First Series, XIII (Boston, 1875),
pp. 171-172.

Just before the dissolution of the meeting, a number of brave and
resolute men, dressed in the Indian manner, approached near the door
of the assembly, gave the war-whoop, which rang through the house,
and was answered by some in the galleries; but silence being commanded, a peaceable deportment was again enjoined till the dissolution. The Indians, as they were then called, repaired to the wharf
where the ships lay that had the tea on board, and were followed by
hundreds of people to see the event of the transactions of those who
made so grotesque an appearance. They, the Indians, immediately
repaired on board Captain Hall's ship, where they hoisted out the
chests of tea, and, when upon deck, stove the chests and emptied the
tea overboard. Having cleared this ship, they proceeded to Captain
Bruce's, and then to Captain Coffin's brig. They applied themselves
so dexterously to the destruction of this commodity that in the space
of three hours they broke up 342 chests, which was the whole number
in those vessels, and discharged their contents into the dock. When
the tide rose, it floated the broken chests and the tea, insomuch that
the surface of the water was filled therewith a considerable way from
the south part of the town to Dorchester Neck, and lodged on the

shores. There was the greatest care taken to prevent the tea from being purloined by the populace. One or two being detected in endeavoring to pocket a small quantity were stripped of their acquisitions and very roughly handled. It is worthy of remark that, although a considerable quantity of goods were still remaining on board the vessels, no injury was sustained. Such attention to private property was observed, that a small padlock belonging to the captain of one of the ships being broke, another was procured and sent to him. The town was very quiet during the whole evening and the night following. Those persons who were from the country returned with a merry heart; and the next day joy appeared in almost every countenance, some on occasion of the destruction of the tea, others on account of the quietness with which it was effected. One of the Monday's papers says, that the masters and owners are well pleased that their ships are thus cleared.

Hutchinson's stubbornness—his refusal to permit the *Dartmouth* to sail without paying the duties—coupled with Sam Adams's incendiary tactics had precipitated a major crisis. News of the Boston Tea Party provoked a wave of shock and indignation in Britain. The new Secretary of State for American Affairs, the Earl of Dartmouth, a friend of the colonies, hoped to avert military coercion, but his colleagues overbore him. The King himself demanded stern action. As he wrote Lord North, February 4, 1774:

Printed: Sir John W. Fortescue, ed., *The Correspondence of King George III from 1760 to December 1783* (6 vols., London, 1927–1928), III, p. 59.

LORD NORTH—Since You left me this day, I have seen Lieutenant General Gage, who came to express his readiness though so lately come from America to return at a day's notice if the conduct of the Colonies should induce the directing coercive measures, his language was very consonant to his Character of an honest determined Man; he says they will be Lyons, whilst we are Lambs but if we take the resolute part they will undoubtedly prove very meek; he thinks the four Regiments intended to Relieve as many Regiments in America if sent to Boston are sufficient to prevent any disturbance; I wish You would see him and hear his ideas as to the mode of compelling Boston to submit to whatever may be thought necessary; indeed all men seem now to feel that the fatal compliance in 1766. has encouraged the Americans annually to encrease in their pretensions that thorough independency which one State has of another, but which is quite subversive of the obedience which a Colony owes to its Mother Country.

Coercion it would be—with Boston the target. On March 14, 1774, Lord North introduced the Boston Port Bill for closing the port of Boston. Edmund Burke led the opposition. In an eloquent speech on March 25, he warned against the folly of coercion:

> Printed: Hansard, *Parliamentary History*, XVII, pp. 1182-1185.

. . . I never knew any thing that has given me a more heart-felt sorrow than the present measure. This Bill is attempted to be hastened through the House in such a manner, that I can by no means assent to it; it is to be carried by force and threats into execution. . . . Persons who oppose this Bill, are immediately put to the same kind of punishment in the public papers which offenders in America are. Look, Sir, into the public papers, you will see Cinna, and a thousand other Roman names, throwing out their invectives, and tarring and feathering all those who dare oppose the Bill. I suppose I shall reap my share for this opposition: but, Sir, at all events, I will enter my protest against this Bill, and will mount my little palfrey, and speak of the injustice which the Bill contains with the greatest confidence. The grievance which is stated in the papers before you on the table, appears to be an universal resistance from all America against any goods or merchandize that shall be loaded with taxes. . . . The disturbances are general; shew me one port in all America where the goods have been landed and vended; the distemper is general, but the punishment is local, by way of exchange.

Whether it will be effectual or not, I do not know; but, Sir, let me paint to this House the impropriety of a measure like this; it is a remedy of the most uncertain operation; view but the consequence, and you will repent the measure; give orders at once to your admirals to burn and destroy the town; that will be both effectual, proper, and moderate, and of a piece with the rest of your proceedings, *eventus tristis.* One town in proscription, the rest in rebellion, can never be a remedial measure for general disturbances. Have you considered whether you have troops and ships sufficient to enforce an universal proscription to the trade of the whole continent of America? If you have not, the attempt is childish, and the operation fruitless. Only, Sir, see the consequence of blocking up one port; for instance, that of Virginia Bay; which, if you do, you will destroy the tobacco trade, and thereby bring, as it were, a certain ruin on your own merchants at Glasgow and Edinburgh. This Bill has been thought a vigorous, but not a rigorous punishment. It is my opinion that you might even punish the individuals who committed the violence, without involving the innocent: I should approve much of that; but, Sir, to take away the trade from the town of Boston, is surely a severe punishment. Would it not be a rigorous measure to take away the trade of the Thames, for instance, and direct the merchandize to be landed at Gravesend? I call this Bill most unjust, for . . . this Bill involves those who have never in the least been guilty. . . .

. . . I cannot think this, by any means, a prudent measure, in blocking up one port after another; the consequence will be dreadful, and I am afraid destructive; you will draw a foreign force upon you, perhaps, at a time when you little expect it; I will not say where that will end; I will be silent upon that head, and go no further; but think, I conjure you, of the consequence. Again, Sir, in one of the clauses of the Bill you proscribe the property of the people, to be governed and measured by the will of the crown. This is a ruinous and dangerous principle to adopt. There is an universal discontent throughout all America, from an internal bad government. There are but two ways to govern America; either to make it subservient to all your laws, or to let it govern itself by its own internal policy. I abhor the measure of taxation where it is only for a quarrel, and not for a revenue; a measure that is teazing and irritating without any good effect; but a revision of this question will one day or other come, wherein I hope to give my opinion. But this is the day, then, that you wish to go to war with all America, in order to conciliate that country to this; and to say that America shall be obedient to all the laws of this country. I wish to see a new regulation and plan of a new legislation in that country, not founded upon your laws and statutes here, but grounded upon the vital principles of English liberty.

But his warning was of no avail. As Burke himself admitted,

"The popular current, both within doors and without, at present sets strongly against America." The bill passed both houses, and on March 31, was signed into law. The measure provided for keeping closed the port of Boston until "full satisfaction" was made by the inhabitants to the East India Company.

This was followed by the adoption of the Massachusetts Government Act. This law made the Massachusetts Council appointive by the king instead of elected by the House of Representatives; gave the governor authority to appoint and remove, "without the consent of the council, all judges of the inferior courts of common pleas, commissioners of *Oyer* and *Terminer*, the attorney general, provosts, marshals, justices of the peace, and other officers to the council or courts of justice belonging"; authorized the governor to appoint, "without the consent of the council," the judges of the superior court, "who shall hold their commissions during the pleasure of his Majesty"; further authorized him "to nominate and appoint the sheriffs without the consent of the council, and to remove such sheriffs with such consent, and not otherwise"; prohibited any town meeting "without leave of the governor," except the regular election meetings; and provided for the selection of jurors by the sheriffs instead of by popular election.

An accompanying measure, the Administration of Justice Act, provided for the trial "in some other of his Majesty's colonies, or in Great Britain" of any royal official in Massachusetts indicted "for murder, or other capital offense" committed in the course of carrying out his official duties when "it shall . . . appear, to the satisfaction of the . . . governor . . ., that an indifferent trial cannot be had within the said province.

A fourth act strengthened the hands of British commanders in finding suitable quarters for their troops.

A fifth act, the Quebec Act, was linked by the colonists with the other four Coercive or Intolerable Acts; but the measure had been long in preparation as a solution to the still vexing western problem. The pressure from land speculators and Indian traders, the necessity for cutting expenses, and the growing revolutionary ferment on the seaboard, had all combined to bring about a revamping of the policy outlined in the Proclamation of 1763. In a report issued March 7, 1768, the Board of Trade stressed two points: the undesirability on mercantilist grounds of encouraging settlement in the interior; and the need to concentrate the army on the seaboard and ease the financial burden upon the mother country. The report, therefore, recommended prompt completion and ratification of a definitive boundary line with the Indians. The colonies "should be required . . . to provide by proper laws for the punishment of all persons, who shall endanger the public peace of the community, by extending settlements or occupying land beyond such line." While royal officers would continue to handle political relations with the tribes, regulation of the Indian trade would be returned to the individual colonies. This change would permit the abandonment of most of the interior posts and the concentration of British troops on the seaboard.

The work of completing the new boundary line was finished by 1770. But the individual colonies failed to take the required action to regulate the Indian trade or prevent frontier troubles. By the end of 1773, the tribes were growing increasingly aroused by the unchecked depredations of land speculators and unscrupulous traders. Only the Canadians—under Governor Sir Guy Carleton—had dealt satisfactorily with the problem. Thus, as Jack Sosin has shown, the ministry determined to solve the Indian question by annexing the territory north and west of the Ohio River to Quebec.

At the same time, another consideration moved British officials. With the growing revolutionary spirit in the American colonies, the ministry felt a pressing need to assure the loyalty of the French inhabitants of Canada. Since these were not thought ready for representative institutions, the Act provided for a military governor and appointive council; but to win the loyalty of the *habitants*, French civil law was retained and Roman Catholics were given complete toleration and full legal rights.

Although later generations hailed the Quebec Act as a wise piece of statesmanship, the colonists thought differently. Western land speculators were furious at the blow to their claims in the interior. Patriots saw the provision for an appointive rather than elective legislative council as a sample of the undemocratic regime to which the ministry would subject all the colonists. Toleration for Roman Catholics excited the always present "no popery" sentiments of the colonists. John Adams set the tone: "Have not," he exclaimed, "the ministry shown, by the Quebec Bill, that we have no security against them for our religion, any more than our property, if we submit to the unlimited claims of Parliament?"

To implement these measures, the ministry appointed General Thomas Gage, the British commander-in-chief for North America, as governor of Massachusetts, with instructions to enforce "a full and absolute submission" by the colonists to "the Sovereignty of the King in His Parliament." Gage faced a formidable task. News of the Boston Port Bill reached that town on May 10, 1774. Three days later, the Boston town meeting adopted a resolution calling upon all the colonies to "come into a joint resolution, to stop all Importations from Great Britain & Exportations to Great Britain, & every part of the West Indies, till the Act for Blocking up this Harbor be repealed. . . ."

But a split became soon apparent between the more conservatively inclined merchants and the radical popular leaders. Things appeared to many men of property to be rapidly getting out of hand. "Our gentry," the wealthy and aristocratic Goveurneur Morris confessed to John Penn, May 20, 1774, had "stimulated some daring coxcombs to rouse the mob into an attack upon the bounds of order and decency" in the fight against the Stamp Act. But now "there is no ruling them." At issue, Morris saw "the future forms of our Government, whether it should be founded upon aristocratic or democratic principles. I see, and I see it with fear and trembling, that if the disputes with *Great Britain* continue, we shall be under the worst of all possible dominions; we shall be under the domination of a riotous mob. It is the interest of all men, therefore, to seek for reunion with the parent State."

Even in Boston a split appeared. The merchants wished to reimburse the East India Company; the radicals in the Boston Committee of Correspondence pushed forward a "Solemn League and Covenant" whereby subscribers pledged "that from and after the first day of *October* next ensuing, we will not . . . purchase or use any goods, wares, manufactures, or merchandise, whensoever or howsoever imported from Great Britain, until the harbors of Boston shall be opened, and our charter rights restored." The showdown came at the town meeting on June 27 and 28, when a motion was presented "for Censuring & annihilating the Committee of Correspondence." Sam Adams again carried the day—the motion was defeated "by a great majority." "A Number of the better Sort of People," General Gage wrote the Earl of Dartmouth, July 5, 1774, "attended a Town-Meeting at Boston with Design to make a Push to pay for the Tea, and annihilate the Committee of Correspondence; but they were outvoted by a great Majority of the lower Class."

The same conflict would rage up and down the continent—and nowhere more bitterly than in New York. There, a pleased Lieutenant Governor Cadwallader Colden informed Dartmouth, June 1, 1774, the merchants succeeded in maintaining the upper hand:

> Printed: E. B. O'Callaghan and B. Fernow, eds., *Documents Relative to the Colonial History of the State of New York* (15 vols., Albany, 1853–1887), VIII, pp. 433-434.

. . . The Act of Parliament shuting up the Port of Boston, was brought to this Place by a Merch' Vessell, a few Days before I received it from your Lordship's Office. The Act was immediately publish'd in all our News Papers, and was the subject of all Conversation. . . .

The Men who at that time call'd themselves the Committee—who dictated, and acted in the name of the People, were many of them, of the lower Rank and all, the warmest zealots of those call'd the Sons of Liberty.—The more considerable Merchants & Citizens seldom or never appeared among them; but I beleive were not displeased with the Clamour and Opposition that was shewn against internal Taxation by Parliament.—The Principal Inhabitants being now afraid that these hot headed men might run the City into dangerous measures, appeard in a considerable body, at the first Meeting of the People after the Boston Port Act was publish'd here.—They dissolved the former Committee, and appointed a new one of 51 Persons, in which care was taken to have a number of the most prudent and considerate People of the Place, some of them have not before join'd in the Public proceedings of the Opposition, and were induced to appear in what they are sensible is an illegal character, from a Consideration that if they did not; the Business would be left in the same rash Hands as before. . . .

The circular letter from Boston asking for a complete stoppage of trade with Britain placed the new Committee of Fifty-One in a dilemma. To agree would mean the financial ruin of the merchants; yet popular sympathy for Boston ran too high for the Committee to refuse outright. So the Committee replied on May 23, 1774, with a proposal for "a Congress of Deputies from the Colonies in general" to deal with "the alarming measures of the *British* Parliament."

Philadelphia made the same reply. There also the moderates, led by John Dickinson, retained the upper hand. On May 21— two days before the New Yorkers did so—the Philadelphia Committee of Nineteen proposed "a general Congress of deputies from the different Colonies" to petition the King. The stoppage of all trade, the Committee held, should "be reserved as our last resource, should the other fail."

The refusal of New York and Philadelphia to join in a nonimportation and non-exportation agreement forced the Massachusetts radicals to beat a partial retreat; on June 17, 1774, the Massachusetts House of Representatives formally called for "a meeting of Committees, from the Several Colonies on the Continent," to be held in Philadelphia on September 1, "to consult upon the present state of the Colonies."

By the time the First Continental Congress met at Philadelphia in September, 1774, a momentous change had taken place in the minds of the colonists. When Benjamin Franklin had, in 1770, came to the conclusion that the colonies and mother country were "so many distinct and separate states," having simply the same king, and were thus not subject to Parliament's authority, his remained a minority view. But events had led more and more colonists to the same conclusion. When early in 1773 Governor Thomas Hutchinson warned that "I know of no line that can be drawn between the supreme authority of Parliament and the total independence of the colonies," the reply of the Massachusetts House of Representatives, written largely by John Adams, did not shrink from the challenge:

> Printed: Bradford, *Speeches of the Governors of Massachusetts,* pp. 351-364.

. . . Your Excellency tells us, "you know of no line that can be drawn between the supreme authority of Parliament and the total independence of the colonies." If there be no such line, the consequence is, either that the colonies are the vassals of the Parliament, or that they are totally independent. As it cannot be supposed to have been the intention of the parties in the compact, that we should be reduced to a state of vassalage, the conclusion is, that it was their sense, that we were thus independent. "It is impossible," your Excellency says, "that there should be two independent Legislatures in one and the same state." May we not then further conclude, that it was their sense, that the colonies were, by their charters, made distinct states from the mother country? Your Excellency adds, "for although there may be but one head, the King, yet the two Legislative bodies will make two governments as distinct as the kingdoms of England and Scotland, before the union." Very true, may it please your Excellency; and if they interfere not with each other, what hinders, but that being united in one head and common Sovereign, they may live happily in that connection, and mutually support and protect each other? Notwithstanding all the terrors which your Excellency has pictured to us as the effects of a total independence, there is more reason to dread the consequences of absolute uncontroled power, whether of a nation or a monarch, than those of a total independence. It would be a misfortune "to know by experience, the difference between the liberties of an English colonist and those of the Spanish, French, and Dutch": and since the British Parliament has passed an act, which is executed even with rigor, though not voluntarily submitted to, for raising a revenue, and appropriating the same, without the consent of the people who pay it, and have claimed a power of making such laws as they please, to order and govern us, your Excellency will excuse us in asking, whether you do not think we already experience too much of such a difference, and have not reason to fear we shall soon be reduced to a worse situation than that of the colonies of France, Spain, or Holland? . . .

After all that we have said, we would be far from being understood to have in the least abated that just sense of allegiance which we owe to the King of Great Britain, our rightful Sovereign; and should the people of this province be left to the free and full exercise of all the liberties and immunities granted to them by charter, there would be no danger of an independence on the Crown. Our charters reserve great power to the Crown in its Representative, fully sufficient to balance, analogous to the English constitution, all the liberties and privileges granted to the people. All this your Excellency knows full well; and whoever considers the power and influence, in all their branches, reserved by our charter, to the Crown, will be far from thinking that the Commons of this province are too independent.

More and more, the colonists based their claims not so much on the rights they enjoyed as British subjects but on the rights belonging to all men under the law of nature. One of the most influential expositions of the argument from natural rights was James Wilson's pamphlet, *Considerations on the Nature and Extent of the Legislative Authority of the British Parliament.* The pamphlet was first written in 1768; now bringing it up to date, Wilson published it in August, 1774. His starting point was:

"All men are, by nature, equal and free"; he concluded by denying the "legislative authority of Parliament over the colonies . . .
in every instance":

Printed: James D. Andrews, ed., *The Works of James
Wilson* (2 vols., Chicago, 1896), II, pp. 501-543.

. . . Many will, perhaps, be surprised to see the legislative authority
of the British parliament over the colonies denied *in every instance*.
Those the writer informs, that, when he began this piece, he would
probably have been surprised at such an opinion himself; for that it
was the *result*, and not the *occasion*, of his disquisitions. He entered
upon them with a view and expectation of being able to trace some
constitutional line between those cases in which we ought, and those
in which we ought not, to acknowledge the power of parliament over
us. In the prosecution of his inquiries, he became fully convinced that
such a line does not exist; and that there can be no medium between
acknowledging and denying that power in *all* cases. . . .

Those who allege that the parliament of Great Britain have power
to make laws binding the American colonies, reason in the following
manner. "That there is and must be in every state a supreme, irresistible, absolute, uncontrolled authority, in which the *jura summi
imperii*, or the rights of sovereignty, reside;" "That this supreme
power is, by the constitution of Great Britain, vested in the king,
lords, and commons:" "That, therefore, the acts of the king, lords,
and commons, or, in other words, acts of parliament, have, by the
British constitution, a binding force on the American colonies, they
composing a part of the British empire."

I admit that the principle, on which this argument is founded, is of
great importance: its importance, however, is derived from its tendency to promote the ultimate end of all government. But if the application of it would, in any instance, destroy, instead of promoting, that
end, it ought, in that instance, to be rejected: for to admit it, would
be to sacrifice the end to the means, which are valuable only so far
as they advance it.

All men are, by nature, equal and free: no one has a right to any
authority over another without his consent: all lawful government is
founded on the consent of those who are subject to it: such consent

was given with a view to ensure and to increase the happiness of the governed, above what they could enjoy in an independent and unconnected state of nature. The consequence is, that the happiness of the society is the *first* law of every government.

This rule is founded on the law of nature: it must control every political maxim: it must regulate the legislature itself. . . .

Let me now be permitted to ask—Will it ensure and increase the happiness of the American colonies, that the parliament of Great Britain should possess a supreme, irresistible, uncontrolled authority over them? Is such an authority consistent with their liberty? Have they any security that it will be employed only for their good? Such a security is absolutely necessary. Parliaments are not infallible: they are not always just. The members, of whom they are composed, are human; and, therefore, they may err; they are influenced by interest; and, therefore, they may deviate from their duty. The acts of the body must depend upon the opinions and dispositions of the members: the acts of the body may, then, be the result of error and of vice. . . .

It will be very material to consider the several securities, which the inhabitants of Great Britain have, that their liberty will not be destroyed by the legislature, in whose hands it is intrusted. If it shall appear, that the same securities are not enjoyed by the colonists; the undeniable consequence will be, that the colonists are not under the same obligations to intrust their liberties into the hands of the same legislature; for the colonists are entitled to all the privileges of Britons. We have committed no crimes to forfeit them: we have too much spirit to resign them. We will leave our posterity as free as our ancestors left us.

To give to anything that passes in parliament the force of a law, the consent of the king, of the lords, and of the commons is absolutely necessary. If, then, the inhabitants of Great Britain possess a sufficient restraint upon any of these branches of the legislature, their liberty is secure, provided they be not wanting to themselves. Let us take a view of the restraints, which they have upon the house of commons.

They elect the members of that house. "Magistrates," says Montesquieu, "are properly theirs, who have the nomination of them." The members of the house of commons, therefore, elected by the people, are the magistrates of the people; and are bound by the ties of gratitude for the honor and confidence conferred upon them, to consult the interest of their constituents. . . .

. . . The interest of the representatives is the same with that of their constituents. Every measure, that is prejudicial to the nation, must be prejudicial to them and their posterity. They cannot betray their electors, without, at the same time, injuring themselves. They must join in bearing the burthen of every oppressive act; and participate in the happy effects of every wise and good law. Influenced by these considerations, they will seriously and with attention examine every measure proposed to them; they will behold it in every light, and extend their views to its most distant consequences. If, after the most mature deliberation, they find it will be conducive to the welfare of their country, they will support it with ardor: if, on the contrary, it appears to be of a dangerous and destructive nature, they will oppose it with firmness. . . .

But lest all these motives, powerful as they are, should be insufficient to animate the representatives of the nation to a vigorous and upright discharge of their duty, and to restrain them from yielding to any temptation that would incite them to betray their trust; their constituents have still a farther security for their liberties in the frequent election of parliaments. . . .

One of the most ancient maxims of the English law is, that no freeman can be taxed at pleasure. But taxes on freemen were absolutely necessary to defray the extraordinary charges of government. The consent of the freemen was, therefore, of necessity to be obtained. Numerous as they were, they could not assemble to give their consent in their proper persons; and for this reason, it was directed by the constitution, that they should give it by their representatives, chosen by and out of themselves. Hence the indisputable and peculiar privilege of the house of commons to grant taxes.

This is the source of that mild but powerful influence, which the commons of Great Britain possess over the crown. In this consists their security, that prerogative, intended for their benefit, will never be exerted for their ruin. By calmly and constitutionally refusing supplies, or by granting them only on certain conditions, they have corrected the extravagancies of some princes, and have tempered the headstrong nature of others; they have checked the progress of arbitrary power. . . .

Such is the admirable temperament of the British constitution! such the glorious fabric of Britain's liberty—the pride of her citizens—the envy of her neighbors—planned by her legislators—erected by her patriots—maintained entire by numerous generations past! may it be maintained entire by numerous generations to come!

Can the Americans, who are descended from British ancestors, and inherit all their rights, be blamed—can they be blamed *by their brethren in Britain*—for claiming still to enjoy those rights? But can they enjoy them, if they are bound by the acts of a British parliament? . . . Are the representatives of the commons of Great Britain the representatives of the Americans? Are they elected by the Americans? Are they such as the Americans, if they had the power of election, would probably elect? Do they know the interest of the Americans? Does their own interest prompt them to pursue the interest of the Americans? If they do not pursue it, have the Americans power to punish them? Can the Americans remove unfaithful members at every new election? Can members, whom the Americans do not elect; with whom the Americans are not connected in interest; whom the Americans cannot remove; over whom the Americans have no influence—can such members be styled, with any propriety, the magistrates of the Americans? Have those, who are bound by the laws of magistrates not their own, any security for the enjoyment of their absolute rights—those rights, "which every man is entitled to enjoy, whether in society or out of it?" Is it probable that those rights will be maintained? Is it "the primary end of government to maintain them?" Shall this primary end be frustrated by a political maxim intended to promote it? . . .

How would the commons of Great Britain startle at a proposal, to deprive them of their share in the legislature, by rendering the house of commons independent of them! With what indignation would they hear it! What resentment would they feel and discover against the authors of it! Yet the commons of Great Britain would suffer less inconvenience from the execution of such a proposal, than the Americans will suffer from the extension of the legislative authority of parliament over them.

The members of parliament, their families, their friends, their posterity must be subject, as well as others, to the laws. Their interest, and that of their families, friends, and posterity, cannot be different from the interest of the rest of the nation. A regard to the former will, therefore, direct to such measures as must promote the latter. But is this the case with respect to America? Are the legislators of Great Britain subject to the laws which are made for the colonies? Is their interest the same with that of the colonies? If we consider it in a large and comprehensive view, we shall discern it to be undoubtedly the same; but few will take the trouble to consider it in that view; and of those who do, few will be influenced by the consideration. Mankind are usually more affected with a near though inferior interest, than with one that is superior, but placed at a greater distance. As the conduct is regulated by the passions, it is not to be wondered at, if they secure the former, by measures which will forfeit the latter. Nay, the latter will frequently be regarded in the same manner as if it were prejudicial to them. It is with regret that I produce some late regulations of parliament as proofs of what I have advanced. We have experienced what an easy matter it is for a minister, with an ordinary share of art, to persuade the parliament and the people, that taxes laid on the colonies will ease the burthens of the mother country; which, if the matter is considered in a proper light, is, in fact, to persuade them, that the stream of national riches will be increased by closing up the fountain, from which they flow.

As the Americans cannot avail themselves of that check, which interest puts upon the members of parliament, and which would operate in favor of the commons of Great Britain, though they possessed no power over the legislature; so the love of reputation, which is a powerful incitement to the legislators to promote the welfare, and obtain the approbation, of those among whom they live, and whose praises or censures will reach and affect them, may have a contrary operation with regard to the colonies. It may become popular and reputable at home to oppress us. A candidate may recommend himself at his election by recounting the many successful instances, in which he has sacrificed the interests of America to those of Great Britain. A member of the house of commons may plume himself upon his ingenuity in inventing schemes to serve the mother country at the expense of the colonies; and may boast of their impotent resentment against him on that account.

Let us pause here a little.—Does neither the love of gain, the love of praise, nor the love of honor influence the members of the British parliament in favor of the Americans? On what principles, then—on what motives of action, can we depend for the security of our liberties, of our properties, of everything dear to us in life, of life itself? Shall we depend on their veneration for the dictates of natural justice? A very little share of experience in the world—a very little degree of knowledge in the history of men, will sufficiently convince us, that a regard to justice is by no means the ruling principle in human nature. He would discover himself to be a very sorry statesman, who would erect a system of jurisprudence upon that slender foundation. "He would make," as my Lord Bacon says, "imaginary laws for imaginary common-wealths; and his discourses, like the stars, would give little light, because they are so high."

But this is not the worst that can justly be said concerning the situation of the colonies, if they are bound by the acts of the British legislature. So far are those powerful springs of action, which we have mentioned, from interesting the members of that legislature in our favor, that, as has been already observed, we have the greatest reason to dread their operation against us. While the happy commons of Great Britain congratulate themselves upon the liberty which they enjoy, and upon the provisions—infallible, as far as they can be rendered so by human wisdom—which are made for perpetuating it to their latest posterity; the unhappy Americans have reason to bewail the dangerous situation to which they are reduced; and to look forward, with dismal apprehension, to those future scenes of woe, which, in all probability, will open upon their descendants.

What has been already advanced will suffice to show, that it is repugnant to the essential maxims of jurisprudence, to the ultimate end of all governments, to the genius of the British constitution, and to the liberty and happiness of the colonies, that they should be bound by the legislative authority of the parliament of Great Britain. . . .

I am sufficiently aware of an objection, that will be made to what I have said concerning the legislative authority of the British parliament. It will be alleged, that I throw off all dependence on Great Britain. . . . I shall take some pains to obviate the objection, and to show that a denial of the legislative authority of the British parliament over America is by no means inconsistent with that connection, which ought to subsist between the mother country and her colonies, and which, at the first settlement of those colonies, it was intended to maintain between them; but that, on the contrary, that connection would be entirely destroyed by the extension of the power of parliament over the American plantations.

Let us examine what is meant by a *dependence* on Great Britain.
. . . [It is] the obedience and loyalty which the colonists owe to the
kings of Great Britain. . . .

Dependence on the mother country seems to have been understood
in this sense, both by the first planters of the colonies, and also by the
most eminent lawyers, at that time, in England.

Those who launched into the unknown deep, in quest of new
countries and habitations, still considered themselves as subjects of
the English monarchs, and behaved suitably to that character; but it
nowhere appears, that they still considered themselves as represented
in an English parliament, or that they thought the authority of the
English parliament extended over them. They took possession of the
country in the *king's* name: they treated, or made war with the
Indians by *his* authority: they held the lands under *his* grants, and
paid *him* the rents reserved upon them: they established governments
under the sanction of *his* prerogative, or by virtue of *his* charters:—
no application for those purposes was made to the parliament: no
ratification of the charters or letters patent was solicited from that
assembly, as is usual in England with regard to grants and franchises
of much less importance. . . .

. . . The only relation, in which . . . the colonists . . . still continue,
is that of subjects: the only dependency, which they ought to acknowledge, is a dependency on the crown.

This is a dependence, which they have acknowledged hitherto;
which they acknowledge now; and which, if it is reasonable to judge
of the future by the past and the present, they will continue to
acknowledge hereafter. . . .

From this dependence, abstracted from every other source, arises
a strict connection between the inhabitants of Great Britain and those
of America. They are fellow-subjects; they are under allegiance to
the same prince; and this union of allegiance naturally produces a
union of hearts. It is also productive of a union of measures through
the whole British dominions. To the king is intrusted the direction
and management of the great machine of government. He therefore
is fittest to adjust the different wheels, and to regulate their motions
in such a manner as to co-operate in the same general designs. He
makes war: he concludes peace: he forms alliances: he regulates
domestic trade by his prerogative, and directs foreign commerce by
his treaties with those nations, with whom it is carried on. He names

the officers of government; so that he can check every jarring movement in the administration. He has a negative on the different legislatures throughout his dominions, so that he can prevent any repugnancy in their different laws.

The connection and harmony between Great Britain and us, which it is her interest and ours mutually to cultivate, and on which her prosperity, as well as ours, so materially depends, will be better preserved by the operation of the legal prerogatives of the crown, than by the exertion of an unlimited authority by parliament.

At about the same time appeared Thomas Jefferson's *A Summary View of the Rights of British America*. Jefferson had prepared the *Summary View* as a resolution to be presented for adoption when the Virginia Convention met in August, 1774, to select delegates to the forthcoming Continental Congress. When Jefferson could not attend the convention because of illness, his friends had it published as a pamphlet. Jefferson started—as did Wilson—with the rights "which nature has given to all men"; his conclusion was the same: "The British parliament has no right to exercise authority over us." But then he gave his argument a striking new twist. When the colonists had migrated to America, Jefferson contended, they had reverted to a state of nature and could adopt whatever form of government they chose. They freely chose to look upon the King of England as their sovereign, but he was bound by the compact between himself and his subjects to exercise his power for the benefit of the people. Has the King fulfilled this compact? Jefferson's answer was a lengthy recital of George III's "deviations from the line of duty." Thus in embryonic form was set forth that the compact theory of the empire which Jefferson would use in the Declaration of Independence to justify the Revolution:

Printed: Julian Boyd, ed., *The Papers of Thomas Jefferson* (16 vols. to date, Princeton, N.J., 1950-   ), I, pp. 121-136.

Resolved that it be an instruction to the said deputies when assembled in General Congress with the deputies from the other states of British America to propose to the said Congress that an humble and dutiful address be presented to his majesty begging leave to lay before him as chief magistrate of the British empire the united complaints of his majesty's subjects in America; complaints which are excited by many unwarrantable incroachments and usurpations, attempted to be made by the legislature of one part of the empire, upon those rights which god and the laws have given equally and independently to all. To represent to his majesty that these his states have often individually made humble application to his imperial throne, to obtain thro' it's intervention some redress of their injured rights; to none of which was ever even an answer condescended. Humbly to hope that this their joint address, penned in the language of truth, and divested of those expressions of servility which would persuade his majesty that we are asking favors and not rights, shall obtain from his majesty a more respectful acceptance. And this his majesty will think we have reason to expect when he reflects that he is no more than the chief officer of the people, appointed by the laws, and circumscribed with definite powers, to assist in working the great machine of government erected for their use, and consequently subject to their superintendance. And in order that these our rights, as well as the invasions of them, may be laid more fully before his majesty, to take a view of them from the origin and first settlement of these countries.

To remind him that our ancestors, before their emigration to America, were the free inhabitants of the British dominions in Europe, and possessed a right, which nature has given to all men, of departing from the country in which chance, not choice has placed them, of going in quest of new habitations, and of there establishing new societies, under such laws and regulations as to them shall seem most likely to promote public happiness. . . . That settlements having been thus effected in the wilds of America, the emigrants thought proper to adopt that system of laws under which they had hitherto lived in the mother country, and to continue their union with her by submitting themselves to the same common sovereign, who was thereby made the central link connecting the several parts of the empire thus newly multiplied.

But that not long were they permitted, however far they thought themselves removed from the hand of oppression, to hold undisturbed the rights thus acquired at the hazard of their lives and loss of their fortunes. A family of princes was then on the British throne, whose treasonable crimes against their people brought on them afterwards the exertion of those sacred and sovereign rights of punishment, re- served in the hands of the people for cases of extreme necessity, and judged by the constitution unsafe to be delegated to any other judica- ture. While every day brought forth some new and unjustifiable exer- tion of power over their subjects on that side the water, it was not to be expected that those here, much less able at that time to oppose the designs of despotism, should be exempted from injury. Accordingly that country which had been acquired by the lives, the labors and the fortunes of individual adventurers, was by these princes at several times parted out and distributed among the favorites and followers of their fortunes; and by an assumed right of the crown alone were erected into distinct and independent governments. . . .

That the exercise of a free trade with all parts of the world, pos- sessed by the American colonists as of natural right, and which no law of their own had taken away or abridged, was next the object of unjust incroachment. . . . The trade of the colonies was laid under such restrictions as shew what hopes they might form from the justice of a British parliament were its uncontrouled power admitted over these states. History has informed us that bodies of men as well as individuals are susceptible of the spirit of tyranny. A view of these acts of parliament for regulation, as it has been affectedly called, of the American trade, if all other evidence were removed out of the case, would undeniably evince the truth of this observation. Besides the duties they impose on our articles of export and import, they prohibit our going to any Markets Northward of cape Finesterra in the kingdom of Spain for the sale of commodities which Great Britain will not take from us, and for the purchase of others with which she cannot supply us; and that for no other than the arbitrary purpose of purchasing for themselves by a sacrifice of our rights and interests, certain privileges in their commerce with an allied state, who, in con- fidence that their exclusive trade with America will be continued while the principles and power of the British parliament be the same, have induldged themselves in every exorbitance which their avarice could dictate, or our necessities extort: have raised their commodities called for in America to the double and treble of what they sold for before such exclusive privileges were given them, and of what better commodities of the same kind would cost us elsewhere; and at the same time give us much less for what we carry thither, than might be had at more convenient ports. That these acts prohibit us from carrying in quest of other purchasers the surplus of our tobaccoes remaining after the consumption of Great Britain is supplied: so that we must leave them with the British merchant for whatever he will please to allow us, to be by him reshipped to foreign markets, where he will reap the benefits of making sale of them for full value. That to heighten still the idea of parliamentary justice, and to shew with what moderation they are like to exercise power, where themselves are to feel no part of it's weight, we take leave to mention to his majesty certain other acts of British parliament, by which they would prohibit us from manufacturing for our own use the articles we raise on our own lands with our own labor. . . .

. . . That we do not point out to his majesty the injustice of these acts with intent to rest on that principle the cause of their nullity, but to shew that experience confirms the propriety of those political principles which exempt us from the jurisdiction of the British parliament. The true ground on which we declare these acts void is that the British parliament has no right to exercise authority over us. . . .

That thus have we hastened thro' the reigns which preceded his majesty's, during which the violation of our rights were less alarming, because repeated at more distant intervals, than that rapid and bold succession of injuries which is likely to distinguish the present from all other periods of American story. Scarcely have our minds been able to emerge from the astonishment into which one stroke of parliamentary thunder has involved us, before another more heavy and more alarming is fallen on us. Single acts of tyranny may be ascribed to the accidental opinion of a day; but a series of oppressions, begun at a distinguished period, and pursued unalterably thro' every change of ministers, too plainly prove a deliberate, systematical plan of reducing us to slavery. . . .

. . . Not only the principles of common sense, but the common feelings of human nature must be surrendered up, before his majesty's subjects here can be persuaded to beleive that they hold their political existence at the will of a British parliament Shall these governments be dissolved, their property annihilated, and their people reduced to a state of nature, at the imperious breath of a body of men whom they never saw, in whom they never confided, and over whom they have no powers of punishment or removal, let their crimes against the American public be ever so great? Can any one reason be assigned why 160,000 electors in the island of Great Britain should give law to four millions in the states of America, every individual of whom is equal to every individual of them in virtue, in understanding, and in bodily strength? Were this to be admitted, instead of being a free people, as we have hitherto supposed, and mean to continue, ourselves, we should suddenly be found the slaves, not of one, but of 160,000 tyrants. . . .

That we next proceed to consider the conduct of his majesty, as holding the executive powers of the laws of these states, and mark out his deviations from the line of duty. . . .

. . . For the most trifling reasons, and sometimes for no conceivable reason at all, his majesty has rejected laws of the most salutary tendency. The abolition of domestic slavery is the great object of desire in those colonies where it was unhappily introduced in their infant state. But previous to the infranchisement of the slaves we have, it is necessary to exclude all further importations from Africa. Yet our repeated attempts to effect this by prohibitions, and by imposing duties which might amount to a prohibition, have been hitherto defeated by his majesty's negative: thus preferring the immediate advantages of a few British corsairs to the lasting interests of the American states, and to the rights of human nature deeply wounded by this infamous practice. Nay the single interposition of an interested individual against a law was scarcely ever known to fail of success, tho' in the opposite scale were placed the interests of a whole country. That this is so shameful an abuse of a power trusted with his majesty for other purposes, as if not reformed would call for some legal restrictions.

With equal inattention to the necessities of his people here, has his majesty permitted our laws to lie neglected in England for years, neither confirming them by his assent, nor annulling them by his negative: so that such of them as have no suspending clause, we hold on the most precarious of all tenures, his majesty's will, and such of them as suspend themselves till his majesty's assent be obtained we have feared might be called into existence at some future and distant period, when time and change of circumstances shall have rendered them destructive to his people here. And to render this grievance still more oppressive, his majesty by his instructions has laid his governors under such restrictions that they can pass no law of any moment unless it have such suspending clause: so that, however immediate may be the call for legislative interposition, the law cannot be executed till it has twice crossed the Atlantic, by which time the evil may have spent it's whole force. . . .

One of the articles of impeachment against Tresilian and the other judges of Westminster Hall in the reign of Richard the second, for which they suffered death as traitors to their country, was that they had advised the king that he might dissolve his parliament at any time: and succeeding kings have adopted the opinion of these unjust judges. Since the establishment however of the British constitution at the glorious Revolution on it's free and antient principles, neither his majesty nor his ancestors have exercised such a power of dissolution in the island of Great Britain. . . . But how different . . . his practice here! To declare as their duty required the known rights of their country, to oppose the usurpation of every foreign judicature, to disregard the imperious mandates of a minister or governor, have been the avowed causes of dissolving houses of representatives in America. . . . Your majesty or your Governors have carried this power beyond every limit known or provided for by the laws. After dissolving one house of representatives, they have refused to call another, so that for a great length of time the legislature provided by the laws has been out of existence. From the nature of things, every society must at all times possess within itself the sovereign powers of legislation. The feelings of human nature revolt against the supposition of a state so situated as that it may not in any emergency provide against dangers which perhaps threaten immediate ruin. While those bodies are in existence to whom the people have delegated the powers of legislation, they alone possess and may exercise those powers. But when they are dissolved by the lopping off one or more of their branches, the power reverts to the people, who may use it to unlimited extent, either assembling together in person, sending deputies, or in any other way they may think proper. We forbear to trace consequences further; the dangers are conspicuous with which this practice is replete.

. . . His majesty has lately taken on him to advance the terms of purchase and of holding [land] to the double of what they were, by which means the acquisition of lands being rendered difficult, the population of our country is likely to be checked. It is time therefore for us to lay this matter before his majesty, and to declare that he has no right to grant lands of himself. From the nature and purpose of civil institutions, all the lands within the limits which any particular society has circumscribed around itself, are assumed by that society, and subject to their allotment only. This may be done by themselves assembled collectively, or by their legislature to whom they may have delegated sovereign authority: and, if they are allotted in neither of these ways, each individual of the society may appropriate to himself such lands as he finds vacant, and occupancy will give him title.

That, in order to inforce the arbitrary measures before complained of, his majesty has from time to time sent among us large bodies of armed forces, not made up of the people here, nor raised by the authority of our laws. Did his majesty possess such a right as this, it might swallow up all our other rights whenever he should think proper. But his majesty has no right to land a single armed man on our shores; and those whom he sends here are liable to our laws for the suppression and punishment of Riots, Routs, and unlawful assemblies, or are hostile bodies invading us in defiance of law. When in the course of the late war it became expedient that a body of Hanoverian troops should be brought over for the defence of Great Britain, his majesty's grandfather, our late sovereign, did not pretend to introduce them under any authority he possessed. Such a measure would have given just alarm to his subjects in Great Britain, whose liberties would not be safe if armed men of another country, and of another spirit, might be brought into the realm at any time without the consent of their legislature. He therefore applied to parliament who passed an act for that purpose, limiting the number to be brought in and the time they were to continue. In like manner is his majesty restrained in every part of the empire. He possesses indeed the executive power of the laws in every state; but they are the laws of the particular state which he is to administer within that state, and not those of any one within the limits of another. Every state must judge for itself the number of armed men which they may safely trust among them, of whom they are to consist, and under what restrictions they are to be laid. To render these proceedings still more criminal against our laws, instead of subjecting the military to the civil power, his majesty has expressly made the civil subordinate to the military. But can his majesty thus put down all law under his feet? Can he erect a power superior to that which erected himself? He has done it indeed by force; but let him remember that force cannot give right.

That these are our grievances which we have thus laid before his majesty with that freedom of language and sentiment which becomes a free people, claiming their rights as derived from the laws of nature, and not as the gift of their chief magistrate. Let those flatter, who fear: it is not an American art. To give praise where it is not due, might be well from the venal, but would ill beseem those who are asserting the rights of human nature. They know, and will therefore say, that kings are the servants, not the proprietors of the people. Open your breast Sire, to liberal and expanded thought. Let not the name of George the third be a blot in the page of history. You are surrounded by British counsellors, but remember that they are parties. You have no ministers for American affairs, because you have none taken from among us, nor amenable to the laws on which they are to give you advice. It behoves you therefore to think and to act for yourself and your people. The great principles of right and wrong are legible to every reader: to pursue them requires not the aid of many counsellors. The whole art of government consists in the art of being honest. Only aim to do your duty, and mankind will give you credit where you fail. No longer persevere in sacrificing the rights of one part of the empire to the inordinate desires of another: but deal out to all equal and impartial right. Let no act be passed by any one legislature which may infringe on the rights and liberties of another. This is the important post in which fortune has placed you, holding the balance of a great, if a well poised empire. This, Sire, is the advice of your great American council, on the observance of which may perhaps depend your felicity and future fame, and the preservation of that harmony which alone can continue both to Great Britain and America the reciprocal advantages of their connection. It is neither our wish nor our interest to separate from her. We are willing on our part to sacrifice every thing which reason can ask to the restoration of that tranquility for which all must wish. On their part let them be ready to establish union on a generous plan. Let them name their terms, but let them be just. Accept of every commercial preference it is in our power to give for such things as we can raise for their use, or they make for ours. But let them not think to exclude us from going to other markets, to dispose of those commodities which they cannot use, nor to supply those wants which they cannot supply. Still less let it be proposed that our properties within our own territories shall be taxed or regulated by any power on earth but our own. The god who gave us life, gave us liberty at the same time: the hand of force may destroy, but cannot disjoin them. This, Sire, is our last, our determined resolution: and that you will be pleased to interpose with that efficacy which your earnest endeavors may insure to procure redress of these our great grievances, to quiet the minds of your subjects in British America against any apprehensions of future incroachment, to establish fraternal love and harmony thro' the whole empire, and that that may continue to the latest ages of time, is the fervent prayer of all British America.

But not all the delegates at the Virginia Convention were ready to go so far. When the *Summary View* was placed before that body, it was tabled. "Tamer statements were preferred," Jefferson noted, "and, I believe, wisely preferred; the leap I proposed being too long, as yet, for the mass of our citizens," and the convention, in its instructions to the delegates took its stand on the rights and privileges of British subjects. But whereas the middle colonies had shied at the proposal for stopping all trade with the mother country, the Virginians resolved to halt all imports from Britain after November 1, 1774, and to stop the export of tobacco after August 10, 1775, "unless American grievances are redressed before."

In September, delegates from all the thirteen colonies except Georgia gathered in Philadelphia. Divided counsels were immediately heard. On the one side stood such men as Joseph Galloway of Pennsylvania, who wished, in his own words, "candidly and carefully to define American rights, and explicitly and dutifully to petition for the remedy which would redress the grievances justly complained of—to form a more solid and constitutional union between the two countries." On the other side stood, in Galloway's jaundiced view, "persons, whose design, from the beginning of their opposition to the Stamp Act, was to throw off all subordination and connexion with Great Britain; who meant by every fiction, falsehood and fraud, to delude the people from their due allegiance, to throw the subsisting governments into anarchy, to incite the ignorant and vulgar into arms, and with those arms to establish American Independence. The one were men of royal principles and possessed of the Greatest fortunes in America; the others were Congregational and Presbyterian republicans, or men of bankrupt fortunes, overwhelmed in debt to British merchants."

The Pennsylvanian oversimplified the situation. Many members of the upper-class did fear that a permanent breach with the mother country would open the door for internal revolution. Many of the radicals did look upon the conflict with Britain as part and parcel of a struggle to break aristocratic control at home. But the planter-aristocrats of Virginia were among the most radical of the delegates. Many of the staunchest radicals vis-à-vis the mother country were politically conservative on other questions—John Adams immediately comes to mind. Nor were the moderates—including Galloway himself, who later became a Loyalist—any less hostile to the British measures taken since 1763 than the radicals. They were as devoted as the radicals to colonial home rule. The conflict between moderates and radicals in the days to follow would revolve around the question of home rule within the British Empire or outside—which would best serve the colonies?

The opening skirmish in this conflict came over the Suffolk Resolves, which Paul Revere brought to Philadelphia on September 16. These resolves, prepared by Sam Adams's lieutenant Dr. Joseph Warren and adopted by an illegal meeting at Milton on September 9, declared that "no obedience is due" to the Coercive Acts, called for total non-intercourse with Britain, and urged the people to prepare to defend their rights by force of arms if need arose:

Printed: Worthington C. Ford, ed., *Journals of the Continental Congress, 1774–1789* (34 vols., Washington, D.C., 1904–1937), I, pp. 32-37.

Whereas the power but not the justice, the vengeance but not the wisdom of Great Britain, which of old persecuted, scourged, and exiled our fugitive parents from their native shores, now pursues us, their guiltless children, with unrelenting severity: And whereas, this, then savage and uncultivated desart, was purchased by the toil and treasure, or acquired by the blood and valor of those our venerable progenitors; to us they bequeathed the dearbought inheritance, to our care and protection they consigned it, and the most sacred obligations are upon us to transmit the glorious purchase, unfettered by power, unclogged with shackles, to our innocent and beloved offspring. On the fortitude, on the wisdom and on the exertions of this important day, is suspended the fate of this new world, and of unborn millions. If a boundless extent of continent, swarming with millions, will tamely submit to live, move and have their being at the arbitrary will of a licentious minister, they basely yield to voluntary slavery, and future generations shall load their memories with incessant execrations. On the other hand, if we arrest the hand which would ransack our pockets, if we disarm the parricide which points the dagger to our bosoms, if we nobly defeat that fatal edict which proclaims a power to frame laws for us in all cases whatsoever, thereby entailing the endless and numberless curses of slavery upon us, our heirs and their heirs forever; if we successfully resist that unparalleled usurpation of unconstitional power, whereby our capital is robbed of the means of life; whereby the streets of Boston are thronged with military executioners; whereby our coasts are lined and harbours crouded with ships of war; whereby the charter of the colony, that sacred barrier against the encroachments of tyranny, is mutilated and, in effect, annihilated; whereby a murderous law is framed to shelter villains from the hands of justice; whereby the unalienable and inestimable inheritance, which we derived from nature, the constitution of Britain, and the privileges warranted to us in the charter of the province, is totally wrecked, annulled, and vacated, posterity will acknowledge that virtue which preserved them free and happy; and while we enjoy the rewards and blessings of the faithful, the torrent of panegyrists will roll our reputations to that latest period, when the streams of time shall be absorbed in the abyss of eternity.—Therefore, we have resolved, and do *resolve*,

1. That whereas his majesty, George the Third, is the rightful successor to the throne of Great-Britain, and justly entitled to the allegiance of the British realm, and agreeable to compact, of the

English colonies in America—therefore, we, the heirs and successors
of the first planters of this colony, do cheerfully acknowledge the said
George the Third to be our rightful sovereign, and that said covenant
is the tenure and claim on which are founded our allegiance and
submission.

2. That it is an indispensable duty which we owe to God, our
country, ourselves and posterity, by all lawful ways and means in our
power to maintain, defend and preserve those civil and religious
rights and liberties, for which many of our fathers fought, bled and
died, and to hand them down entire to future generations.

3. That the late acts of the British parliament for blocking up the
harbour of Boston, for altering the established form of government
in this colony, and for screening the most flagitious violators of the
laws of the province from a legal trial, are gross infractions of those
rights to which we are justly entitled by the laws of nature, the
British constitution, and the charter of the province.

4. That no obedience is due from this province to either or any
part of the acts above-mentioned, but that they be rejected as the
attempts of a wicked administration to enslave America.

5. That so long as the justices of our superior court of judicature,
court of assize, &c. and inferior court of common pleas in this county
are appointed, or hold their places, by any other tenure than that
which the charter and the laws of the province direct, they must be
considered as under undue influence, and are therefore unconstitutional officers, and, as such, no regard ought to be paid to them by
the people of this county.

6. That if the justices of the superior court of judicature, assize,
&c. justices of the court of common pleas, or of the general sessions
of the peace, shall sit and act during their present disqualified state,
this county will support, and bear harmless, all sheriffs and their
deputies, constables, jurors and other officers who shall refuse to
carry into execution the orders of said courts. . . .

7. That it be recommended to the collectors of taxes, constables
and all other officers, who have public monies in their hands, to
retain the same, and not to make any payment thereof to the
provincial county treasurer until the civil government of the province
is placed upon a constitutional foundation, or until it shall otherwise
be ordered by the proposed provincial Congress. . . .

10. That the late act of parliament for establishing the Roman Catholic religion and the French laws in that extensive country, now called Canada, is dangerous in an extreme degree to the Protestant religion and to the civil rights and liberties of all America; and, therefore, as men and Protestant Christians, we are indispensably obliged to take all proper measures for our security.

11. That whereas our enemies have flattered themselves that they shall make an easy prey of this numerous, brave and hardy people, from an apprehension that they are unacquainted with military discipline; we, therefore, for the honour, defence and security of this county and province, advise, as it has been recommended to take away all commissions from the officers of the militia, that those who now hold commissions, or such other persons, be elected in each town as officers in the militia, as shall be judged of sufficient capacity for that purpose, and who have evidenced themselves the inflexible friends to the rights of the people; and that the inhabitants of those towns and districts, who are qualified, do use their utmost diligence to acquaint themselves with the art of war as soon as possible, and do, for that purpose, appear under arms at least once every week.

12. That during the present hostile appearances on the part of Great-Britain, notwithstanding the many insults and oppressions which we most sensibly resent, yet, nevertheless, from our affection to his majesty, which we have at all times evidenced, we are determined to act merely upon the defensive, so long as such conduct may be vindicated by reason and the principles of self-preservation, but no longer.

13. That, as we understand it has been in contemplation to apprehend sundry persons of this county, who have rendered themselves conspicuous in contending for the violated rights and liberties of their countrymen; we do recommend, should such an audacious measure be put in practice, to seize and keep in safe custody, every servant of the present tyrannical and unconstitutional government throughout the county and province, until the persons so apprehended be liberated from the hands of our adversaries, and restored safe and uninjured to their respective friends and families.

14. That until our rights are fully restored to us, we will, to the utmost of our power, and we recommend the same to the other counties, to withhold all commercial intercourse with Great-Britain, Ireland, and the West-Indies, and abstain from the consumption of

British merchandise and manufactures, and especially of East-India teas and piece goods, with such additions, alterations, and exceptions only, as the General Congress of the colonies may agree to. . . .

The tide was running in a radical direction. The "Powder Alarm"— a rumor that the British had begun a "horrid butchery" in Massachusetts—helped to swing opinion toward radical measures. Along with the copy of the Resolves, Paul Revere brought inflammatory accounts of England's military preparations in Boston. With feeling running high, the Congress voted approval of the Resolves—unanimously, according to the official record; after "long and warm debates," according to Galloway—on September 17, 1774.

Having thus placed the Congress on record in favor of absolute non-intercourse, the radicals pushed forward. On September 27, Congress voted for non-importation effective December 1, 1774. But stiff opposition came from the southern colonies against non-exportation. As exporters of rice and tobacco, the southern colonies feared that non-exportation would mean their financial ruin. To meet their protests, the Congress finally voted on September 30, to postpone non-exportation until September 10, 1775.

Two days earlier, Galloway had made a last ditch bid to stem the radical tide. On that day, he presented a Plan of Union that would, he explained, guarantee the colonies home rule within the empire. He proposed:

Printed: Ford, *Journals of the Continental Congress*, I, pp. 49-51.

Resolved, That the Congress will apply to his Majesty for a redress of grievances under which his faithful subjects in America labour; and assure him, that the Colonies hold in abhorrence the idea of being considered independent communities on the British government, and most ardently desire the establishment of a Political Union, not only among themselves, but with the Mother State, upon those principles of safety and freedom which are essential in the constitution of all free governments, and particularly that of the British Legislature; and as the Colonies from their local circumstances, cannot be represented in the Parliament of Great-Britain, they will humbly propose to his Majesty and his two Houses of Parliament, the following plan, under which the strength of the whole Empire may be drawn together on any contingency, the interest of both countries advanced, and the rights and liberties of America secured.

A Plan of a proposed Union between Great Britain and the Colonies

That a British and American legislature, for regulating the administration of the general affairs of America, be proposed and established in America, including all the said colonies; within, and under which government, each colony shall retain its present constitution, and powers of regulating and governing its own internal police, in all cases what[so]ever.

That the said government be administered by a President General, to be appointed by the King, and a grand Council, to be chosen by the Representatives of the people of the several colonies, in their respective assemblies, once in every three years. . . .

That the Grand Council shall meet once in every year, if they shall think it necessary, and oftener, if occasions shall require, at such time and place as they shall adjourn to, at the last preceding meeting, or as they shall be called to meet at, by the President-General, on any emergency.

That the grand Council shall have power to choose their Speaker, and shall hold and exercise all the like rights, liberties and privileges, as are held and exercised by and in the House of Commons of Great Britain.

That the President-General shall hold his office during the pleasure of the King, and his assent shall be requisite to all acts of the Grand Council, and it shall be his office and duty to cause them to be carried into execution.

That the President-General, by and with the advice and consent of the Grand-Council, hold and exercise all the legislative rights, powers, and authorities, necessary for regulating and administering all the general police and affairs of the colonies, in which Great-Britain and the colonies, or any of them, the colonies in general, or more than one colony, are in any manner concerned, as well civil and criminal as commercial.

That the said President-General and the Grand Council, be an inferior and distinct branch of the British legislature, united and incorporated with it, for the aforesaid general purposes; and that any of the said general regulations may originate and be formed and digested, either in the Parliament of Great Britain, or in the said Grand Council, and being prepared, transmitted to the other for their approbation or dissent; and that the assent of both shall be requisite to the validity of all such general acts or statutes.

That in time of war, all bills for granting aid to the crown, prepared by the Grand Council, and approved by the President General, shall be valid and passed into a law, without the assent of the British Parliament.

Galloway introduced the plan with an eloquent speech. In a bid to disarm radical opposition, Galloway conceded the constitutional argument against British taxation. The colonists, he acknowledged, had "complained of the Stamp Act . . . with the greatest reason and justice." But reminding the delegates that "protection and allegiance are reciprocal duties," he pleaded for reconciliation with the mother country. The following notes of what he said were taken by John Adams:

Printed: *The Works of John Adams,* II, pp. 387-389.

. . . A general non-importation from Great Britain and Ireland has been adopted, but I think this will be too gradual in its operation for the relief of Boston. A general non-exportation I have ever looked on as an undigested proposition. It is impossible America can exist under a total non-exportation. We, in this Province, should have tens of thousands of people thrown upon the cold hand of charity. Our ships would lie by the walls, our seamen would be thrown out of bread, our shipwrights, &c. out of employ, and it would affect the landed interest. It would weaken us in another struggle, which I fear is too near.

To explain my plan, I must state a number of facts relative to

Great Britain and relative to America. I hope no facts which I shall state will be disagreeable.

In the last war, America was in the greatest danger of destruction. This was held up by the Massachusetts, and by the Congress in 1754. They said we are disunited among ourselves. There is no indifferent arbiter between us.

Requisitions came over. A number of the Colonies gave most extensively and liberally; others gave nothing or late. Pennsylvania gave late, not for want of zeal or loyalty, but owing to their disputes with proprietors, their disunited state. These delinquencies were handed up to the parent State, and these gave occasion to the Stamp Act. America, with the greatest reason and justice, complained of the Stamp Act.

Had they proposed some plan of policy, some negotiation been set afoot, it would have terminated in the most happy harmony between the two countries. They repealed the Stamp Act, but they passed the Declaratory Act.

Without some supreme legislature, some common arbiter, you are not, say they, part of the State.

I am as much a friend of liberty as exists; and no man shall go further in point of fortune, or in point of blood, than the man who now addresses you.

Burlamaqui, Grotius, Puffendorf, Hooker. There must be a union of wills and strength; distinction between a State and a multitude; a State is animated by one soul.

As we are not within the circle of the supreme jurisdiction of the Parliament, we are independent States. The law of Great Britain does not bind us in any case whatever.

We want the aid and assistance and protection of the arm of our mother country. Protection and allegiance are reciprocal duties. Can we lay claim to the money and protection of Great Britain upon any principles of honor or conscience? Can we wish to become aliens to the mother state?

We must come upon terms with Great Britain.

Some gentlemen are not for negotiation. I wish I could hear some reason against it.

The minister must be at twenty or thirty millions [expense] to enforce his measures.

I propose this proposition. The plan,—two classes of laws. 1. Laws of internal policy. 2. Laws in which more than one Colony are concerned,—raising money for war. No one act can be done without the assent of Great Britain. No one without the assent of America. A British American Legislature.

After a spirited debate in which such moderates as John Jay and James Duane of New York backed the proposal, the plan was entered on the minutes, with an order referring it to future consideration; "but," Lieutenant Governor Cadwallader Colden of New York learned from Galloway, "[it] was afterwards not only totally rejected without proposing a substitute but expunged from the minutes. . . . The Delegates from Virginia were the most violent of any—those of Maryland and some of the Carolinas were little less so. These Southern Gentlemen exceeded even the New England Delegates:—they together made a majority that the others could have very little effect on."

Amid these maneuvers, debate continued in committee over the framing of a Declaration of Rights. In later years, John Adams related in his *Autobiography* the crux of the difficulty:

Printed: *The Works of John Adams,* II, pp. 373-377.

. . . The two points which labored the most were: 1. Whether we should recur to the law of nature, as well as to the British constitution, and our American charters and grants. Mr. Galloway and Mr. Duane were for excluding the law of nature. I was very strenuous for retaining and insisting on it, as a resource to which we might be driven by Parliament much sooner than we were aware. 2. The other great question was, what authority we should concede to Parliament; whether we should deny the authority of Parliament in all cases; whether we should allow any authority to it in our internal affairs; or whether we should allow it to regulate the trade of the empire with or without any restrictions. These discussions spun into great length, and nothing was decided. After many fruitless essays, the committee determined to appoint a sub-committee to make a draught of a set of articles that might be laid in writing before the grand committee, and become the foundation of a more regular debate and final decision. I was appointed on the sub-committee, in which, after going over the ground again, a set of articles were drawn and debated one by one. After several days deliberation, we agreed upon all the articles excepting one, and that was the authority of Parliament, which was indeed the essence of the whole controversy; some were for a flat denial of all authority; others for denying the power of taxation only; some for denying internal, but admitting external, taxation. After a multitude of motions had been made, discussed, negatived, it seemed as if we should never agree upon any thing. Mr. John Rutledge of South Carolina, one of the committee, addressing himself to me, was pleased to say, "Adams, we must agree upon something; you appear to be as familiar with the subject as any of us, and I like your expressions,— *'the necessity of the case,'* and *'excluding all ideas of taxation, external and internal;'* I have a great opinion of that same idea of the necessity of the case, and I am determined against all taxation for revenue. Come, take the pen and see if you can't produce something that will unite us." Some others of the committee seconding Mr. Rutledge, I took a sheet of paper and drew up an article. When it was read, I believe not one of the committee was fully satisfied with it; but they all soon acknowledged that there was no hope of hitting on any thing in which we could all agree with more satisfaction. All therefore agreed to this, and upon this depended the union of the Colonies. The sub-committee reported their draught to the grand committee, and another long debate ensued, especially on this article, and various changes and modifications of it were attempted, but none adopted.

The articles were then reported to Congress, and debated, paragraph by paragraph. The difficult article was again attacked and defended. Congress rejected all amendments to it, and the general sense of the members was, that the article demanded as little as could be demanded, and conceded as much as could be conceded with safety, and certainly as little as would be accepted by Great Britain; and that the country must take its fate, in consequence of it. When Congress had gone through the articles, I was appointed to put them into form and report a fair draught for their final acceptance. This was done, and they were finally accepted.

The Declaration, as adopted October 14, represented a triumph for the radicals. The rights the colonists claimed were said to derive from "the immutable laws of nature, the principles of the English constitution, and the several charters or compacts." As for the authority of Parliament, the Declaration stated that inasmuch as the colonies cannot, "from their local and other circumstances," be represented in the British Parliament, "they are entitled to a free and exclusive power of legislation in their several provincial legislatures"; but to satisfy the moderates, a qualifying proviso based upon a draft prepared by James Duane of New York was added. This proviso declared that "from the necessity of the case," the colonies "cheerfully consent" to regulation of trade by Parliament:

> Printed: Ford, *Journals of the Continental Congress*, I, pp. 63-73.

Whereas, since the close of the last war, the British parliament, claiming a power of right to bind the people of America, by statute in all cases whatsoever, hath in some acts expressly imposed taxes on them, and in others, under various pretences, but in fact for the purpose of raising a revenue, hath imposed rates and duties payable in these colonies, established a board of commissioners, with unconstitutional powers, and extended the jurisdiction of courts of Admiralty, not only for collecting the said duties, but for the trial of causes merely arising within the body of a county.

And whereas, in consequence of other statutes, judges, who before held only estates at will in their offices, have been made dependant on the Crown alone for their salaries, and standing armies kept in times of peace:

And it has lately been resolved in Parliament, that by force of a statute, made in the thirty-fifth year of the reign of king Henry the eighth, colonists may be transported to England, and tried there upon accusations for treasons, and misprisions, or concealments of treasons committed in the colonies; and by a late statute, such trials have been directed in cases therein mentioned.

And whereas, in the last session of parliament, three statutes were made [the Coercive Acts]. . . . All which statutes are impolitic, unjust, and cruel, as well as unconstitutional, and most dangerous and destructive of American rights.

And whereas, Assemblies have been frequently dissolved, contrary to the rights of the people, when they attempted to deliberate on grievances; and their dutiful, humble, loyal, & reasonable petitions to the crown for redress, have been repeatedly treated with contempt, by his majesty's ministers of state:

The good people of the several Colonies of New-hampshire, Massachusetts-bay, Rhode-island and Providence plantations, Connecticut, New-York, New-Jersey, Pennsylvania, Newcastle, Kent and Sussex on Delaware, Maryland, Virginia, North Carolina, and South Carolina, justly alarmed at these arbitrary proceedings of parliament and administration, have severally elected, constituted, and appointed deputies to meet and sit in general congress, in the city of Philadelphia, in order to obtain such establishment, as that their religion, laws, and liberties may not be subverted:

Whereupon the deputies so appointed being now assembled, in a full and free representation of these Colonies, taking into their most serious consideration, the best means of attaining the ends aforesaid, do, in the first place, as Englishmen, their ancestors in like cases have usually done, for asserting and vindicating their rights and liberties, declare,

That the inhabitants of the English Colonies in North America, by the immutable laws of nature, the principles of the English constitution, and the several charters or compacts, have the following Rights:

Resolved, N.C.D. 1. That they are entitled to life, liberty, & property, and they have never ceded to any sovereign power whatever, a right to dispose of either without their consent.

Resolved, N.C.D. 2. That our ancestors, who first settled these colonies, were at the time of their emigration from the mother country, entitled to all the rights, liberties, and immunities of free and natural-born subjects, within the realm of England.

Resolved, N.C.D. 3. That by such emigration they by no means forfeited, surrendered, or lost any of those rights, but that they were, and their descendants now are, entitled to the exercise and enjoyment of all such of them, as their local and other circumstances enable them to exercise and enjoy.

Resolved, 4. That the foundation of English liberty, and of all free government, is a right in the people to participate in their legislative council: and as the English colonists are not represented, and from their local and other circumstances, cannot properly be represented in the British parliament, they are entitled to a free and exclusive power of legislation in their several provincial legislatures, where their right of representation can alone be preserved, in all cases of taxation and internal polity, subject only to the negative of their sovereign, in such manner as has been heretofore used and accustomed. But, from the necessity of the case, and a regard to the mutual interest of both countries, we cheerfully consent to the operation of such acts of the British parliament, as are bona fide, restrained to the regulation of our external commerce, for the purpose of securing the commercial advantages of the whole empire to the mother country, and the commercial benefits of its respective members; excluding every idea of taxation, internal or external, for raising a revenue on the subjects in America, without their consent.

Resolved, N.C.D. 5. That the respective colonies are entitled to the common law of England, and more especially to the great and inestimable privilege of being tried by their peers of the vicinage, according to the course of that law. . . .

Resolved, N.C.D. 8. That they have a right peaceably to assemble, consider of their grievances, and petition the King; and that all prosecutions, prohibitory proclamations, and commitments for the same, are illegal.

Resolved, N.C.D. 9. That the keeping a Standing army in these colonies, in times of peace, without the consent of the legislature of that colony, in which such army is kept, is against law.

Resolved, N.C.D. 10. It is indispensably necessary to good government, and rendered essential by the English constitution, that the constituent branches of the legislature be independent of each other; that, therefore, the exercise of legislative power in several colonies, by a council appointed, during pleasure, by the crown, is unconstitutional, dangerous, and destructive to the freedom of American legislation.

All and each of which the aforesaid deputies, in behalf of themselves and their constituents, do claim, demand, and insist on, as their indubitable rights and liberties; which cannot be legally taken from them, altered or abridged by any power whatever, without their own consent, by their representatives in their several provincial legislatures.

In the course of our inquiry, we find many infringements and violations of the foregoing rights, which, from an ardent desire, that harmony and mutual intercourse of affection and interest may be restored, we pass over for the present, and proceed to state such acts and measures as have been adopted since the last war, which demonstrate a system formed to enslave America.

Resolved, N.C.D. That the following acts of Parliament are infringements and violations of the rights of the colonists; and that the repeal of them is essentially necessary in order to restore harmony between Great-Britain and the American colonies, viz:

The several acts . . . which impose duties for the purpose of raising a revenue in America, extend the powers of the admiralty courts beyond their ancient limits, deprive the American subject of trial by jury, authorize the judges' certificate to indemnify the prosecutor from damages, that he might otherwise be liable to, requiring oppressive security from a claimant of ships and goods seized, before he shall be allowed to defend his property, . . . are subversive of American rights. . . .

Also the three acts passed in the last session of parliament, for stopping the port and blocking up the harbour of Boston, for altering the charter & government of the Massachusetts-bay, and that which is entituled "An act for the better administration of Justice," &c.

Also the act passed in the same session for establishing the Roman Catholick Religion in the province of Quebec, abolishing the equitable system of English laws, and erecting a tyranny there, to the great danger, from so total a dissimilarity of Religion, law, and government of the neighbouring British colonies, by the assistance of whose blood and treasure the said country was conquered from France.

Also the act passed in the same session for the better providing suitable quarters for officers and soldiers in his Majesty's service in North-America.

Also, that the keeping a standing army in several of these colonies, in time of peace, without the consent of the legislature of that colony in which such army is kept, is against law.

To these grievous acts and measures, Americans cannot submit, but in hopes that their fellow subjects in Great-Britain will, on a revision of them, restore us to that state in which both countries

found happiness and prosperity, we have for the present only resolved to pursue the following peaceable measures:

1st. To enter into a non-importation, non-consumption, and non-
exportation agreement or association.

2. To prepare an address to the people of Great-Britain, and a
memorial to the inhabitants of British America, &

3. To prepare a loyal address to his Majesty; agreeable to Resolutions already entered into.

With the Declaration of Rights approved, the Congress proceeded to implement its non-importation and non-exportation resolves by adopting, on October 20, the following "Association":

> Printed: Ford, *Journals of the Continental Congress*, I,
> pp. 75-81.

We, his majesty's most loyal subjects, the delegates of the several
colonies of New-Hampshire, Massachusetts-Bay, Rhode-Island, Connecticut, New-York, New-Jersey, Pennsylvania, the three lower
counties of New-Castle, Kent and Sussex, on Delaware, Maryland,
Virginia, North-Carolina, and South-Carolina, deputed to represent
them in a continental Congress, held in the city of Philadelphia, on
the 5th day of September, 1774, avowing our allegiance to his
majesty, our affection and regard for our fellow-subjects in Great-
Britain and elsewhere, affected with the deepest anxiety, and most
alarming apprehensions, at those grievances and distresses, with
which his Majesty's American subjects are oppressed; and having
taken under our most serious deliberation, the state of the whole
continent, find, that the present unhappy situation of our affairs is
occasioned by a ruinous system of colony administration, adopted
by the British ministry about the year 1763, evidently calculated for
inslaving these colonies, and, with them, the British empire. In
prosecution of which system, various acts of parliament have been
passed, for raising a revenue in America, for depriving the American
subjects, in many instances, of the constitutional trial by jury, exposing their lives to danger, by directing a new and illegal trial beyond

the seas, for crimes alleged to have been committed in America: and in prosecution of the same system, several late, cruel, and oppressive acts have been passed, respecting the town of Boston and the Massachusetts-Bay, and also an act for extending the province of Quebec, so as to border on the western frontiers of these colonies, establishing an arbitrary government therein, and discouraging the settlement of British subjects in that wide extended country; thus, by the influence of civil principles and ancient prejudices, to dispose the inhabitants to act with hostility against the free Protestant colonies, whenever a wicked ministry shall chuse so to direct them.

To obtain redress of these grievances, which threaten destruction to the lives, liberty, and property of his majesty's subjects, in North America, we are of opinion, that a non-importation, non-consumption, and non-exportation agreement, faithfully adhered to, will prove the most speedy, effectual, and peaceable measure: and, therefore, we do, for ourselves, and the inhabitants of the several colonies, whom we represent, firmly agree and associate, under the sacred ties of virtue, honour and love of our country, as follows:

1. That from and after the first day of December next, we will not import, into British America, from Great-Britain or Ireland, any goods, wares, or merchandise whatsoever, or from any other place, any such goods, wares, or merchandise, as shall have been exported from Great-Britain or Ireland; nor will we, after that day, import any East-India tea from any part of the world; nor any molasses, syrups, paneles, coffee, or pimento, from the British plantations or from Great-Britain or Ireland; nor will we, after that day, import any East India tea from any part of the world; nor any molasses, syrups, paneles, coffee, or pimento, from the British plantations. . . .

4. The earnest desire we have, not to injure our fellow-subjects in Great-Britain, Ireland, or the West Indies, induces us to suspend a non-exportation, until the tenth day of September, 1775; at which time, if the said acts and parts of acts of the British parliament herein after mentioned are not repealed, we will not, directly or indirectly, export any merchandise or commodity whatsoever to Great-Britain, Ireland, or the West Indies, except rice to Europe. . . .

9. Such as are venders of goods or merchandise will not take advantage of the scarcity of goods, that may be occasioned by this association, but will sell the same at the rates we have been respectively accustomed to do, for twelve months last past. . . .

11. That a committee be chosen in every county, city, and town, by those who are qualified to vote for representatives in the legislature, whose business it shall be attentively to observe the conduct of all persons touching this association; and when it shall be made to appear, to the satisfaction of a majority of any such committee, that any person within the limits of their appointment has violated this association, that such majority do forthwith cause the truth of the case to be published in the gazette; to the end, that all such foes to the rights of British-America may be publicly known, and universally contemned as the enemies of American liberty; and thenceforth we respectively will break off all dealings with him or her. . . .

And we do solemnly bind ourselves and our constituents, under the ties aforesaid, to adhere to this association, until such parts of the several acts of parliament passed since the close of the last war, as impose or continue duties on tea, wine, molasses, syrups, paneles, coffee, sugar, pimento, indigo, foreign paper, glass, and painters' colours, imported into America, and extend the powers of the admiralty courts beyond their ancient limits, deprive the American subject of trial by jury, authorize the judge's certificate to indemnify the prosecutor from damages, that he might otherwise be liable to from a trial by his peers, require oppressive security from a claimant of ships or goods seized, before he shall be allowed to defend his property, are repealed. . . .

The adoption of the "Association" forced the colonists to make their decision: they could support the boycott, or refusing, affirm their allegiance to the mother country. The question of allegiance was thus brought to the forefront, and in Carl Becker's words, "loyalty to America was rapidly becoming incompatible with adherence to the laws of the Empire."

The Association set into motion the administrative machinery to carry through the revolution that was underway. Each county and town was to have a Committee of Safety "to the end, that all such foes to the rights of British America may be publicly known, and universally contemned as the enemies of American liberty." In each colony sprang up new extra-legal agencies of coercion that took over the functions of government. Dissidents were silenced by ostracism and even violence. The royal authority,

Virginia's governor Lord Dunmore complained to the Earl of Dartmouth, December 24, 1774, stood paralyzed:

Printed: Historical Manuscripts Commission, *Dartmouth Papers* (3 vols., London, 1887–1896), II, p. 243.

. . . The Associations first in part entered into by the Colony and adopted by the Continental Congress are now enforcing throughout the country with great vigour. A committee is chosen in every county to carry the Association of the Congress into execution. They inspect the trade and correspondence of any merchant, watch the conduct of any inhabitant, may send for, catechize, and stigmatize him if he does not appear to follow the laws of their Congress. Every city besides is arming an independent Company to protect their Committees and to be employed against Government should occasion require. As to the power of Government which Lord Dartmouth in his letter of November 11th directs should be exerted to counteract the dangerous measures pursuing here, it is entirely disregarded if not wholly overturned. Not a Justice of the Peace acts except as a Committee-man. Abolishing the Courts of Justice was the first step taken. The General Court is much the same, for the lawyers refuse to attend, nor would the people allow them. Interposition of Government in its present feeble state would only suffer the disgrace of a disappointment. . . .

The Congress adjourned on October 26, after having resolved that another Congress meet at Philadelphia in May, 1775, unless the colonists' grievances had been redressed. Well could Sam Adams gloat that "things went in the Continental Congress . . . as perfectly to his liking as if he were the sole director." As John Dickinson wrote to Arthur Lee, October 27, 1774, the day after the Congress adjourned, the hour of decision lay at hand:

Printed: Peter Force, ed., *American Archives, Fourth Series* (6 vols., Washington, D.C., 1837–1846), I, p. 947.

Philadelphia, October 27, 1774.

DEAR SIR: Yesterday the Congress broke up. You will immediately know their Proceedings from publications.

The Colonists have now taken such grounds that *Great Britain* must relax, or inevitably involve herself in a civil war, likely in all human probability to overwhelm her with a weight of calamities, in comparison of which, the contentions between the Houses of *York* and *Lancaster,* or the distractions of the last century, were gentle misfortunes.

A determined and unanimous resolution animates this Continent, firmly and faithfully to support the common cause to the utmost extremity, in this great struggle for the blessing of liberty—a blessing that can alone render life worth holding.

I grieve for the fate of a brave and generous Nation, plunged by a few profligate men into such scenes of unmerited and inglorious distress. Let her rouse her noble spirit, be true to herself, and she cannot fail of being true to us. Let her not so far adopt the schemes of base yet visionary men and knaves, that she may think her dignity concerned to maintain the projects of those whom her justice commands her to punish.

Give up the *Butes, Mansfields, Norths, Bernards,* and *Hutchinsons,* whose falsehoods and misrepresentations have inflamed the people; call not their cause the cause of *Great Britain;* throw all errours and occasions of dissatisfactions on their guilty heads. A new Ministry of such a character that *England* and *America* both can trust, may do great things; especially if a considerable change be made at the next general election. Why should Nations meet with hostile eyes, because villains and ideots have acted like villains and ideots?

I wish for peace ardently; but must say, delightful as it is, it will come more grateful by being unexpected. The first act of violence on the part of Administration in *America,* or the attempt to reinforce General *Gage* this winter or next year, will put the whole Continent in arms, from *Nova Scotia* to *Georgia.*

May *God* of his infinite mercy grant a happy event to these afflicting agitations.   Your friend,

JOHN DICKINSON.

VI. The Colonies Declare their Independence

"GREAT BRITAIN must relax, or inevitably involve herself in a civil war"—but any retreat on the question of parliamentary supremacy was unthinkable to most politically conscious Britons of the day. George III set the tone. "The dye is now cast," he wrote North, September 11, 1774, "the colonies must either submit or triumph; I do not wish to come to severer measures but we must not retreat. . . ."

In his address from the throne at the opening of Parliament at the end of November, the King reaffirmed his "firm and steadfast resolution to withstand every attempt to weaken or impair the supreme authority of this legislature over all the dominions of my crown." Both houses replied favorably by overwhelming margins. The temper of Parliament was clearly demonstrated by the following joint address to the King adopted on February 9, 1775:

Printed: William A. Whitehead, *et al.*, eds., *Archives of the State of New Jersey, First Series: Documents Relating to the Colonial History of the State of New Jersey* (42 vols., Newark, Patterson, Somerville, and Trenton, 1880–1949), X, pp. 553-554. Hereafter referred to as *New Jersey Archives*.

. . . We find, that a part of Your Majesty's subjects, in the province of Massachusett's-Bay, have proceeded so far as to resist the authority of the supreme legislature; that rebellion at this time actually exists within the said province; and we see, with the utmost concern, that they have been countenanced and encouraged by unlawful combinations and engagements, entered into by Your Majesty's subjects in several of the other colonies, to the injury and oppression of many of their innocent fellow-subjects, resident within the kingdom of Great-Britain, and the rest of Your Majesty's dominions: This conduct, on their part, appears to us the more inexcusable, when we consider with how much temper Your Majesty, and the two Houses of Parliament, have acted in support of the laws and constitution of Great Britain. We can never so far desert the trust reposed in us, as to relinquish any part of the sovereign authority over all Your Majesty's dominions, which, by the law, is vested in Your Majesty and the two Houses of Parliament; and the conduct of many persons, in several of the colonies, during the late disturbances, is alone sufficient to convince us how necessary this power is for the protection of the lives and fortunes of Your Majesty's subjects.

We ever have been, and always shall be, ready to pay attention and regard to any real grievances of any of Your Majesty's subjects, which shall, in a dutiful and constitutional manner, be laid before us; and, whenever any of the colonies shall make a proper application to us, we shall be ready to afford them every just and reasonable indulgence: At the same time, we consider it as our indispensable duty humbly to beseech Your Majesty, that you will take the most effectual measures to enforce due obedience to the laws and authority of the supreme legislature; and we beg leave, in the most solemn manner, to assure Your Majesty, that it is our fixed resolution, at the hazard of our lives and properties, to stand by Your Majesty against all rebellious attempts in the maintenance of the just rights of Your Majesty and the two Houses of Parliament.

Only a small minority challenged the dominant mood. On January 20, 1775, Chatham moved a resolution calling for the immediate removal of British troops from Boston. He warned that any delay might bring "years of calamity"; reaffirmed his distinction between regulation of trade and taxation; called colonial resistance to parliamentary taxation "necessary as it was just"; sketched the difficulties involved in military coercion; and pleaded for reconcilation lest "the kingdom be undone."

Printed: Hansard, *Parliamentary History*, XVIII, pp. 149-156.

. . . I wish, my lords, not to lose a day in this urgent, pressing crisis; an hour now lost in allaying ferments in America, may produce years of calamity: for my own part, I will not desert, for a moment, the conduct of this weighty business, from the first to the last; unless nailed to my bed by the extremity of sickness, I will give it unremitted attention; I will knock at the door of this sleeping and confounded ministry, and will rouse them to a sense of their important danger.

When I state the importance of the colonies to this country, and the magnitude of danger hanging over this country, from the present plan of mis-administration practised against them, I desire not to be understood to argue for a reciprocity of indulgence between England and America. I contend not for indulgence, but justice to America; and I shall ever contend, that the Americans justly owe obedience to us in a limited degree—they owe obedience to our ordinances of trade and navigation; but let the line be skillfully drawn between the objects of those ordinances, and their private, internal property; let the sacredness of their property remain inviolate; let it be taxable only by their own consent, given in their provincial assemblies, else it will cease to be property. As to the metaphysical refinements, attempting to shew that the Americans are equally free from obedience and commercial restraints, as from taxation for revenue, as being unrepresented here, I pronounce them futile, frivolous, and groundless.

When I urge this measure of recalling the troops from Boston, I urge it on this pressing principle, that it is necessarily preparatory to the restoration of your peace, and the establishment of your prosperity. It will then appear that you are disposed to treat amicably and equitably; and to consider, revise, and repeal, if it should be found necessary, as I affirm it will, those violent acts and declarations which have disseminated confusion throughout your empire.

Resistance to your acts was necessary as it was just; and your vain declarations of the omnipotence of parliament, and your imperious doctrines of the necessity of submission, will be found equally impotent to convince, or to enslave your fellow-subjects in America, who feel that tyranny, whether ambitioned by an individual part of the legislature, or the bodies who compose it, is equally intolerable to British subjects.

The means of enforcing this thraldom are found to be as ridiculous and weak in practice, as they are unjust in principle. Indeed I cannot but feel the most anxious sensibility for the situation of general Gage, and the troops under his command; thinking him, as I do, a man of humanity and understanding; and entertaining, as I ever will, the highest respect, the warmest love, for the British troops. Their situation is truly unworthy; penned up—pining in inglorious inactivity. They are an army of impotence. You may call them an army of safety and of guard; but they are in truth an army of impotence and contempt: and, to make the folly equal to the disgrace, they are an army of irritation and vexation. . . .

I therefore urge and conjure your lordships, immediately to adopt this conciliating measure. I will pledge myself for its immediately producing conciliatory effects, by its being thus well-timed: but if you delay till your vain hope shall be accomplished, of triumphantly dictating reconciliation, you delay for ever. But, admitting that this hope, which in truth is desperate, should be accomplished, what do you gain by the imposition of your victorious amity?—you will be untrusted and unthanked. Adopt, then, the grace, while you have the opportunity of reconcilement; or at least prepare the way. Allay the ferment prevailing in America, by removing the obnoxious hostile cause—obnoxious and unserviceable; for their merit can be only inaction: *Non dimicare et vincere,*—their victory can never be by exertions. Their force would be most disproportionately exerted against a brave, generous, and united people, with arms in their hands, and courage in their hearts: three millions of people, the genuine descendants of a valiant and pious ancestry, driven to those deserts by the narrow maxims of a superstitious tyranny. And is the spirit of persecution never to be appeased? Are the brave sons of those brave forefathers to inherit their sufferings, as they have inherited their virtues? Are they to sustain the infliction of the most oppressive and unexampled severity, beyond the accounts of history, or description of poetry: *'Rhadamanthus habet durissima regna, castigatque, auditque.'* So says the wisest poet, and perhaps the wisest statesman and politician. But our ministers say, the Americans must not be heard. They have been condemned unheard. The indiscriminate hand of vengeance has lumped together innocent and guilty; while all the formalities of hostility, has blocked up the town (Boston), and reduced to beggary and famine thirty thousand inhabitants.

But his majesty is advised, that the union in America cannot last. Ministers have more eyes than I, and should have more ears; but with all the information I have been able to procure, I can pronounce it—an union, solid, permanent, and effectual. . . .

If illegal violences have been, as it is said, committed in America; prepare the way, open the door of possibility, for acknowledgment and satisfaction: but proceed not to such coercion, such proscription; cease your indiscriminate inflictions; amerce not thirty thousand; oppress not three millions, for the fault of forty or fifty individuals. Such severity of injustice must for ever render incurable the wounds you have already given your colonies; you irritate them to unappeasable rancour. What though you march from town to town, and from province to province; though you should be able to enforce a temporary and local submission, which I only suppose, not admit—how shall you be able to secure the obedience of the country you leave behind you in your progress, to grasp the dominion of eighteen hundred miles of continent, populous in numbers, possessing valour, liberty and resistance?

This resistance to your arbitrary system of taxation might have been foreseen: it was obvious from the nature of things, and of mankind; and above all, from the Whiggish spirit flourishing in that country. The spirit which now resists your taxation in America, is the same which formerly opposed loans, benevolences, and ship-money, in England: the same spirit which called all England on its legs, and by the Bill of Rights vindicated the English constitution: the same spirit which established the great fundamental, essential maxim of your liberties—*that no subject of England shall be taxed but by his own consent.*

This glorious spirit of Whiggism animates three millions in America; who prefer poverty with liberty, to gilded chains and sordid affluence; and who will die in defence of their rights as men, as freemen. What shall oppose this spirit, aided by the congenial flame glowing in the breasts of every Whig in England, to the amount, I hope, of double the American numbers? Ireland they have to a man. In that country, joined as it is with the cause of colonies, and placed at their head, the distinction I contend for is and must be observed. This country superintends and controuls their trade and navigation; but they tax themselves. And this distinction between external and internal controul is sacred and insurmountable; it is involved in the abstract nature of things. Property is private, individual, absolute. Trade is an extended and complicated consideration: it reaches as far as ships can sail or winds can blow: it is a great and various machine. To regulate the numberless movements of its several parts, and combine them into effect, for the good of the whole, requires the superintending wisdom and energy of the supreme power in the empire. But this supreme power has no effect towards internal taxation; for it does not exist in that relation; there is no such thing, no such idea in this constitution, as a supreme power operating upon property. Let this distinction then remain for ever ascertained; taxation is theirs, commercial regulation is ours. As an American I would recognize to England her supreme right of regulating commerce and navigation: as an Englishman by birth and principle, I recognize to the Americans their supreme unalienable right in their property; a right which they are justified in the defence of to the last extremity. To maintain this principle is the common cause of the Whigs on the other side of the Atlantic, and on this. ' 'Tis liberty to liberty engaged,' that they will defend themselves, their families, and their country. In this great cause they are immoveably allied: it is the alliance of God and nature—immutable, eternal—fixed as the firmament of heaven.

To such united force, what force shall be opposed?—What, my lords?—A few regiments in America, and seventeen or eighteen thousand men at home!—The idea is too ridiculous to take up a moment of your lordships' time. . . .

. . . I trust it is obvious to your lordships, that all attempts to impose servitude upon such men, to establish despotism over such a mighty continental nation, must be vain, must be fatal. We shall be forced ultimately to retract; let us retract while we can, not when we must. I say we must necessarily undo these violent oppressive acts: they must be repealed—you will repeal them; I pledge myself for it, that you will in the end repeal them; I stake my reputation on it:— I will consent to be taken for an idiot, if they are not finally repealed. —Avoid, then, this humiliating, disgraceful necessity. With a dignity becoming your exalted situation, make the first advances to concord, to peace, and happiness: for that is your true dignity, to act with prudence and justice. That you should first concede, is obvious, from sound and rational policy. Concession comes with better grace and more salutary effect from superior power; it reconciles superiority of power with the feelings of men; and establishes solid confidence on the foundations of affection and gratitude.

So thought a wise poet and a wise man in political sagacity; the friend of Mecænas, and the eulogist of Augustus.—To him, the adopted son and successor, the first Cæsar, to him, the master of the world, he wisely urged this conduct of prudence and dignity; *"Tuque prior, tu parce;—projice tela manu."*

Every motive, therefore, of justice and of policy, of dignity and of prudence, urges you to allay the ferment in America—by a removal of your troops from Boston—by a repeal of your acts of parliament —and by demonstration of amicable dispositions towards your colonies. On the other hand, every danger and every hazard impend, to deter you from perseverance in your present ruinous measures.— Foreign war hanging over your heads by a slight and brittle thread: France and Spain watching your conduct, and waiting for the maturity of your errors;—with a vigilant eye to America, and the temper of your colonies, more than to their own concerns, be they what they may.

To conclude, my lords; if the ministers thus persevere in misadvising and misleading the King, I will not say, that they can alienate the affections of his subjects from his crown; but I will affirm, that they will make the crown not worth his wearing—I will not say that the King is betrayed; but I will pronounce,—that the kingdom is undone.

The Lords voted down his motion by 68 to 18. Undaunted, he introduced, on February 1, his plan "for settling the Troubles in America"—a proposal that showed Chatham groping toward a federal solution whereby Parliament would legislate "in all matters touching the general weal of the whole dominion of the imperial crown of Great Britain," while leaving all matters of internal legislation—including taxation—solely to the colonial assemblies. But Chatham was too far in advance of most of his colleagues. The Lords rejected the proposal by a two to one margin—61-30.

Equally unsuccessful was another conciliatory proposal introduced on March 22, 1775, in the Commons by Edmund Burke. As a Rockinghamite, Burke continued to adhere to the principle of the Declaratory Act; he simply proposed that on grounds of expediency that Parliament should refrain from exercising its power in taxing the colonies. Burke, in essence, wished to return to the days before 1763, ignoring the whole question of right versus rights that arisen. Although the proposal was inadequate to the exigencies of the day, Burke accompanied his plan with an eloquent plea for conciliation that has become a classic:

Printed: Hansard, *Parliamentary History*, XVIII, pp. 478-538.

The proposition is peace. Not peace through the medium of war; not peace to be hunted through the labyrinth of intricate and endless negociations; not peace to arise out of universal discord, fomented from principle, in all parts of the empire; not peace to depend on the juridical determination of perplexing questions; or the precise marking [of] the shadowy boundaries of a complex government. It is simple peace; sought in its natural course, and in its ordinary haunts. —It is peace sought in the spirit of peace; and laid in principles purely pacific. I propose, by removing the ground of the difference, . . . [to restore] the *former unsuspecting confidence of the colonies in the mother country.* . . .

The capital leading questions on which you must this day decide, are these two. First, whether you ought to concede; and secondly, what your concession ought to be. . . .

First, Sir, permit me to observe, that the use of force alone is but *temporary.* It may subdue for a moment; but it does not remove the necessity of subduing again: and a nation is not governed, which is perpetually to be conquered.

My next objection is *uncertainty.* Terror is not always the effect of force; and an armament is not a victory. If you do not succeed, you are without resource; for, conciliation failing, force remains; but, force failing, no further hope of reconciliation is left. Power and authority are sometimes bought by kindness; but they can never be begged as alms, by an impoverished and defeated violence.

A further objection to force is, that you *impair the object* by your very endeavours to preserve it. The thing you fought for is not the thing which you recover; but depreciated, sunk, wasted, and consumed in the contest. Nothing less will content me, than *whole America*. I do not choose to consume its strength along with our own; because in all parts it is the British strength that I consume. I do not choose to be caught by a foreign enemy at the end of this exhausting conflict; and still less in the midst of it. I may escape; but I can make no insurance against such an event. Let me add, that I do not choose wholly to break the American spirit, because it is the spirit that has made the country.

Lastly, we have no sort of *experience* in favour of force as an instrument in the rule of our colonies. Their growth and their utility has been owing to methods altogether different. Our ancient indulgence has been said to be pursued to a fault. It may be so. But we know, if feeling is evidence, that our fault was more tolerable than our attempt to mend it; and our sin far more salutary than our penitence. These, Sir, are my reasons for not entertaining that high opinion of untried force, by which many gentlemen, for whose sentiments in other particulars I have great respect, seem to be so greatly captivated. But there is still behind a third consideration concerning this object, which serves to determine my opinion on the sort of policy, which ought to be pursued in the management of America, even more than its population and its commerce, I mean its *temper and character*.

In this character of the Americans, a love of freedom is the predominating feature which marks and distinguishes the whole: and as an ardent is always a jealous affection, your colonies become suspicious, restive, and untractable, whenever they see the least attempt to wrest from them by force, or shuffle from them by chicane, what they think the only advantage worth living for. This fierce spirit of liberty is stronger in the English colonies probably than in any other people of the earth; and this from a great variety of powerful causes; which, to understand the true temper of their minds, and the direction which this spirit takes, it will not be amiss to lay open somewhat more largely.

First, the people of the colonies are descendants of Englishmen. . . . The colonies draw from you, . . . as a fundamental principle, that the people must in effect themselves mediately or immediately possess the power of granting their own money, or no shadow of liberty could subsist. . . . Their love of liberty, as with you, is fixed and attached on this specific point of taxing. Liberty might be safe, or might be endangered in twenty other particulars, without their being much pleased or alarmed. Here they felt its pulse; and as they found that beat, they thought themselves sick or sound. . . .

They were further confirmed in this pleasing error, by the form of their provincial legislative assemblies. Their governments are popular in a high degree. . . .

If any thing were wanting to this necessary operation of the form of government, religion would have given it a complete effect. . . . The people are Protestants: and of that kind, which is the most adverse to all implicit submission of mind and opinion. This is a persuasion not only favourable to liberty, but built upon it. . . . All Protestantism, even of the most cold and passive, is a sort of dissent. But the religion most prevalent in our northern colonies is a refinement on the principle of resistance; it is the dissidence of dissent; and the Protestantism of the Protestant religion. This religion, under a variety of denominations, agreeing in nothing but in the communion of the spirit of liberty, is predominant in most of the northern provinces. . . .

Sir, I can perceive by their manner, that some gentlemen object to the latitude of this description; because in the southern colonies the church of England forms a large body, and has a regular establishment. It is certainly true. There is however a circumstance attending these colonies, which, in my opinion, fully counterbalances this difference, and makes the spirit of liberty still more high and haughty than in those to the northward. It is that in Virginia and the Carolinas, they have a vast multitude of slaves. Where this is the case in any part of the world, those who are free, are by far the most proud and jealous of their freedom. Freedom is to them not only an enjoyment, but a kind of rank and privilege. . . .

Permit me, Sir, to add another circumstance in our colonies, which contributes no mean part towards the growth and effect of this untractable spirit. I mean their education. In no country perhaps in the world is the law so general a study. . . . This study renders men acute, inquisitive, dexterous, prompt in attack, ready in defence, full of resources. In other countries, the people, more simple, and of a less mercurial cast, judge of an ill principle in government only by an actual grievance; here they anticipate the evil, and judge of the pressure of the grievance by the badness of the principle. They augur misgovernment at a distance; and sniff the approach of tyranny in every tainted breeze.

The last cause of this disobedient spirit in the colonies is hardly less powerful than the rest, as it is not merely moral, but laid deep in the natural constitution of things. Three thousand miles of ocean lie between you and them. No contrivance can prevent the effect of this distance, in weakening government. . . .

Then, Sir, from these six capital sources; of descent; of form of government; of religion in the northern provinces; of manners in the southern; of education; of the remoteness of situation from the first mover of government; from all these causes a fierce spirit of liberty has grown up. It has grown with the growth of the people in your colonies, and increased with the increase of their wealth; a spirit, that unhappily meeting with an exercise of power in England, which, however lawful, is not reconcileable to any ideas of liberty, much less with theirs, has kindled this flame, that is ready to consume us.

I do not mean to commend either the spirit in this excess, or the moral causes which produce it. . . . But the question is, not whether their spirit deserves praise or blame;—what, in the name of God, shall we do with it? . . .

. . . As far as I am capable of discerning, there are but three ways of proceeding relative to this stubborn spirit, which prevails in your colonies and disturbs your government. These are—To change that spirit, as inconvenient, by removing the causes. To prosecute it as criminal. Or, to comply with it as necessary. I would not be guilty of an imperfect enumeration; I can think of but these three. Another has indeed been started, that of giving up the colonies; but it met so slight a reception, that I do not think myself obliged to dwell a great while upon it. It is nothing but a little sally of anger, like the forwardness of peevish children, who, when they cannot get all they would have, are resolved to take nothing.

The first of these plans, to change the spirit as inconvenient, by removing the causes, I think is the most like a systematic proceeding. It is radical in its principle; but it is attended with great difficulties, some of them little short, as I conceive, of impossibilities. . . .

The temper and character, which prevail in our colonies, are, I am afraid, unalterable by any human art. We cannot, I fear, falsify the pedigree of this fierce people, and persuade them that they are not sprung from a nation, in whose veins the blood of freedom circulates. . . .

If then, Sir, it seems almost desperate to think of any . . . course, for changing the . . . causes . . . which produce prejudices irreconcilable to the late exercise of our authority; but that the spirit, infallibly will continue; and, continuing, will produce such effects, as now embarrass us; the second mode under consideration is, to prosecute that spirit in its overt acts, as *criminal*.

At this proposition, I must pause a moment. The thing seems a great deal too big for my ideas of jurisprudence. . . . It looks to me narrow and pedantic, to apply the ordinary ideas of criminal justice to this great public contest. I do not know the method of drawing up an indictment against a whole people. . . . I really think, that for wise men this is not judicious; for sober men, not decent; for minds tinctured with humanity, not mild and merciful. . . .

There is, Sir, also a circumstance which convinces me, that this mode of criminal proceeding is not (at least in the present stage of our contest) altogether expedient. . . . What is it we have got by all our menaces, which have been many and ferocious? What advantage have we derived from the penal laws we have passed, and which, for the time, have been severe and numerous? What advances have we made towards our object, by the sending of a force, which, by land and sea, is no contemptible strength? Has the disorder abated? Nothing less.—When I see things in this situation, after such confident hopes, bold promises, and active exertions, I cannot, for my life, avoid a suspicion, that the plan itself is not correctly right.

If then the removal of the causes of this spirit of American liberty be, for the greater part, or rather entirely, impracticable; if the ideas of criminal process be inapplicable, or, if applicable, are in the highest degree inexpedient, what way yet remains? No way is open, but the third and last—to comply with the American spirit as necessary; or, if you please to submit to it, as a necessary evil.

If we adopt this mode; if we mean to conciliate and concede; let us see of what nature the concession ought to be: to ascertain the nature of our concession, we must look at their complaint. The colonies complain, that they have not the characteristic mark and seal of British freedom. They complain, that they are taxed in a parliament, in which they are not represented. If you mean to satisfy them at all, you must satisfy them with regard to this complaint. . . .

Sir, I think you must perceive, that I am resolved this day to have nothing at all to do with the question of the right of taxation. Some gentlemen startle—but it is true: I put it totally out of the question.

It is less than nothing in my consideration. . . . My consideration is narrow, confined, and wholly limited to the policy of the question. I do not examine, whether . . . a right of taxation is necessarily involved in the general principle of legislation, and inseparable from the ordinary supreme power. These are deep questions, where great names militate against each other; where reason is perplexed; and an appeal to authorities only thickens the confusion. . . . The question with me is, not whether you have a right to render your people miserable; but whether it is not your interest to make them happy. It is not, what a lawyer tells me, I may do; but what humanity, reason, and justice, tell me, I ought to do. Is a politic act the worse for being a generous one? Is no concession proper, but that which is made from your want of right to keep what you grant? Or does it lessen the grace or dignity of relaxing in the exercise of an odious claim, because you have your evidence-room full of titles, and your magazines stuffed with arms to enforce them? What signify all those titles, and all those arms? Of what avail are they, when the reason of the thing tells me, that the assertion of my title is the loss of my suit; and that I could do nothing but wound myself by the use of my own weapons.

. . . I am not determining a point of law; I am restoring tranquillity; and the general character and situation of a people must determine what sort of government is fitted for them. That point nothing else can or ought to determine.

My idea therefore, without considering whether we yield as matter of right, or grant as matter of favour, is *to admit the people of our colonies into an interest in the constitution*; and, by recording that admission in the journals of parliament, to give them as strong an assurance as the nature of the thing will admit, that we mean for ever to adhere to that solemn declaration of systematic indulgence. . . .

. . . The more moderate among the opposers of parliamentary concession freely confess, that they hope no good from taxation; but they apprehend the colonists have further views; and if this point were conceded, they would instantly attack the trade laws. . . .

. . . [But I do not] discern how the revenue laws form any security whatsoever to the commercial regulations; or that these commercial regulations are the true ground of the quarrel; or, that the giving way in any one instance of authority, is to lose all that may remain unconceded.

One fact is clear and indisputable. The public and avowed origin of this quarrel was on taxation. This quarrel has indeed brought on new disputes on new questions; but certainly the least bitter and the fewest of all, on trade laws. To judge which of the two be the real radical cause of quarrel, we have to see whether the commercial dispute did, in order of time, precede the dispute on taxation? There is not a shadow of evidence for it. . . . And I would, Sir, recommend to your serious consideration, whether it be prudent to form a rule for punishing people, not on their own acts, but on your conjectures? Surely it is preposterous at the very best. It is not justifying your anger, by their misconduct; but it is converting your ill-will into their delinquency.

But the colonies will go further.—Alas! alas! when will this speculating against fact and reason end? What will quiet these panic fears which we entertain of the hostile effect of the conciliatory conduct? Is it true, that no case can exist, in which it is proper for the sovereign to accede to the desires of his discontented subjects? Is there any thing peculiar in this case, to make a rule for itself? Is all authority of course lost, when it is not pushed to the extreme? Is it a certain maxim, that, the fewer causes of dissatisfaction are left by government, the more the subject will be inclined to resist and rebel?

All these objections being in fact no more than suspicions, conjectures, divinations, formed in defiance of fact and experience; they did not, Sir, discourage me from entertaining the idea of a conciliatory concession, founded on the principles which I have just stated. . . .

You will now, Sir, perhaps imagine, that I am on the point of proposing to you a scheme for a representation of the colonies in parliament. Perhaps I might be inclined to entertain some such thought; but a great flood stops me in my course. *Opposuit natura*—I cannot remove the eternal barriers of the creation. The thing in that mode, I do not know to be possible. As I meddle with no theory, I do not absolutely assert the impracticability of such a representation. But I do not see my way to it; and those who have been more confident, have not been more successful. However, the arm of public benevolence is not shortened; and there are often several means to the same end. What nature has disjoined in one way, wisdom may unite in another. When we cannot give the benefit as we would wish, let us not refuse it altogether. If we cannot give the principal, let us find a substitute. But how? Where? What substitute?

. . . I only wish you . . . to return to that mode which an uniform experience has marked out to you as best; and in which you walked with security, advantage, and honour, until the year 1763.

My resolutions therefore mean to establish the equity and justice of a taxation of America, by *grant* and not by *imposition*. To mark the *legal competency* of the colony assemblies for the support of their government in peace, and for public aids in time of war. To acknowledge that this legal competency has had *a dutiful and beneficial exercise;* and that experience has shewn the *benefit of their grants,* and the *futility of parliamentary taxation as a method of supply.*

These solid truths compose six fundamental propositions. . . . I have no more doubt than I entertain of my existence, that, if you admitted these, you would command an immediate peace; and with but tolerable future management, a lasting obedience in America. I am not arrogant in this confident assurance. The propositions are all mere matters of fact; and if they are such facts as draw irresistible conclusions even in the stating, this is the power of truth, and not any management of mine.

. . . The first is a resolution—"That the colonies and plantations of Great Britain in North America, consisting of fourteen separate governments, and containing two millions and upwards of free inhabitants, have not had the liberty and privilege of electing and sending any knights and burgesses, or others to represent them in the high court of parliament."—This is a plain matter of fact, necessary to be laid down. . . .

The second is like unto the first—"That the said colonies and plantations have been liable to, and bounden by, several subsidies, payments, rates, and taxes, given and granted by parliament, though the said colonies and plantations have not their knights and burgesses, in the said high court of parliament, of their own election, to represent the condition of their country; by lack whereof they have been oftentimes touched and grieved by subsidies, given, granted, and assented to, in the said court, in a manner prejudicial to the commonwealth, quietness, rest, and peace of the subjects inhabiting within the same." . . .

The next proposition is—"That, from the distance of the said colonies, and from other circumstances, no method hath hitherto been devised for procuring a representation in parliament for the said colonies." . . .

The fourth resolution is—"That each of the said colonies hath within itself a body, chosen in part, or in the whole, by the freemen, freeholders, or other free inhabitants thereof, commonly called the General Assembly, or general court, with powers, legally to raise, levy, and assess, according to the several usage of such colonies, duties and taxes towards defraying all sorts of public services." . . .

The fifth resolution is also a resolution of fact—"That the said general assemblies, general courts, or other bodies legally qualified as aforesaid, have at sundry times freely granted several large subsidies and public aids for his Majesty's service, according to their abilities, when required thereto by letter from one of his Majesty's principal secretaries of state; and that their right to grant the same, and their cheerfulness and sufficiency, in the said grants, have been at sundry times acknowledged by parliament." . . .

I think then I am . . . justified in the sixth and last resolution, which is—"That it hath been found by experience, that the manner of granting the said supplies and aids, by the said general assemblies, hath been more agreeable to the said colonies, and more beneficial, and conducive to the public service, than the mode of giving and granting aids in parliament, to be raised and paid in the said colonies." This makes the whole of the fundamental part of the plan. . . .

The question now, on all this accumulated matter, is;—whether you will chuse to abide by a profitable experience, or a mischievous theory; whether you chuse to build on imagination or fact; whether you prefer enjoyment or hope; satisfaction in your subjects, or discontent?

. . . [Some may object] that the grievance from a want of representation . . . goes to the whole of legislation as well as to taxation. And that the colonies grounding themselves upon that doctrine, will apply it to all parts of legislative authority. . . .

I do not know, that the colonies have, in any general way, or in any cool hour, gone much beyond the demand of immunity in relation to taxes. It is not fair to judge of the temper or dispositions of any man, or any set of men, when they are composed and at rest, from their conduct, or their expressions, in a state of disturbance and irritation. It is besides a very great mistake to imagine, that mankind follow up practically any speculative principle, either of government or of freedom, as far as it will go in argument and logic. . . . Man acts from adequate motives relative to his interest; and not on metaphysical speculations. Aristotle, the great master of reasoning, cautions us, and with great weight and propriety, against this species of delusive geometrical accuracy in moral arguments, as the most fallacious of all sophistry.

The Americans will have no interest contrary to the grandeur and glory of England, when they are not oppressed by the weight of it; and they will rather be inclined to respect the acts of a superintending legislature; when they see them the acts of that power, which is itself the security, not the rival, of their secondary importance. In this assurance, my mind most perfectly acquiesces; and I confess, I feel not the least alarm, from the discontents which are to arise, from putting people at their ease; nor do I apprehend the destruction of this empire, from giving, by an act of free grace and indulgence, to two millions of my fellow citizens, some share of those rights, upon which I have always been taught to value myself. . . .

. . . May you decide with wisdom! For my part, I feel my mind greatly disburthened by what I have done to day. I have been the less fearful of trying your patience, because on this subject I mean to spare it altogether in future. I have this comfort, that in every stage of the American affairs, I have steadily opposed the measures that have produced the confusion, and may bring on the destruction of this empire. I now go so far as to risk a proposal of my own. If I cannot give peace to my country, I give it to my conscience.

But what (says the financier) is peace to us without money? Your plan gives us no revenue. No! But it does—For it secures to the subject the power of refusal; the first of all revenues. Experience is a cheat, and fact a liar, if this power in the subject of proportioning his grant, or of not granting at all, has not been found the richest mine of revenue ever discovered by the skill or by the fortune of man. . . . What is the soil or climate where experience has not uniformly proved, that the voluntary flow of heaped-up plenty, bursting from the weight of its own rich luxuriance, has ever run with a more copious stream of revenue, than could be squeezed from the dry husks of oppressed indigence, by the straining of all the politic machinery in the world? . . .

. . . My trust . . . is in the close affection which grows from common names, from kindred blood, from similar privileges, and equal protection. These are ties, which, though light as air, are as strong as links of iron. Let the colonies always keep the idea of their civil rights associated with your government;—they will cling and grapple to you; and no force under heaven will be of power to tear them from their allegiance. But let it be once understood, that your government may be one thing, and their privileges another; that these two things may exist without any mutual relation; the cement is gone; the cohesion is loosened; and everything hastens to decay and dissolution. As long as you have the wisdom to keep the sovereign authority of this country as the sanctuary of liberty, the sacred temple consecrated to our common faith, wherever the chosen race and sons of England worship freedom, they will turn their faces towards you. The more they multiply, the more friends you will have; the more ardently they love liberty, the more perfect will be their obedience. Slavery they can have any where. It is a weed that grows in every soil. They may have it from Spain, they may have it from Prussia. But until you become lost to all feeling of your true interest and your natural dignity, freedom they can have from none but you. This is the commodity of price, of which you have the monopoly. This is the true act of navigation, which binds to you the commerce of the colonies, and through them secures to you the wealth of the world. Deny them this participation of freedom, and you break that sole bond, which originally made, and must still preserve, the unity of the empire. Do not entertain so weak an imagination, as that your registers and your bonds, your affidavits and your sufferances, your cockets and your clearances, are what form the great securities of your commerce. Do not dream that your letters of office, and your instructions, and your suspending clauses, are the things that hold together the great contexture of this mysterious whole. These things do not make your government. Dead instruments, passive tools as they are, it is the spirit of the English communion, that gives all their life and efficacy to them. It is the spirit of the English constitution, which, infused through the mighty mass, pervades, feeds, unites, invigorates, vivifies, every part of the empire, even down to the minutest member.

Is it not the same virtue which does every thing for us here in England? Do you imagine then, that it is the Land Tax Act which raises your revenue; that it is the annual vote in the committee of supply, which gives you your army? or that it is the Mutiny Bill which

inspires it with bravery and discipline? No! surely no! It is the love of
the people; it is their attachment to their government from the sense
of the deep stake they have in such a glorious institution, which gives
you your army and your navy, and infuses into both that liberal
obedience, without which your army would be a base rabble, and your
navy nothing but rotten timber.

All this, I know well enough, will sound wild and chimerical to the
profane herd of those vulgar and mechanical politicians, who have
no place among us; a sort of people who think that nothing exists but
what is gross and material; and who therefore, far from being qualified
to be directors of the great movement of empire, are not fit to turn a
wheel in the machine. But to men truly initiated and rightly taught,
these ruling and master principles, which, in the opinion of such men
as I have mentioned, have no substantial existence, are in truth
every thing, and all in all. Magnanimity in politics is not seldom the
truest wisdom; and a great empire and little minds go ill together. If
we are conscious of our situation, and glow with zeal to fill our places
as becomes our station and ourselves, we ought to auspicate all our
public proceedings on America, with the old warning of the church,
Sursum corda! We ought to elevate our minds to the greatness of that
trust to which the order of Providence has called us. By adverting to
the dignity of this high calling, our ancestors have turned a savage
wilderness into a glorious empire; and have made the most extensive,
and the only honourable conquests; not by destroying, but by promoting, the wealth, the number, the happiness of the human race.
Let us get an American revenue as we have got an American empire.
English privileges have made it all that it is; English privileges alone
will make it all it can be.

His eloquence notwithstanding, his resolutions went down to
a resounding defeat. The rank-and-file of Parliament stood over-
whelmingly for coercion.

Why the weakness of the forces favoring conciliation? Part of
the reason lay in the division of the opposition. Chatham would
have nothing to do with the Rockinghamites; he saw in the
Declaratory Act the root of all subsequent troubles. The forces
favoring conciliation were further weakened by the growing
anti-Americanism among British merchants and manufacturers.

The opening of new markets in Spain, Russia, and Turkey had largely nullified the impact of the colonial boycott; more importantly, the merchants had become increasingly fearful that the colonists were aiming at the complete overthrow of British authority including the Acts of Trade and Navigation.

Most importantly, public opinion in Britain had swung against the colonists. The Declaration of Rights voted by the Continental Congress made sweeping demands. Parliament would have to renounce all authority over the colonies; even its regulation of trade would rest upon their consent; and the sole bond of union would be a common king. Such terms were unacceptable to most politically conscious Britons of the day. Even Chatham, in his final plea for reconciliation, insisted upon "due Recognition of the Supreme Authority and superintending Powers of Parliament."

The traditional Whig legend that George III maintained the North ministry in power by corruption and bribery is a myth. The disorders in America coupled with the Wilkes agitation in Britain itself had produced a conservative reaction in support of the government. As a Scottish M.P. friendly to the American cause acknowledged in June, 1775: "When you never see more than eighty in Parliament opposing the measure, you may depend upon it, the measure is not thought a bad one; for corruption does not reach so deep. Many members support the minister who are not supported by him." Rockingham himself recognized the weakness of the opposition in the country at large; "the real fact is," he wrote Burke, September 24, 1775, "that the generality of the people of England are now led away by the misrepresentations and arts of the ministry, the court, and their abettors, so that the violent measures toward America, are fairly adopted and countenanced by a majority of individuals of all ranks, professions, or occupations in this country."

Supported by a solid majority, the government itself resolved to follow what Lord North regarded as a judicious mixture of the carrot and the stick. Early in January, 1775, orders went out to the royal governors and General Gage to exert their "utmost Endeavors" to block the election of delegates to the Second Continental Congress. On January 27, the Earl of Dartmouth drew up a "secret" dispatch to General Gage informing him that reinforcements were on their way and instructing him to meet force with force. "It is the opinion of The King's Servants in which His Majesty concurs," the dispatch informed Gage, "that the first & essential step to be taken towards re-establishing Government" was the arrest of the revolutionary leaders in Massachusetts even if that meant the beginning of open warfare:

Printed: Carter, *The Correspondence of General Thomas Gage,* II, pp. 179-183.

. . . Your Dispatches . . . relate to Facts, and state Proceedings, that amount to actual Revolt, and shew a Determination in the People to commit themselves at all Events in open Rebellion.

The King's Dignity, & the Honor and Safety of the Empire, require, that, in such a Situation, Force should be repelled by Force; and it has been His Majesty's Care not only to send you from hence such Reinforcement of the Army under your Command as general Considerations of public Safety would admit, but also to authorize you to collect together every Corps that could be spared from necessary Duty in every other part of America. It is hoped therefore that by this time your Force will amount to little less than 4,000. effective Men, including the Detachment of Marines that went out in the Men of War that sailed in October last, and I have the Satisfaction to acquaint you that Orders have been given this day for the immediate Embarkation of a further Detachment of Seven Hundred Marines, and of three Regiments of Infantry, & One of light Dragoons, from Ireland. . . .

It appears that your Object has hitherto been to act upon the Defensive, & to avoid the hazard of weakening your Force by sending out Detachments of your Troops upon any Occasion whatsoever; & I should do Injustice to Your Conduct, and to my own Sentiments of your Prudence & Discretion, if I could suppose that such Precaution was not necessary.

It is hoped however that this large Reinforcement to your Army will enable you to take a more active & determined part. . . .

I have already said, in more Letters than one, that the Authority of this Kingdom must be supported, & the Execution of its Laws inforced, & you will have seen in His Maty's Speech to both Houses of Parliament, & in the Addresses which they have presented to His Majesty, the firm Resolution of His Majesty and Parliament to act upon those Principles; and as there is a strong Appearance that the Body of the People in at least three of the New England Governments are determined to cast off their Dependence upon the Government of this Kingdom, the only Consideration that remains is, in what manner the Force under your Command may be exerted to defend the Constitution & to restore the Vigour of Government.

It seems to be your Idea that Matters are come to such a State that this is no otherwise attainable than by an absolute Conquest of the People of the three Governments of Massachuset's Bay, Connecticut & Rhode Island, & that such Conquest cannot be effected by a less Force than 20,000. Men.

. . . Yet I am unwilling to believe that matters are as yet come to that Issue.

I have stated that the violences committed by those who have taken up arms in Massachusetts Bay, have appeared to me as the acts of a rude Rabble without plan, without concert, & without conduct, and therefore I think that a smaller Force now, if put to the Test, would be able to encounter them with greater probability of Success than might be expected from a greater Army, if the people should be suffered to form themselves upon a more regular plan, to acquire confidence from discipline, and to prepare those resources without which every thing must be put to the issue of a single Action.

In this view therefore of the situation of The King's Affairs, it is the Opinion of The King's Servants in which His Majesty concurs, that the first & essential step to be taken towards re-establishing Government, would be to arrest and imprison the principal actors & abettors in the Provincial Congress (whose proceedings appear in every light to be acts of treason & rebellion) if regardless of your Proclamation & in defiance of it they should presume again to assemble for such rebellious purposes; and if the steps taken upon this occasion be accompanied with due precaution, and every means be devised to keep the Measure Secret until the moment of Execution, it can hardly fail of Success, and will perhaps be accomplished without bloodshed; but however that may be I must again repeat that any efforts of the People, unprepared to encounter with a regular force, cannot be very formidable; and though such a proceeding should be, according to your own idea of it, a Signal for Hostilities yet, for the reasons I have already given, it will surely be better that the Conflict should be brought on, upon such ground, than in a riper state of Rebellion.

It must be understood, however, after all I have said, that this is a matter which must be left to your own Discretion to be executed or not as you shall, upon weighing all Circumstances, and the advantages and disadvantages on one side, and the other, think most advisable.

I have fully exposed to you the Grounds upon which the Proposition has been adopted here, & unless the situation of things shall be very different from what they at present appear to be, it is considered as the best & most effectual means of vindicating the authority of this Kingdom. . . .

I sincerely wish that the Information which we have received of the State of the Province, would enable me to instruct you upon every Case, in which you may wish to receive such Instruction; but in a Situation where every thing depends so much upon the Events of the Day, and upon local Circumstances, your Conduct must be governed very much by your own Judgement and Discretion.

What I have said will point out to you with precision the Idea entertained here, of the manner in which the Military Force under your Command may be employed with effect. . . .

With regard to the state of America in general, affairs there are now come to a Crisis in which the Government of this Country must act with firmness and decision. . . .

But even while thus preparing for a military showdown, the ministry decided upon a conciliatory gesture. The Conciliatory Proposition which North introduced on February 20, provided that if the colonies would make adequate provision for their defense and government, Parliament would refrain from taxation. North had few illusions about the results, but he hoped that such a conciliatory gesture might win back the loyalty of wavering moderates. Despite back-bench mutterings against even as modest a concession, the resolution passed, February 27, 1775, by a vote of 274 to 88:

Printed: *New Jersey Archives,* X, pp. 556-557.

That when the Governor, Council, and Assembly, or General Court, of any of His Majesty's Provinces or Colonies in America, shall propose to make Provision, according to the Condition, Circumstances, and Situation, of such Province or Colony, for contributing their Proportion to the Common Defence (such Proportion to be raised under the Authority of the General Court, or General Assembly, of such Province or Colony, and disposable by Parliament) and shall engage to make Provision also for the Support of the Civil Government, and the Administration of Justice, in such Province or Colony, it will be proper, if such Proposal shall be approved by His Majesty and the Two Houses of Parliament, and for so long as such Provision shall be made accordingly, to forbear, in respect of such Province or Colony, to levy any Duty, Tax, or Assessment, or to impose any farther Duty, Tax, or Assessment, except only such Duties as it may be expedient to continue to levy or to impose for the Regulation of Commerce; the Nett Produce of the Duties last mentioned to be carried to the Account of such Province or Colony respectively.

Whatever effect the resolution might have had in swaying American opinion was nullified by events in Massachusetts. For the Proposition reached New York the day after the news of the fighting at Lexington and Concord.

Tension had been rising in Massachusetts since the news of the Coercive Acts. Gage's attempt to enforce the new Government of Massachusetts Act met with violent resistance. After the meeting of the First Continental Congress, the situation rapidly worsened. The Massachusetts radicals, emboldened by the promise of support against British aggression, established the first colonial revolutionary assembly in October, 1774. This Provincial Congress set up a full-fledged revolutionary government that collected taxes, raised an army, and superseded the royal authority throughout the province. Sam Adams and his fellow radicals were ready for a showdown provided they could convince the rest of the colonies that they had acted defensively. Arms were collected, the militia drilled, and a close watch was kept for any movement of British troops from their stronghold in Boston.

Gage was determined to avoid premature hostilities. He fully agreed that the supremacy of Parliament must be maintained at all costs, but knowing the weakness of his forces, he took pains to avoid an open clash until sufficient reinforcements arrived. This cautious policy brought Gage much criticism in British official circles. Discounting the gravity of the situation, and contemptuous of the fighting capacities of the colonists, the ministers were eager for forceful action.

On April 14, 1775, Gage received the "secret" dispatch of January 27. Although the instructions indicated that "in a Situation where everything depends as much upon the Events of the Day, and upon local Circumstances, your Conduct must be governed very much by your own Judgement and Discretion," Gage correctly read the dispatch to be an order for him to take decisive action. The dispatch had in mind the arrest of the patriot leaders; Gage decided instead to send a detachment to Concord to destroy the military supplies which his spies told him had been gathered there.

The detachment set forth on the night of April 18; but observant eyes in Boston had noted the preparations for the expedition and the patriots were able to send out messengers that eluded the British guards and alerted the countryside. The outlines of what happened are not in dispute. The British troops crossed by water from Boston to a point near Cambridge and marched to Lexington. Arriving there at dawn, April 19, the British forces were faced by a hastily assembled band of minute men under Captain John Parker. A skirmish ensued with the British advance units led by Major John Pitcairn in which the minute men lost eight killed and ten wounded. The British then marched on to Concord, where they destroyed whatever military supplies they could find. But returning to Boston, they suffered withering

fire from American militiamen along the route. What is disputed
is who fired first at Lexington. Each side blamed the other.
Acting swiftly, the Massachusetts radicals circulated their account of the clash throughout the colonies and even in Britain
itself before the official British version arrived.

The news of the clash ran like an electric shock through the
colonists. The severest blow was to moderates such as John
Dickinson who still hoped to restore harmony between mother
country and colonies. "The *'immedicable vulnas'* is at length
struck," the Pennsylvanian wrote to Arthur Lee, April 29, 1775.
"The rescript to our Petition is written in blood. The impious
war of tyranny against innocence has commenced in the neigh-
borhood of *Boston*":

> Printed: Force, *American Archives, Fourth Series,* II, pp.
> 443-445.

. . . What human policy can divine the prudence of precipitating
us into these shocking scenes? Why have we rashly been declared
rebels? Why have directions been sent to disarm us? Why orders to
commence hostilities? Why was not General *Gage* at least restrained
from hostilities until the sense of another Congress could be collected? It was the determined resolution of some, already appointed
Delegates for it, to have strained every nerve at that meeting to attempt bringing the unhappy dispute to terms of accommodation, safe
for the Colonies, and honourable and advantageous for our Mother
Country, in whose prosperity and glory our hearts take as large a
share as any Minister's of State, and from as just and as generous
motives, to say no more of them.

But what topicks of reconciliation are now left for men who think
as I do, to address our countrymen? To recommend reverence for the
Monarch, or affection for the Mother Country? Will the distinctions
between the Prince and his Ministers, between the People and their
Representatives, wipe out the stain of blood? Or have we the slightest
reason to hope that those Ministers and Representatives will not be
supported throughout the tragedy, as they have been through the first
act? No. While we revere and love our Mother Country, her sword is
opening our veins. The same delusions will still prevail, till *France*

and *Spain,* if not other Powers, long jealous of *Britain's* force and fame, will fall upon her, embarrassed with an exhausting civil war, and crush, or at least depress her; then turn their arms on these Provinces, which must submit to wear their chains, or wade through seas of blood to a dear-bought and at best a frequently convulsed and precarious independence.

All the ministerial intelligence concerning us is false. We are a united, resolved people; are, or quickly shall be, well armed and disciplined; our smiths and powder-mills are at work day and night; our supplies from foreign parts continually arriving. Good officers, that is, well-experienced ones, we shall soon have, and the Navy of *Great Britain* cannot stop our whole trade. Our Towns are but brick and stone, and mortar and wood; they, perhaps, may be destroyed; they are only the hairs of our heads; if sheared ever so close, they will grow again. We compare them not with our rights and liberties. We worship as our fathers worshipped, not idols which our hands have made. . . .

In colony after colony, excited patriots swore to defend their liberties by force of arms. In South Carolina no less than in New England, the revolutionary fervor ran high:

Printed: Hezekiah Niles, *Principles and Acts of the Revolution in America* (New York, Chicago, and New Orleans, 1876), p. 321.

The actual commencement of hostilities against this continent, by the British troops, in the bloody scene on the 19th of April last, near Boston; the increase of arbitrary impositions, from a wicked and despotic ministry, and the dread of instigated insurrections in the colonies, are causes sufficient to drive an oppressed people to the use of arms:—We, therefore, the subscribers, inhabitants of South Carolina, holding ourselves bound, by that most sacred of all obligations, the duty of good citizens towards an injured country, and thoroughly convinced, that, under our present distressed circumstances, we shall be justified before God and man, in resisting force by force, *do unite* ourselves under every tie of religion and honor, and associate as a band in her defence, against every foe; hereby solemnly engaging that whenever our continental and provincial councils shall decree it necessary, we will go forth, and be ready to sacrifice our lives, and fortunes, to secure her freedom and safety.—This obligation to continue in full force until a reconciliation shall take place between Great Britain and America, upon constitutional principles; an event which we most ardently desire. And we will hold all those persons inimical to the liberties of the colonies, who shall refuse to subscribe to this association.

Subscribed by every member present, and certified by

HENRY LAURENS, *President.*

June, 1775.

The reaction in British official circles was equally resolute. The King called for swift action, insisting that "when once those rebels have felt a small blow, they will submit." The fighting at Lexington and Concord followed by the seizure of Ticonderoga and Crown Point, Dartmouth wrote to Gage, July, 1775, "evinces the Necessity, and will manifest to the World the Justice of the Measures which the King has adopted, for supporting the Constitution, and on which His Majesty will firmly persevere." Writing the same day to Governor William Tryon of New York, he reiterated "that it is His Majesty's firm Resolution to exert every power which the constitution has placed in His hands to compel obedience to the Laws and authority of the supreme Legislature. To that end orders have been already given for augmenting our Naval Forces in America, and we think we shall soon be able to make such addition to the Army under General Gage as will enable him to withstand the utmost efforts of that Rebellion into which the People of the four New England Provinces have so rashly plunged."

What would the Congress do? When that body met at Philadelphia on May 10, 1775, the lines of battle were drawn. The membership ran the gamut from advocates of outright independence such as Sam Adams to conservatively inclined supporters of reconciliation such as John Dickinson; the majority stood in between. The conflicting emotions tugging at the delegates were reflected in the resolution adopted May 26, 1775. That resolution provided, on the one hand, that "these colonies be immediately put into a state of defence"; on the other, that "measures be entered into for opening a Negotiation, in order to accommodate the unhappy disputes subsisting between Great Britain and these colonies":

Printed: Ford, *Journals of the Continental Congress,* II, pp. 64-66.

Resolved unanimously, 1, That his Majesty's most faithful subjects, in these colonies, are reduced to a dangerous and critical situation, by the attempts of the british Ministry to carry into execution, by force of arms, several unconstitutional and oppressive acts of the british parliament for laying taxes in America; to enforce the collection of those taxes, and for altering and changing the constitution and internal police of some of these colonies, in violation of the natural and civil rights of the colonists.

Unanimously 2. Hostilities being actually commenced in the Massachusetts bay, by the British troops, under the command of General Gage, and the lives of a number of the inhabitants of that colony destroyed, the town of Boston having not only been long occupied as a garrisoned town in an enemy's country, but the inhabitants thereof treated with a severity and cruelty not to be justifyed even towards declared enemies; large re-inforcements too being ordered and soon expected, for the declared purpose of compelling these colonies to submit to the operation of the s^d acts; *Resolved,* therefore, that for the purpose of securing and defending these colonies, and preserving them in safety against all attempts to carry the s^d acts into execution by force of arms, these colonies be immediately put into a state of defence.

Unanimously 3. But, as we most ardently wish for a restoration of the harmony formerly subsisting between our Mother country and these colonies, the interruption of which must, at all events, be exceedingly injurious to both countries, *Resolved,* that with a sincere design of contributing by all the means in our power, not incompatible with a just regard for the undoubted rights and true interests

of these colonies, to the promotion of this most desireable reconciliation, an humble and dutiful petition be presented to his Majesty.

4. *Resolved,* That measures be entered into for opening a Negotiation, in order to accomodate the unhappy disputes subsisting between
Great Britain and these colonies, and that this be made a part of the
petition to the King.

In the days that followed, the Congress devoted itself mainly
to carrying out that part of the resolution calling for placing
the colonies in a state of defense. After Lexington and Concord,
a hastily assembled army of 15,000 men besieged Boston, and
on May 16, the Massachusetts Provincial Congress asked that
the Continental Congress take over its direction. In reply, the
Congress voted, on June 15, to appoint a general "to command
all the continental forces, raised or to be raised, for the defense
of American liberty." After much behind-the-scenes bickering,
George Washington was named commander-in-chief. Gradually
taking over all the functions of government, the Congress provided for the recruiting of additional troops, adopted a plan of
military organization, and undertook to raise money by issuing
paper currency.

While these steps were being taken in Philadelphia, open warfare flared anew in Massachusetts. On June 12, Gage decided to
have his troops occupy the heights on Dorchester Peninsula and
Charlestown Peninsula. If the colonists succeeded in fortifying
these positions, their artillery could bombard the town below
and force the British to evacuate Boston. But news of Gage's
plans leaked out before the British could act, and on June 16, the
American militiamen seized and fortified Breed's Hill on the
Charlestown Peninsula. The next day a British force under Major
General William Howe made a frontal assault upon the American
positions. Twice the ill-trained and badly-organized militiamen
drove back the attackers with heavy losses. The third charge
carried the day, but the capture of the hill was a Pyrrhic victory
for the British, who lost over a thousand men killed or wounded.

The Continental Congress heard the news of what has become
known as the battle of Bunker Hill on June 26. But even then

the hope for reconciliation would not down. A radical such as John Adams might privately fume and fuss; but, as he complained to James Warren, July 6, 1775, the time was not ripe for a declaration of independence:

> Printed: *Warren-Adams Letters,* Massachusetts Historical Society *Collections,* vols. 72-73 (2 vols., Boston, 1917–1925), I, pp. 73-75.

Secret and Confidential, as the Saying is.

The Congress is not yet so much alarmed as it ought to be. There are still hopes, that Ministry and Parliament, will immediately receed as soon as they hear of the Battle of Lexington, the Spirit of New York and Phyladelphia, the Permanency of the Union of the Colonies etc.: I think they are much deceived and that we shall have nothing but Deceit and Hostility, Fire, Famine, Pestilence and Sword from Administration and Parliament. Yet the Colonies like all Bodies of Men must and will have their Way and their Humour, and even their Whims.

These opinions of Some Colonies which are founded I think in their Wishes and passions, their Hopes and Fears, rather than in Reason and Evidence will give a whimsical Cast to the Proceedings of this Congress. You will see a strange Oscillation between love and hatred, between War and Peace—Preparations for War and Negociations for Peace. We must have a Petition to the King and a delicate Proposal of Negociations, etc. This Negociation I dread like Death: But it must be proposed. We cant avoid it. Discord and total Disunion would be the certain Effect of a resolute Refusal to petition and negociate. My Hopes are that Ministry will be afraid of Negociation as well as We and therefore refuse it. If they agree to it, We shall have Occasion for all our Wit Vigilance and Virtue to avoid being deceived, wheedled threatened or bribed out of our Freedom. If we Strenuously insist upon our Liberties, as I hope and am pretty sure We shall however, a Negotiation, if agreed to, will terminate in Nothing. it will effect nothing. We may possibly gain Time and Powder and Arms.

You will see an Address to the People of G. Britain, another to those of Ireland, and another to Jamaica.

You will also see a Spirited Manifesto. We ought immediately to dissolve all Ministerial Tyrannies, and Custom houses, set up Governments of our own, like that of Connecticutt in all the Colonies, confederate together like an indissoluble Band, for mutual defence, and open our Ports to all Nations immediately. This is the system that your Friend has arrived at promoting from first to last: But the Colonies are not yet ripe for it—a Bill of Attainder, etc., may soon ripen them.

The "Spirited Manifesto" Adams mentioned was adopted that very day, July 6, 1775. The first draft of this "Declaration on Taking Arms" was prepared by Thomas Jefferson; but John Dickinson, still hopeful for reconciliation, rewrote it to remove the harsher language. Even with this pruning, however, the Declaration remained a forceful indictment of British policy:

> Printed: Ford, *Journals of the Continental Congress*, II, pp. 140-157.

A declaration by the Representatives of the United Colonies of North America, now met in General Congress at Philadelphia, setting forth the causes and necessity of their taking up arms.

If it was possible for men, who exercise their reason, to believe, that the Divine Author of our existence intended a part of the human race to hold an absolute property in, and an unbounded power over others, marked out by his infinite goodness and wisdom, as the objects of a legal domination never rightfully resistible, however severe and oppressive, the Inhabitants of these Colonies might at least require from the Parliament of Great Britain some evidence, that this dreadful authority over them, has been granted to that body. But a reverence for our great Creator, principles of humanity, and the dictates of common sense, must convince all those who reflect upon the subject, that government was instituted to promote the welfare of mankind, and ought to be administered for the attainment of that end. The legislature of Great Britain, however, stimulated by an inordinate passion for a power, not only unjustifiable, but which they know to be peculiarly reprobated by the very constitution of that kingdom, and desperate of success in any mode of contest, where regard should be had to truth, law, or right, have at length, deserting those, attempted to effect their cruel and impolitic purpose of enslaving these Colonies by violence, and have thereby rendered it necessary for us to close with their last appeal from Reason to Arms. . . .

. . . They have undertaken to give and grant our money without our consent, though we have ever exercised an exclusive right to dispose of our own property; statutes have been passed for extending the jurisdiction of courts of Admiralty and Vice-Admiralty beyond their ancient limits; for depriving us of the accustomed and inestimable privilege of trial by jury, in cases affecting both life and property; for suspending the legislature of one of the colonies; for interdicting all commerce to the capital of another; and for altering fundamentally the form of government established by charter, and secured by acts of its own legislature solemnly confirmed by the crown; for exempting the "murderers" of colonists from legal trial, and in effect, from punishment; for erecting in a neighboring province, acquired by the joint arms of Great Britain and America, a despotism dangerous to our very existence; and for quartering soldiers upon the colonists in time of profound peace. It has also been resolved in parliament, that colonists charged with committing certain offences, shall be transported to England to be tried.

But why should we enumerate our injuries in detail? By one statute it is declared, that parliament can "of right make laws to bind us IN ALL CASES WHATSOEVER." What is to defend us against so enormous, so unlimited a power? Not a single man of those who assume it, is chosen by us; or is subject to our controul or influence; but, on the contrary, they are all of them exempt from the operation of such laws, and an American revenue, if not diverted from the ostensible purposes for which it is raised, would actually lighten their own burdens in proportion as they increase ours. We saw the misery to which such despotism would reduce us. We for ten years incessantly and ineffectually besieged the Throne as suppliants; we reasoned, we remonstrated with parliament, in the most mild and decent language. But Administration, sensible that we should regard these oppressive measures as freemen ought to do, sent over fleets and armies to enforce them. The indignation of the Americans was roused, it is true; but it was the indignation of a virtuous, loyal, and affectionate people. A Congress of Delegates from the United Colonies was assembled at Philadelphia, on the fifth day of last September. We resolved again to offer an humble and dutiful petition to the King, and also addressed our fellow-subjects of Great Britain. We have pursued every temperate, every respectful measure: we have even proceeded to break off our commercial intercourse with our fellow-subjects, as the last peaceable admonition, that our attachment to no nation upon earth should supplant our attachment to liberty.— This, we flattered ourselves, was the ultimate step of the controversy: But subsequent events have shewn, how vain was this hope of finding moderation in our enemies. . . .

. . . A part of these colonies now feels, and all of them are sure of feeling, as far as the vengance of administration can inflict them, the complicated calamities of fire, sword, and famine.—We are reduced to the alternative of chusing an unconditional submission to the tyranny of irritated ministers, or resistance by force.—The latter is our choice.—We have counted the cost of this contest, and find nothing so dreadful as voluntary slavery.—Honor, justice, and humanity, forbid us tamely to surrender that freedom which we received from our gallant ancestors, and which our innocent posterity have a right to receive from us. We cannot endure the infamy and guilt of resigning succeeding generations to that wretchedness which inevitably awaits them, if we basely entail hereditary bondage upon them.

Our cause is just. Our union is perfect. Our internal resources are great, and if necessary, foreign assistance is undoubtedly attainable.— We gratefully acknowledge, as signal instances of the Divine favour towards us, that his Providence would not permit us to be called into this severe controversy, until we were grown up to our present strength, had been previously exercised in warlike operation, and possessed of the means of defending ourselves.—With hearts fortified with these animating reflections, we most solemnly, before God and the world, declare, that, exerting the utmost energy of those powers, which our beneficent Creator hath graciously bestowed upon us, the arms we have been compelled by our enemies to assume, we will, in defiance of every hazard, with unabating firmness and perseverance, employ for the presevation of our liberties; being with our [one] mind resolved to dye Free-men rather than live Slaves.

Lest this declaration should disquiet the minds of our friends and fellow-subjects in any part of the empire, we assure them that we mean not to dissolve that Union which has so long and so happily

subsisted between us, and which we sincerely wish to see restored.—
Necessity has not yet driven us into that desperate measure, or induced us to excite any other nation to war against them.—We have
not raised armies with ambitious designs of separating from Great
Britain, and establishing independent states. We fight not for glory or
for conquest. We exhibit to mankind the remarkable spectacle of a
people attacked by unprovoked enemies, without any imputation or
even suspicion of offence. They boast of their privileges and civilization, and yet proffer no milder conditions than servitude or death.

In our own native land, in defence of the freedom that is our
birth-right, and which we ever enjoyed till the late violation of it—
for the protection of our property, acquired solely by the honest
industry of our fore-fathers and ourselves, against violence actually
offered, we have taken up arms. We shall lay them down when
hostilities shall cease on the part of the aggressors, and all danger of
their being renewed shall be removed, and not before.

With an humble confidence in the mercies of the supreme and
impartial Judge and Ruler of the universe, we most devoutly implore
his divine goodness to protect us happily through this great conflict,
to dispose our adversaries to reconciliation on reasonable terms, and
thereby to relieve the empire from the calamities of civil war.

Forceful as was its indictment of British policy, the Declaration explicitly denied that the colonies sought their independence.
In a last-ditch bid for reconciliation, Dickinson took the lead in
writing and winning support for a final petition to the King. The
so-called Olive Branch Petition was agreed to on July 5, and
was signed by the members on July 8, 1775:

Printed: Ford, *Journals of the Continental Congress*, II,
pp. 158-161.

. . . Your Majesty's Ministers, persevering in their measures, and
proceeding to open hostilities for enforcing them, have compelled us
to arm in our own defence, and have engaged us in a controversy so
peculiarly abhorrent to the affections of your still faithful colonists,
that when we consider whom we must oppose in this contest, and if

it continues, what may be the consequences, our own particular misfortunes are accounted by us only as parts of our distress.

Knowing to what violent resentments and incurable animosities, civil discords are apt to exasperate and inflame the contending parties, we think ourselves required by indispensable obligations to Almighty God, to your Majesty, to our fellow subjects, and to ourselves, immediately to use all the means in our power, not incompatible with our safety, for stopping the further effusion of blood, and for averting the impending calamities that threaten the British Empire. . . .

Attached to your Majesty's person, family, and government, with all devotion that principle and affection can inspire, connected with Great Britain by the strongest ties that can unite societies, and deploring every event that tends in any degree to weaken them, we solemnly assure your Majesty, that we not only most ardently desire the former harmony between her and these colonies may be restored, but that a concord may be established between them upon so firm a basis as to perpetuate its blessings, uninterrupted by any future dissentions, to succeeding generations in both countries, and to transmit your Majesty's Name to posterity, adorned with that signal and lasting glory, that has attended the memory of those illustrious personages, whose virtues and abilities have extricated states from dangerous convulsions, and, by securing happiness to others, have erected the most noble and durable monuments to their own fame. . . .

We, therefore, beseech your Majesty, that your royal authority and influence may be graciously interposed to procure us relief from our afflicting fears and jealousies, occasioned by the system before mentioned, and to settle peace through every part of your dominions, with all humility submitting to your Majesty's wise consideration whether it may not be expedient for facilitating those important purposes, that your Majesty be pleased to direct some mode, by which the united applications of your faithful colonists to the throne, in pursuance of their common councils, may be improved into a happy and permanent reconciliation; and that, in the mean time, measures may be taken for preventing the further destruction of the lives of your Majesty's subjects; and that such statutes as more immediately distress any of your Majesty's colonies may be repealed.

For by such arrangements as your Majesty's wisdom can form, for collecting the united sense of your American people, we are convinced your Majesty would receive such satisfactory proofs of the disposition of the colonists towards their sovereign and parent state, that the wished for opportunity would soon be restored to them, of evincing the sincerity of their professions, by every testimony of devotion becoming the most dutiful subjects, and the most affectionate colonists.

That your Majesty may enjoy a long and prosperous reign, and that your descendants may govern your dominions with honor to themselves and happiness to their subjects, is our sincere and fervent prayer. . . .

Dickinson believed that the Petition offered grounds for a reconciliation. Writing to Arthur Lee, July 7, 1775, he explained:

> Printed: Edmund C. Burnett, ed., *Letters of the Members of the Continental Congress* (8 vols., Washington, D.C., 1921–1938), I, p. 157.

Before this comes to hand, you will have received, I presume, the Petition to the King. You will perhaps at first be surpriz'd, that we make no *Claim*, and mention no *Right*. But I hope, [on] considering all Circumstances, you will be [of] opinion, that this Humility in an address [to] the Throne is at present proper.

Our Rights [have] been already stated—our Claims made—W[ar] is actually begun, and we are carrying it on Vigor[ously]. This conduct and our other Publications will shew, [that our] spirits are not lowered. If Administration [be] desirous of stopping the Effusion of British [blood,] the Opportunity is now offered to them [by an] unexceptionable Petition, praying for [an] accommodation. If they reject this appl[ication] with Contempt, the more humble it is, [the more] such Treatment will confirm the Minds of [our] Countrymen, to endure all the Misfortunes [that] may attend the Contest. . . .

But the ground upon which reconciliation could come were becoming steadily narrower. At the end of the month, the Congress formally rejected Lord North's Conciliatory Proposition as "unreasonable and insidious: Unreasonable, because, if we declare we accede to it, we declare, without reservation, we will purchase the favor of parliament, not knowing at the same time at what price they will please to estimate their favor; it is insidious, because, individual colonies, having bid and bidden again, till they find the avidity of the seller too great for all their powers to satisfy; are then to return into opposition, divided from their sister colonies whom the minister will have previously detached by a grant of easier terms, or by an artful procrastination of a definitive answer."

As the radicals hoped, the continued intransigence of the British government played into the hands of those favoring independence. The pious and peace-loving Lord Dartmouth, the Secretary of State for the Colonies, was eager for conciliation, and even Lord North leaned in that direction. But the war party in the ministry was too strong, and North lacked the strengh of character to resist their importunities. The news of Bunker Hill gave further impetus to the demand for coercion: British military honor demanded vindication. North gave way, and on August 23—one day before the Olive Branch Petition reached Lord Dartmouth—the Proclamation of Rebellion was published The government was thus committed to war:

Printed: Brigham, *Royal Proclamations Relating to America*, pp. 228-229.

Whereas many of Our Subjects in divers Parts of Our Colonies and Plantations in North America, misled by dangerous and ill-designing Men, and forgetting the Allegiance which they owe to the Power that has protected and sustained them, after various disorderly Acts committed in Disturbance of the Publick Peace, to the Obstruction of lawful Commerce, and to the Oppression of Our loyal Subjects carrying on the same, have at length proceeded to an open and avowed Rebellion, by arraying themselves in hostile Manner to withstand the Execution of the Law, and traitorously preparing, ordering, and levying War against Us; And whereas there is Reason to apprehend that such Rebellion hath been much promoted and encouraged by the traitorous Correspondence, Counsels, and Comfort of divers wicked and desperate Persons within this Realm: To the End therefore that none of Our Subjects may neglect or violate their Duty through

Ignorance thereof, or through any Doubt of the Protection which the Law will afford to their Loyalty and Zeal; We have thought fit, by and with the Advice of Our Privy Council, to issue this Our Royal Proclamation, hereby declaring that not only all Our Officers Civil and Military are obliged to exert their utmost Endeavours to suppress such Rebellion, and to bring the Traitors to Justice; but that all Our Subjects of this Realm and the Dominions thereunto belonging are bound by Law to be aiding and assisting in the Suppression of such Rebellion, and to disclose and make known all traitorous Conspiracies and Attempts against Us, Our Crown and Dignity; And We do accordingly strictly charge and command all Our Officers as well Civil as Military, and all other Our obedient and loyal Subjects, to use their utmost Endeavours to withstand and suppress such Rebellion, and to disclose and make known all Treasons and traitorous Conspiracies which they shall know to be against Us, Our Crown and Dignity; and for that Purpose, that they transmit to One of Our Principal Secretaries of State, or other proper Officer, due and full Information of all Persons who shall be found carrying on Correspondence with, or in any Manner or Degree aiding or abetting the Persons now in open Arms and Rebellion against Our Government within any of Our Colonies and Plantations in North America, in order to bring to condign Punishment the Authors, Perpetrators, and Abettors of such traitorous Designs.

The King contemptuously refused even to answer the Petition, and in his address from the throne when Parliament reassembled in October, accused the colonies of a "desperate conspiracy" to establish "an independent empire." Parliament supported by majorities of more than two to one the government measures looking to suppress the rebellion by force. The most important of these measures was the American Prohibitory Act of December 22, 1775, which prohibited "all manner of trade and commerce" with the colonies and directed seizure and forfeiture of all colonial vessels found.

Having thus appeased the war party, North resolved to make one last bid for an accommodation. His plan was to send special commissioners to America to negotiate a settlement. But wrangling first over who should be named and then over the terms to be offered delayed final action until May, 1776. Even then the commissioners' instructions envisaged a settlement on the basis of North's Conciliatory Proposition—terms which the colonists had already rejected. The commissioners finally named were Admiral Lord Howe and his brother, General William Howe; but the Admiral did not reach America until June of 1776. By that late date the tide was running too strongly for independence to be reversed.

Throughout 1775, the declared purpose of the revolutionaries remained the defense of American liberties within the empire. The mere mention of independence brought excited denials. The radicals chafed at the continued hesitancy of their colleagues. As John Adams complained to James Warren, July 24, 1775: "We ought to have had in our Hands a month ago the whole Legislative, executive and judicial of the whole Continent, and have completely modeled a Constitution; to have raised a naval Power, and opened all our Ports wide." But the majority feared lest such action lead inevitably to independence. The same fear inspired the tabling of Benjamin Franklin's proposal for a permanent union of the colonies. As late as November, 1775, the Pennsylvania Assembly instructed its delegates to the Congress to "dissent from, and utterly reject, any propositions, should such be made, that may cause or lead to a separation from our Mother Country, or a changing the form of this Government." That same month, the Congress, in its letter to the colonial agents in London, reaffirmed its hope that "the spirit and virtue of a sensible nation will soon be exerted to procure justice for the innocent oppressed colonies and to restore harmony and peace to the British Empire."

Most hostile to independence were the Tories. Many were members of the upper-class who feared lest independence would open the way for the leveling influence of democracy. In the Carolinas and Georgia, on the other hand, the antagonism between the western frontiersman and the pro-revolutionary tidewater made the westerners hostile to the revolution. But the violence of the revolutionary committees of safety intimidated into silence all but the boldest spirits. Only a foolhardy man would bring down upon himself such treatment as was meted out to the disaffected in Philadelphia:

Printed: Alexander Graydon, *Memoirs of His Own Time* (Philadelphia, 1846), pp. 126-127.

Among the disaffected in Philadelphia, Doctor Kearsley was pre-eminently ardent and rash. An extremely zealous loyalist, and impetuous in his temper, he had given much umbrage to the whigs; and if I am not mistaken, he had been detected in some hostile machinations. Hence he was deemed a proper subject for the fashionable punishment of tarring, feathering and carting. He was seized at his own door by a party of the militia, and, in the attempt to resist them, received a wound in his hand from a bayonet. Being overpowered, he was placed in a cart provided for the purpose, and amidst a multitude of boys and idlers, paraded through the streets to the tune of the rogue's march. I happened to be at the coffee-house when the concourse arrived there. They made a halt, while the Doctor foaming with rage and indignation, without his hat, his wig dishevelled and bloody from his wounded hand, stood up in the cart and called for a bowl of punch. It was quickly handed to him; when, so vehement was his thirst, that he drained it of its contents before he took it from his lips. What were the feelings of others on this lawless proceeding, I know not, but mine, I must confess, revolted at the spectacle. I was shocked at seeing a lately respected citizen so cruelly vilified, and was imprudent enough to say, that had I been a magistrate, I would, at every hazard, have interposed my authority in suppression of the outrage. But this was not the only instance which convinced me, that I wanted nerves for a revolutionist. It must be admitted, however, that the conduct of the populace was marked by a lenity which peculiarly distinguished the cradle of our republicanism. Tar and feathers had been dispensed with, and excepting the injury he had received in his hand, no sort of violence was offered by the mob to their victim. But to a man of high spirit, as the Doctor was, the indignity in its lightest form was sufficient to madden him: it probably had this effect, since his conduct became so extremely outrageous, that it was thought necessary to confine him. From the city he was soon after removed to Carlisle, where he died during the war.

A few days after the carting of Mr. Kearsley, Mr. Isaac Hunt, the attorney, was treated in the same manner, but he managed the matter much better than his precursor. Instead of braving his conductors like the Doctor, Mr. Hunt was a pattern of meekness and humility; and at every halt that was made, he rose and expressed his acknowledgments to the crowd for their forbearance and civility. After a parade of an hour or two, he was set down at his own door, as uninjured in body as in mind. He soon after removed to one of the islands, if I mistake not, to Barbadoes, where, it was understood, he took orders.

Even many staunch patriots, however, who would support independence after July, 1776, as the sole way in which American rights and liberties could be safeguarded, moved only reluctantly and hesitantly to that decision. Upper-class Whigs shared their Tory cousins' fear of the virus of democracy. Over and above such fears, deep ties of affection and sentiment continued to bind the colonists to the mother country. Recognizing the depth of this feeling, the radicals moved warily. "We must be content," Sam Adams agreed, "to wait till the Fruit is ripe before we gather it."

To hasten that day, radical propagandists went to work. The colonists were warned that they could hope for no mercy from Britain; the mother country was pictured as hopelessly corrupt and doomed to destruction; American prowess at arms was said to guarantee a quick and painless triumph. The vision of a powerful American empire, free from British fetters, stretching across the continent, and destined to rule the world, was held up before men's eyes.

The most effective stroke of propaganda for independence came from the English radical Thomas Paine. The son of a poor Quaker corset maker, Paine had been discharged from the British excise service because of his agitation for raises for the excise men. He came to America in October, 1774, with a letter of introduction from Benjamin Franklin, worked as a free-lance journalist, and published in January, 1776, an anonymous pamphlet entitled *Common Sense* urging an immediate declaration of independence. In appealing to the King against Parliament, the colonists themselves had created the myth of good King George. The King's wicked ministers were blamed for the American grievances, not the King himself, and this reverence for George III became a major stumbling-block to independence. Paine boldly assailed George as the principal author to blame for the wrongs done the colonies. He went even further: whereas the colonists had repeately expressed their devotion to the principles of the British Constitution, Paine denounced that constitution as the "base remains of two ancient tyrannies, compounded with some new Republican materials." He condemned the very principle of monarchy as hostile to the liberties of free men. The colonists could fulfill their glorious mission in the world, he proclaimed, only by cutting loose from the decaying mother country:

Printed: Moncure D. Conway, ed., *The Writings of Thomas Paine* (4 vols., 1894–1896), I, pp. 67-111.

SOME writers have so confounded society with government, as to leave little or no distinction between them; whereas they are not only different, but have different origins. Society is produced by our wants, and government by our wickedness; the former promotes our happiness *possitively* by uniting our affections, the latter *negatively* by restraining our vices. The one encourages intercourse, the other creates distinctions. The first is a patron, the last a punisher.

Society in every state is a blessing, but Government, even in its best state, is but a necessary evil; in its worst state an intolerable one: for when we suffer, or are exposed to the same miseries *by a Government,* which we might expect in a country *without Government,* our calamity is heightened by reflecting that we furnish the means by which we suffer. Government, like dress, is the badge of lost innocence; the palaces of kings are built upon the ruins of the bowers of paradise. For were the impulses of conscience clear, uniform and irresistibly obeyed, man would need no other lawgiver; but that not being the case, he finds it necessary to surrender up a part of his property to furnish means for the protection of the rest; and this he is induced to do by the same prudence which in every other case advises him, out of two evils to choose the least. Wherefore, security being the true design and end of government, it unanswerably follows that whatever form thereof appears most likely to ensure it to us, with the least expence and greatest benefit, is preferable to all others. . . .

Here then is the origin and rise of government; namely, a mode rendered necessary by the inability of moral virtue to govern the world; here too is the design and end of government, viz. Freedom and security. And however our eyes may be dazzled with show, or our ears deceived by sound; however prejudice may warp our wills, or interest darken our understanding, the simple voice of nature and reason will say, 'tis right.

I draw my idea of the form of government from a principle in nature which no art can overturn, viz. that the more simple any thing is, the less liable it is to be disordered, and the easier repaired when disordered; and with this maxim in view I offer a few remarks on the so much boasted constitution of England. That it was noble for the dark and slavish times in which it was erected, is granted. When the world was overrun with tyranny the least remove therefrom was a glorious rescue. But that it is imperfect, subject to convulsions, and incapable of producing what it seems to promise, is easily demonstrated.

Absolute governments, (tho' the disgrace of human nature) have this advantage with them, they are simple; if the people suffer, they know the head from which their suffering springs; know likewise the remedy; and are not bewildered by a variety of causes and cures. But the constitution of England is so exceedingly complex, that the nation may suffer for years together without being able to discover in which part the fault lies; some will say in one and some in another, and every political physician will advise a different medicine.

I know it is difficult to get over local or long standing prejudices, yet if we will suffer ourselves to examine the component parts of the English constitution, we shall find them to be the base remains of two ancient tyrannies, compounded with some new Republican materials.

First.—The remains of Monarchical tyranny in the person of the King.

Secondly.—The remains of Aristocratical tyranny in the persons of the Peers.

Thirdly.—The new Republican materials, in the persons of the Commons, on whose virtue depends the freedom of England.

The two first, by being hereditary, are independant of the People; wherefore in a *constitutional sense* they contribute nothing towards the freedom of the State.

To say that the constitution of England is an *union* of three powers, reciprocally *checking* each other, is farcical . . . [for] the provision is unequal to the task; the means either cannot or will not accomplish the end, and the whole affair is a *Felo de se:* for as the greater weight will always carry up the less, and as all the wheels of a machine are put in motion by one, it only remains to know which power in the constitution has the most weight, for that will govern: and tho' the others, or a part of them, may clog, or, as the phrase is, check the rapidity of its motion, yet so long as they cannot stop it, their endeavours will be ineffectual: The first moving power will at last have its way, and what it wants in speed is supplied by time.

That the crown is this overbearing part in the English constitution needs not be mentioned, and that it derives its whole consequence merely from being the giver of places and pensions is self-evident; wherefore, though we have been wise enough to shut and lock a door against absolute Monarchy, we at the same time have been foolish enough to put the Crown in possession of the key.

The prejudice of Englishmen, in favour of their own government, by King, Lords and Commons, arises as much or more from national pride than reason. Individuals are undoubtedly safer in England than in some other countries: but the will of the king is as much the law of the land in Britain as in France, with this difference, that instead of proceeding directly from his mouth, it is handed to the people under the formidable shape of an act of parliament. For the fate of Charles the First hath only made kings more subtle—not more just. . . .

MANKIND being originally equals in the order of creation, the equality could only be destroyed by some subsequent circumstance: the distinctions of rich and poor may in a great measure be accounted for, and that without having recourse to the harsh ill-sounding names of oppression and avarice. . . .

But there is another and greater distinction for which no truly natural or religious reason can be assigned, and that is the distinction of men into KINGS and SUBJECTS. Male and female are the distinctions of nature, good and bad the distinctions of Heaven; but how a race of men came into the world so exalted above the rest, and distinguished like some new species, is worth inquiring into, and whether they are the means of happiness or of misery to mankind.

In the early ages of the world, according to the scripture chronology there were no kings; the consequence of which was, there were no wars; it is the pride of kings which throws mankind into confusion. . . .

Government by kings was first introduced into the world by the Heathens, from whom the children of Israel copied the custom. It was the most prosperous invention the Devil ever set on foot for the promotion of idolatry. The Heathens paid divine honours to their deceased kings, and the Christian World hath improved on the plan by doing the same to their living ones. How impious is the title of sacred Majesty applied to a worm, who in the midst of his splendor is crumbling into dust! . . .

To the evil of monarchy we have added that of hereditary succession; and as the first is a degradation and lessening of ourselves, so the second, claimed as a matter of right, is an insult and imposition on posterity. For all men being originally equals, no one by birth could have a right to set up his own family in perpetual preference to all others for ever, and tho' himself might deserve some decent degree of honours of his contemporaries, yet his descendants might be far too unworthy to inherit them. One of the strongest natural proofs of the folly of hereditary right in Kings, is that nature disapproves it, otherwise she would not so frequently turn it into ridicule, by giving mankind an *Ass for a Lion*. . . .

. . . Could we take off the dark covering of antiquity and trace [the present race of kings] to their first rise, we should find the first of them nothing better than the principal ruffian of some restless gang, whose savage manners or pre-eminence in subtilty obtained him the title of chief among plunderers: and who by increasing in power and extending his depredations, overawed the quiet and defenceless to purchase their safety by frequent contributions. . . .

But it is not so much the absurdity as the evil of hereditary succession which concerns mankind. Did it ensure a race of good and wise men it would have the seal of divine authority, but as it opens a door to the *foolish,* the *wicked,* and the *improper,* it hath in it the nature of oppression. Men who look upon themselves born to reign, and others to obey, soon grow insolent. Selected from the rest of mankind, their minds are early poisoned by importance; and the world they act in differs so materially from the world at large, that they have but little opportunity of knowing its true interests, and when they succeed to the government are frequently the most ignorant and unfit of any throughout the dominions. . . .

In short, monarchy and succession have laid (not this or that kingdom only) but the world in blood and ashes. 'Tis a form of government which the word of God bears testimony against. . . .

The nearer any government approaches to a Republic, the less business there is for a King. It is somewhat difficult to find a proper name for the government of England. Sir William Meredith calls it a Republic; but in its present state it is unworthy of the name, because the corrupt influence of the Crown, by having all the places in its disposal, hath so effectually swallowed up the power, and eaten out the virtue of the House of Commons (the Republican part in the constitution) that the government of England is nearly as monarchical as that of France or Spain. Men fall out with names without understanding them. For 'tis the Republican and not the Monarchical part of the constitution of England which Englishmen glory in, viz. the liberty of choosing an House of Commons from out of their own body —and it is easy to see that when Republican virtues fails, slavery ensues. Why is the constitution of England sickly, but because monarchy hath poisoned the Republic; the Crown hath engrossed the Commons. . . .

Volumes have been written on the subject of the struggle between England and America. Men of all ranks have embarked in the controversy, from different motives, and with various designs; but all have been ineffectual, and the period of debate is closed. Arms as the last resource decide the contest; the appeal was the choice of the King, and the Continent has accepted the challenge. . . .

The Sun never shined on a cause of greater worth. 'Tis not the affair of a City, a County, a Province, or a Kingdom; but of a Continent—of at least one eighth part of the habitable Globe. 'Tis not the concern of a day, a year, or an age; posterity are virtually involved in the contest, and will be more or less affected even to the end of time, by the proceedings now. . . .

By referring the matter from argument to arms, a new æra for politics is struck—a new method of thinking hath arisen. All plans, proposals, &c. prior to the nineteenth of April, *i. e.* to the commencement of hostilities, are like the almanacks of the last year; which tho' proper then, are superceded and useless now. Whatever was advanced by the advocates on either side of the question then, terminated in one and the same point, viz. a union with Great Britain; the only difference between the parties was the method of effecting it; the one proposing force, the other friendship; but it hath so far happened that the first hath failed, and the second hath withdrawn her influence.

As much hath been said of the advantages of reconciliation, which, like an agreeable dream, hath passed away and left us as we were, it is but right that we should examine the contrary side of the argument, and enquire into some of the many material injuries which these Colonies sustain, and always will sustain, by being connected with and dependant on Great-Britain. To examine that connection and dependance, on the principles of nature and common sense, to see what we have to trust to, if separated, and what we are to expect, if dependant.

I have heard it aserted by some, that as America has flourished under her former connection with Great-Britain, the same connection is necessary towards her future happiness, and will always have the same effect. Nothing can be more fallacious than this kind of argument. We may as well assert that because a child has thrived upon milk, that it is never to have meat, or that the first twenty years of our lives is to become a precedent for the next twenty. But even this is admitting more than is true; for I answer roundly, that America would have flourished as much, and probably much more, had no European power taken any notice of her. The commerce by which she hath enriched herself are the necessaries of life, and will always have a market while eating is the custom of Europe.

But she has protected us, say some. That she hath engrossed us is true, and defended the Continent at our expense as well as her own, is admitted; and she would have defended Turkey from the same motive, *viz.* for the sake of trade and dominion.

Alas! we have been long led away by ancient prejudices and made large sacrifices to superstition. We have boasted the protection of Great Britain, without considering, that her motive was *interest* not *attachment;* and that she did not protect us from *our enemies* on *our account;* but from *her enemies* on *her own account,* from those who had no quarrel with us on any *other account,* and who will always be our enemies on the *same account.* Let Britain waive her pretensions to the Continent, or the Continent throw off the dependance, and we should be at peace with France and Spain, were they at war with Britain. . . . France and Spain never were, nor perhaps ever will be, our enemies as *Americans,* but as our being the *subjects of Great Britain.*

But Britain is the parent country, say some. Then the more shame upon her conduct. Even brutes do not devour their young, nor savages make war upon their families; Wherefore, the assertion, if true, turns to her reproach; but it happens not to be true, or only partly so, and the phrase *parent* or *mother country* hath been jesuitically adopted by the King and his parasites, with a low papistical design of gaining an unfair bias on the credulous weakness of our minds. Europe, and not England, is the parent country of America. This new World hath been the asylum for the persecuted lovers of civil and religious liberty from *every part* of Europe. Hither have they fled, not from the tender embraces of the mother, but from the cruelty of the monster; and it is so far true of England, that the same tyranny which drove the first emigrants from home, pursues their descendants still. . . .

Much hath been said of the united strength of Britain and the Colonies, that in conjunction they might bid defiance to the world: But this is mere presumption; the fate of war is uncertain, neither do the expressions mean any thing; for this continent would never suffer itself to be drained of inhabitants, to support the British arms in either Asia, Africa, or Europe.

Besides, what have we to do with setting the world at defiance? Our plan is commerce, and that, well attended to, will secure us the peace and friendship of all Europe; because it is the interest of all Europe to have America a free port. Her trade will always be a protection, and her barrenness of gold and silver secure her from invaders.

I challenge the warmest advocate for reconciliation to show a single advantage that this continent can reap by being connected with Great Britain. I repeat the challenge; not a single advantage is derived. Our corn will fetch its price in any market in Europe, and our imported goods must be paid for buy them where we will.

But the injuries and disadvantages which we sustain by that connection, are without number; and our duty to mankind at large, as well as to ourselves, instruct us to renounce the alliance: because, any submission to, or dependance on, Great Britain, tends directly to involve this Continent in European wars and quarrels, and set us at variance with nations who would otherwise seek our friendship, and against whom we have neither anger nor complaint. As Europe is our market for trade, we ought to form no partial connection with any part of it. It is the true interest of America to steer clear of European contentions, which she never can do, while, by her dependance on Britain, she is made the make-weight in the scale of British politics.

Europe is too thickly planted with Kingdoms to be long at peace, and whenever a war breaks out between England and any foreign power, the trade of America goes to ruin, *because of her connection with Britain.* The next war may not turn out like the last, and should it not, the advocates for reconciliation now will be wishing for separation then, because neutrality in that case would be a safer convoy than a man of war. Every thing that is right or reasonable pleads for separation. The blood of the slain, the weeping voice of nature cries, 'TIS TIME TO PART. Even the distance at which the Almighty hath placed England and America is a strong and natural proof that the authority of the one over the other, was never the design of Heaven. The time likewise at which the Continent was discovered, adds weight to the argument, and the manner in which it was peopled, encreases the force of it. The Reformation was preceded by the discovery of America: As if the Almighty graciously meant to open a sanctuary to the persecuted in future years, when home should afford neither friendship nor safety. . . .

'Tis repugnant to reason, to the universal order of things, to all examples from former ages, to suppose that this Continent can long remain subject to any external power. The most sanguine in Britain doth not think so. The utmost stretch of human wisdom cannot, at this time, compass a plan, short of separation, which can promise the continent even a year's security. Reconciliation is *now* a fallacious dream. Nature hath deserted the connection, and art cannot supply her place. For, as Milton wisely expresses, "never can true reconcilement grow where wounds of deadly hate have pierced so deep." . . .

. . . 'Tis not in the power of Britain to do this continent justice: the business of it will soon be too weighty and intricate to be managed with any tolerable degree of convenience, by a power so distant from us, and so very ignorant of us; for if they cannot conquer us, they cannot govern us. To be always running three or four thousand miles with a tale or a petition, waiting four or five months for an answer, which, when obtained, requires five or six more to explain it in, will in a few years be looked upon as folly and childishness. There was a time when it was proper, and there is a proper time for it to cease.

Small islands not capable of protecting themselves are the proper objects for government to take under their care; but there is something absurd, in supposing a Continent to be perpetually governed by an island. In no instance hath nature made the satellite larger than its primary planet; and as England and America, with respect to each other, reverse the common order of nature, it is evident that they belong to different systems. England to Europe: America to itself.

I am not induced by motives of pride, party, or resentment to espouse the doctrine of separation and independence; I am clearly, positively, and conscientiously persuaded that it is the true interest of this Continent to be so; that every thing short of *that* is mere patchwork, that it can afford no lasting felicity,—that it is leaving the sword to our children, and shrinking back at a time when a little more, a little further, would have rendered this Continent the glory of the earth. . . .

. . . No man was a warmer wisher for a reconciliation than myself, before the fatal nineteenth of April, 1775, but the moment the event of that day was made known, I rejected the hardened, sullen-tempered Pharaoh of England for ever; and disdain the wretch, that with the pretended title of FATHER OF HIS PEOPLE can unfeelingly hear of their slaughter, and composedly sleep with their blood upon his soul.

But admitting that matters were now made up, what would be the event? I .answer, the ruin of the Continent. And that for several reasons.

First. The powers of governing still remaining in the hands of the King, he will have a negative over the whole legislation of this Continent. And as he hath shown himself such an inveterate enemy to liberty, and discovered such a thirst for arbitrary power, is he, or is he not, a proper person to say to these colonies, *You shall make no laws but what I please!?* . . .

America is only a secondary object in the system of British politics. England consults the good of this country no further than it answers her own purpose. Wherefore, her own interest leads her to suppress the growth of ours in every case which doth not promote her advantage, or in the least interferes with it. A pretty state we should soon be in under such a second hand government, considering what has happened! Men do not change from enemies to friends by the alteration of a name: And in order to show that reconciliation now is a dangerous doctrine, I affirm, *that it would be policy in the King at this time to repeal the acts, for the sake of reinstating himself in the government of the provinces;* In order that HE MAY ACCOMPLISH BY CRAFT AND SUBTLETY, IN THE LONG RUN, WHAT HE CANNOT DO BY FORCE AND VIOLENCE IN THE SHORT ONE. Reconciliation and ruin are nearly related. . . .

But the most powerful of all arguments is, that nothing but independance, *i. e.* a Continental form of government, can keep the peace of the Continent and preserve it inviolate from civil wars. I dread the event of a reconciliation with Britain now, as it is more than probable that it will be followed by a revolt some where or other, the consequences of which may be far more fatal than all the malice of Britain.

Thousands are already ruined by British barbarity; (thousands more will probably suffer the same fate.) . . . All they now possess is liberty; what they before enjoyed is sacrificed to its service, and having nothing more to lose they disdain submission. . . . I make the sufferer's case my own, and I protest, that were I driven from house and home, my property destroyed, and my circumstances ruined, that as a man, sensible of injuries, I could never relish the doctrine of reconciliation, or consider myself bound thereby.

. . . Let a Continental Conference be held. . . . Let their business be to frame a Continental Charter, or Charter of the United Colonies;

(answering to what is called the Magna Charta of England) fixing the number and manner of choosing Members of Congress, Members of Assembly, with their date of sitting; and drawing the line of business and jurisdiction between them: Always remembering, that our strength is Continental, not Provincial. Securing freedom and property to all men, and above all things, the free exercise of religion, according to the dictates of conscience; with such other matter as it is necessary for a charter to contain. Immediately after which, the said conference to dissolve, and the bodies which shall be chosen conformable to the said charter, to be the Legislators and Governors of this Continent for the time being: Whose peace and happiness, may GOD preserve. AMEN. . . .

But where, say some, is the King of America? I'll tell you, friend, he reigns above, and doth not make havoc of mankind like the Royal Brute of Great Britain. Yet that we may not appear to be defective even in earthly honours, let a day be solemnly set apart for proclaiming the Charter; let it be brought forth placed on the Divine Law, the Word of God; let a crown be placed thereon, by which the world may know, that so far as we approve of monarchy, that in America the law is king. For as in absolute governments the King is law, so in free countries the law ought to be king; and there ought to be no other. But lest any ill use should afterwards arise, let the Crown at the conclusion of the ceremony be demolished, and scattered among the people whose right it is.

A government of our own is our natural right: and when a man seriously reflects on the precariousness of human affairs, he will become convinced, that it is infinitely wiser and safer, to form a constitution of our own in a cool deliberate manner, while we have it in our power, than to trust such an interesting event to time and chance. . . .

To talk of friendship with those in whom our reason forbids us to have faith, and our affections wounded thro' a thousand pores instruct us to detest, is madness and folly. Every day wears out the little remains of kindred between us and them; and can there be any reason to hope, that as the relationship expires, the affection will encrease, or that we shall agree better when we have ten times more and greater concerns to quarrel over than ever?

Ye that tell us of harmony and reconciliation, can ye restore to us the time that is past? Can ye give to prostitution its former innocence? neither can ye reconcile Britain and America. The last cord now is broken, the people of England are presenting addresses against us. There are injuries which nature cannot forgive; she would cease to be nature if she did. As well can the lover forgive the ravisher of his mistress, as the Continent forgive the murders of Britain. The Almighty hath implanted in us these unextinguishable feelings for good and wise purposes. They are the Guardians of his Image in our hearts. They distinguish us from the herd of common animals. The social compact would dissolve, and justice be extirpated from the earth, or have only a casual existence were we callous to the touches of affection. The robber and the murderer would often escape unpunished, did not the injuries which our tempers sustain, provoke us into justice.

O! ye that love mankind! Ye that dare oppose not only the tyranny but the tyrant, stand forth! Every spot of the old world is overrun with oppression. Freedom hath been hunted round the Globe. Asia and Africa have long expelled her. Europe regards her like a stranger, and England hath given her warning to depart. O! receive the fugitive, and prepare in time an asylum for mankind. . . .

To CONCLUDE, however strange it may appear to some, or however unwilling they may be to think so, matters not, but many strong and striking reasons may be given to show, that nothing can settle our affairs so expeditiously as an open and determined declaration for independance. Some of which are,

First—It is the custom of Nations, when any two are at war, for some other powers, not engaged in the quarrel, to step in as mediators, and bring about the preliminaries of a peace: But while America calls herself the subject of Great Britain, no power, however well disposed she may be, can offer her mediation. Wherefore, in our present state we may quarrel on for ever.

Secondly—It is unreasonable to suppose, that France or Spain will give us any kind of assistance, if we mean only to make use of that assistance for the purpose of repairing the breach, and strengthening the connection between Britain and America; because, those powers would be sufferers by the consequences.

Thirdly—While we profess ourselves the subjects of Britain, we must, in the eyes of foreign nations, be considered as Rebels. The precedent is somewhat dangerous to their peace, for men to be in arms under the name of subjects: we, on the spot, can solve the paradox; but to unite resistance and subjection, requires an idea much too refined for common understanding.

Fourthly—Were a manifesto to be published, and despatched to foreign Courts, setting forth the miseries we have endured, and the peaceful methods which we have ineffectually used for redress; declaring at the same time, that not being able any longer to live happily or safely under the cruel disposition of the British Court, we had been driven to the necessity of breaking off all connections with her; at the same time, assuring all such Courts of our peaceable disposition towards them, and of our desire of entering into trade with them: such a memorial would produce more good effects to this Continent, than if a ship were freighted with petitions to Britain.

Under our present denomination of British subjects, we can neither be received nor heard abroad: the custom of all Courts is against us, and will be so, until by an independance we take rank with other nations.

These proceedings may at first seem strange and difficult, but like all other steps which we have already passed over, will in a little time become familiar and agreeable: and until an independance is declared, the Continent will feel itself like a man who continues putting off some unpleasant business from day to day, yet knows it must be done, hates to set about it, wishes it over, and is continually haunted with the thoughts of its necessity.

The success of the pamphlet was enormous. Paine estimated that 120,000 copies were sold in less than three months. Although horrified conservatives rushed to answer Paine, *Common Sense* made "independence" a word to be conjured with. As General Charles Lee wrote Washington, January 24, 1776: "I never saw such a masterly, irresistible performance. It will, if I mistake not, in concurrence with the transcendent folly and wickedness of the Ministry, give the coup-de-grace to Great Britain. In short, I own myself convinced, by the arguments of the necessity of separation."

Events worked in the same direction. Each step taken by the British to bring the colonists back to obedience further alienated them. In Virginia, Lord Dunmore's call for a slave rebellion excited bitter resentment; the British recruitments of Indians to fight against the colonists outraged frontiersmen; and the hiring of mercenaries offended all Americans. The passage of the American Prohibitory Act played into the hands of the radicals. Calling the measure an "Act of Independency," John Adams rejoiced that "King Lords and Commons have united in sundering this country from that I think forever. It is a compleate Dismemberment of the British Empire. It throws thirteen Colonies out of the Royal Protection, levels all Distinctions, and makes us independent in spite of our supplications and entreaties."

Washington, as commander-in-chief of the army, threw his influence on the side of independence. The reports of British plans to push vigorously forward the war had convinced him as early as October, 1775, that conciliation was no longer possible. Realizing that public opinion in Britain stood behind the ministry, he had no illusions about the possibility of a British retreat. In November, 1775, he warned his troops to prepare to overcome "the diabolical designs of administration to prosecute, with unrelenting fury, the most cruel and savage war that ever a civilized nation engaged in." Early in 1776, as Curtis Nettels has shown, Washington began a letter writing campaign in favor of independence. The high point of this campaign was his letter of February 10, to Joseph Reed:

Printed: John C. Fitzpatrick, ed., *The Writings of George Washington* (39 vols., Washington, D.C., 1931–1941), IV, pp. 318-323.

. . . I have never entertained an idea of an accommodation, since I heard of the measures, which were adopted in consequence of the Bunker's Hill fight. The king's speech has confirmed the sentiments I entertained upon the news of that affair; and if every man was of my mind, the ministers of Great Britain should know, in a few words, upon what issue the cause should be put. I would not be deceived by artful declarations, nor specious pretences; nor would I be amused by unmeaning propositions; but in open, undisguised, and manly terms proclaim our wrongs, and our resolution to be redressed. I would tell them, that we had borne much, that we had long and ardently sought for reconciliation upon honorable terms, that it had been denied us, that all our attempts after peace had proved abortive, and had been grossly misrepresented, that we had done every thing which could be expected from the best of subjects, that the spirit of freedom beat too high in us to submit to slavery, and that, if nothing else could satisfy a tyrant and his diabolical ministry, we are determined to shake off all connexions with a state so unjust and unnatural. This I would tell them, not under covert, but in words as clear as the sun in its meridian brightness. . . .

Step by step, almost imperceptibly, the Continental Congress moved toward independence. In July, 1775, the Congress voted to import arms and ammunition. Another step taken that same month was the establishment of a continental postal system. That fall American troops invaded Canada, transforming the conflict from a defensive to an offensive war. On November 19, 1775, Congress appointed what became known as the Committee of Secret Correspondence "for the sole purpose of corresponding with our friends in Great Britain, Ireland, and other parts of the world," and in the following months the growing conviction that a French alliance was indispensable for victory gave further impetus to the demand for independence. By January, the radicals were sufficiently powerful to force postponement of action on a motion by James Wilson disavowing any thought of independence. On April 6, 1776, the ports of the colonies were opened to the entire world except Britain. Then came the most important step of all. On May 10, the Congress, sitting as a committee of the whole, approved the following resolution, introduced by John Adams in conjunction with Richard Henry Lee of Virginia, calling upon all the colonies to set up new revolutionary governments to replace the old:

Printed: Ford, *Journals of the Continental Congress,* IV, p. 342.

Resolved, That it be recommended to the respective assemblies and conventions of the United Colonies, where no government sufficient to the exigencies of their affairs have been hitherto established, to adopt such government as shall, in the opinion of the representatives of the people, best conduce to the happiness and safety of their constituents in particular, and America in general.

John Adams termed this action in his Autobiography "an Epocha, a decisive Event," and the language of the preamble adopted May 15, 1776, was even stronger.

Printed: Ford, *Journals of the Continental Congress,* IV, pp. 357-358.

Wheras his Britannic Majesty, in conjunction with the lords and commons of Great Britain, has, by a late act of Parliament, excluded the inhabitants of these United Colonies from the protection of his crown; And whereas, no answer, whatever, to the humble petitions of the colonies for redress of grievances and reconciliation with Great Britain has been or is likely to be given; but the whole force of that kingdom, aided by foreign mercenaries, is to be exerted for the destruction of the good people of these colonies; And whereas, it appears absolutely irreconciliable to reason and good Conscience for the people of these colonies now to take oaths and affirmations necessary for the support of any government under the crown of Great Britain, and it is necessary that the exercise of every kind of authority under the said crown should be totally suppressed, and all the powers of government exerted, under the authority of the people of the colonies, for the preservation of internal peace, virtue, and good order, as well as for the defence of their lives, liberties, and properties, against the hostile invasions and cruel depredations of their enemies.

A bitter debate raged over the preamble, with James Duane of New York and James Wilson of Pennsylvania leading the opposition. But the resolution and preamble were formally adopted on May 15. John Adams rejoiced that "Congress has passed the most important Resolution that was ever taken in

America." A major step, he exulted to his wife, May 17, 1776, had been taken toward independence:

Printed: Burnett, *Letters of Members of the Continental Congress*, I, p. 453.

. . . Great Britain has at last driven America to the last step, a complete separation from her; a total absolute independence, not only of her Parliament, but of her crown, for such is the amount of the resolve of the 15th. Confederation among ourselves, or alliances with foreign nations are not necessary to a perfect separation from Britain. That is effected by extinguishing all authority under the crown, Parliament, and nation, as the resolution for instituting governments has done, to all intents and purposes. Confederation will be necessary for our internal concord, and alliances may be so for our external defence.

I have reasons to believe that no colony, which shall assume a government under the people, will give it up. There is something very unnatural and odious in a government a thousand leagues off. A whole government of our own choice, managed by persons whom we love, revere, and can confide in, has charms in it, for which men will fight. . . .

The last major obstacles to independence were the instructions binding the delegates from New York, Maryland, and Pennsylvania to oppose separation. Pennsylvania represented the most serious stumbling block. When the Pennsylvania Assembly refused to rescind its instructions against independence, the radicals seized upon the resolve of May 15 and staged a coup to replace the Assembly with a new, revolutionary provincial convention. In the other colonies, the radicals were active in securing adoption of positive instructions in favor of independence. The North Carolina Provincial Congress took the lead, and on April 12, authorized its delegates to Congress "to concur with the delegates of the other Colonies in declaring Independency." On May 4, Rhode Island declared its independence. And on May 15,

1776, the Virginia convention instructed its delegates to introduce a resolution to declare the colonies independent:

Printed: Boyd, *The Papers of Thomas Jefferson*, I, pp.
290-291.

FORASMUCH as all the endeavours of the United Colonies by the
most decent representations and petitions to the king and parliament
of Great Britain to restore peace and security to America under the
British government and a re-union with that people upon just and
liberal terms instead of a redress of grievances have produced from
an imperious and vindictive administration increased insult oppression and a vigorous attempt to effect our total destruction. By a late
act, all these colonies are declared to be in rebellion, and out of the
protection of the British crown our properties subjected to confisca-
tion, our people, when captivated, compelled to join in the murder
and plunder of their relations and countrymen, and all former rapine
and oppression of Americans declared legal and just. Fleets and
armies are raised, and the aid of foreign troops engaged to assist these
destructive purposes: The king's representative in this colony hath
not only withheld all the powers of government from operating for
our safety, but, having retired on board an armed ship, is carrying on
a piratical and savage war against us tempting our slaves by every
artifice to resort to him, and training and employing them against
their masters. In this state of extreme danger, we have no alternative
left but an abject submission to the will of those over-bearing tyrants,
or a total separation from the crown and government of Great Britain,
uniting and exerting the strength of all America for defence, and
forming alliances with foreign powers for commerce and aid in war:
Wherefore, appealing to the SEARCHER OF HEARTS for the
sincerity of former declarations, expressing our desire to preserve the
connection with that nation, and that we are driven from that inclination by their wicked councils, and the eternal laws of self-preservation.
RESOLVED unanimously, that the delegates appointed to represent this colony in General Congress be instructed to propose to that
respectable body to declare the United Colonies free and independent
states, absolved from all allegiance to, or dependence upon, the crown
or parliament of Great Britain; and that they give the assent of this

colony to such declaration, and to whatever measures may be thought proper and necessary by the Congress for forming foreign alliances and a confederation of the colonies, at such time, and in the manner, as to them shall seem best: Provided, that the power of forming government for, and the regulations of the internal concerns of each colony, be left to the respective colonial legislatures.

RESOLVED unanimously, that a committee be appointed to prepare a DECLARATION OF RIGHTS, and such a plan of government as will be most likely to maintain peace and order in this colony, and secure substantial and equal liberty to the people.

Acting in accordance with these instructions, Richard Henry Lee introduced, on June 7, 1776, the following resolution for independence:

> Printed: Ford, *Journals of the Continental Congress*, V, p. 425.

Resolved, That these United Colonies are, and of right ought to be, free and independent States, that they are absolved from all allegiance to the British Crown, and that all political connection between them and the state of Great Britain is, and ought to be, totally dissolved.

That it is expedient forthwith to take the most effectual measures for forming foreign Alliances.

That a plan of confederation be prepared and transmitted to the respective Colonies for their consideration and approbation.

The motion was debated on the following day, Saturday, June 8, and then again on June 10. On that day, the Congress resolved that a final decision should be postponed until July 1, but that a committee be appointed to prepare a declaration of independence "in case the Congress agree thereto." This postponement of the final decision was made necessary by the continued hesitancy on the part of the delegates from the middle colonies to agree to independence. The following notes of the debate were made by Thomas Jefferson:

Printed: Ford, *Journals of the Continental Congress*, VI, pp. 1087-1092.

IN CONGRESS, *Friday, June 7, 1776.*

The delegates from Virginia moved in obedience to instructions from their constituents that the Congress should declare that these United colonies are and of right ought to be free and independent states, that they are absolved from all obedience to the British crown, and that all political connection between them and the state of Great Britain is and ought to be totally dissolved: that measures should be immediately taken for procuring the assistance of foreign powers, and a Confederation be formed to bind the colonies more closely together.

The house being obliged to attend at that time to some other business, the proposition was referred to the next day when the members were ordered to attend punctually at ten o'clock.

Saturday June 8th they proceeded to take it into Consideration, and referred it to a Committee of the whole, into which they immediately resolved themselves, and passed that day and Monday the 10th in debating on the subject.

It was argued by [James] Wilson, Robert R. Livingston, E. Rutlege, [John] Dickinson and others

That tho they were friends to the measures themselves, and saw the impossibility that we should ever again be united with Great Britain, yet they were against adopting them at this time:

That the conduct we had formerly observed was wise and proper now, of deferring to take any capital step till the voice of the people drove us into it:

That they were our power and without them our declarations could not be carried into effect:

That the people of the middle colonies (Maryland, Delaware, Pennsylvania, the Jersies and N. York) were not yet ripe for bidding adieu to British connection; but that they were fast ripening, and in a short time would join in the general voice of America:

That the resolution entered into by this house on the 15th of May, for suppressing the exercise of all powers derived from the crown, had shewn, by the ferment into which it had thrown these middle colonies that they had not yet accomodated their minds to a separation from the mother country.

That some of them had expressly forbidden their delegates to consent to such a declaration, and others had given no instructions, and consequently no powers to give such consent:

That if the delegates of any particular colony had no power to declare such colony independant, certain they were the others could not declare it for them; the colonies being as yet perfectly independant of each other:

That the assembly of Pennsylvania was now sitting above stairs, their convention would sit within a few days, the convention of New York was now sitting, and those of the Jersies and Delaware counties would meet on the Monday following, and it was probable these bodies would take up the question of Independance, and would declare to their delegates the voice of their state:

That if such a declaration should now be agreed to, these delegates must retire and possibly their colonies might secede from the Union:

That such a secession would weaken us more than could be compensated by any foreign alliance:

That in the event of such a division foreign powers would either refuse to join themselves to our fortunes, or having us so much in their power as that desperate declaration would place us they would insist on terms proportionably more hard and prejudicial:

That we had little reason to expect an alliance with those to whom alone as yet we had cast our eyes:

That France and Spain had reason to be jealous of that rising power which would one day certainly strip them of all their American possessions:

That it was more likely they should form a connection with the British court, who, if they should find themselves unable otherwise to extricate themselves from their difficulties, would agree to a partition of our territories, restoring Canada to France, and the Floridas to Spain, to accomplish for themselves a recovery of these colonies:

That it would not be long before we should receive certain information of the disposition of the French court, from the agent whom we had sent to Paris for that purpose.

That if this disposition should be favourable, by waiting the event of the present campaign, which we all hoped would be successful, we should have reason to expect an alliance on better terms:

That this would in fact work no delay of any effectual aid from such ally, as, from the advance of the season, and distance of our situation, it was impossible we could receive any assistance during this campaign:

That it was prudent to fix among ourselves the terms on which we would form alliance, before we declared we would form one at all events:

And that if these were agreed on and our Declaration of Independance ready by the time our Ambassador should be ready to sail, it would be as well as to go into that Declaration at this day.

On the other side it was urged by J. Adams, Lee, Wythe and others

That no gentleman had argued against the policy or the right of separation from Britain, nor had supposed it possible we should ever renew our connection; that they had only opposed it's being now declared:

That the question was not whether, by a declaration of Independance, we should make ourselves what we are not; but whether we should declare a fact which already exists:

That as to the people or parliament of England, we had alwais been independant of them, their restraints on our trade deriving efficacy from our acquiescence only, and not from any rights they possessed of imposing them, and that so far our connection had been federal only, and was now dissolved by the commencement of hostilities:

That as to the king, we had been bound to him by allegiance, but that this bond was now dissolved by his assent to the late act of parliament, by which he declares us out of his protection, and by his levying war on us, a fact which had long ago proved us out of his protection; it being a certain position in law that allegiance and protection are reciprocal, the one ceasing when the other is withdrawn:

That James the II^d never declared the people of England out of his protection; yet his actions proved it, and the parliament declared it:

No delegates then can be denied, or ever want a power of declaring an existent truth:

That the delegates from the Delaware counties having declared their constituents ready to join, there are only two colonies Pennsylvania and Maryland, whose delegates are absolutely tied up, and that these had by their instructions only reserved a right of confirming or rejecting the measure:

That the instructions from Pennsylvania might be accounted for from the times in which they were drawn, near a twelvemonth ago, since which the face of affairs has totally changed:

That within that time it had become apparent that Britain was determined to accept nothing less than a carte blanche, and that the king's answer to the Lord Mayor, Aldermen and common council of London, which had come to hand four days ago, must have satisfied every one of this point:

That the people wait for us to lead the way:

That *they* are in favor of the measure, tho' the instructions given by some of their *representatives* are not:

That the voice of the representatives is not alwais consonant with the voice of the people, and that this is remarkably the case in these middle colonies:

That the effect of the resolution of the 15th of May has proved this, which, raising the murmurs of some in the colonies of Pennsylvania and Maryland, called forth the opposing voice of the freer part of the people, and proved them to be the majority, even in these colonies:

That the backwardness of these two colonies might be ascribed partly to the influence of proprietary power and connections, and partly to their having not yet been attacked by the enemy:

That these causes were not likely to be soon removed, as there seemed no probability that the enemy would make either of these the seat of this summer's war:

That it would be vain to wait either weeks or months for perfect unanimity, since it was impossible that all men should ever become of one sentiment on any question:

That the conduct of some colonies, from the beginning of this contest, had given reason to suspect it was their settled policy to keep in the rear of the confederacy, that their particular prospect might be better, even in the worst event:

That therefore it was necessary for those colonies who had thrown themselves forward and hazarded all from the beginning, to come forward now also, and put all again to their own hazard:

That the history of the Dutch revolution, of whom three states only confederated at first proved that a secession of some colonies would not be so dangerous as some apprehended:

That a declaration of Independence alone could render it consistent with European delicacy for European powers to treat with us, or even to receive an Ambassador from us:

That till this they would not receive our vessels into their ports, nor acknowledge the adjudications of our courts of Admiralty to be legitimate, in cases of capture of British vessels:

That tho' France and Spain may be jealous of our rising power, they must think it will be much more formidable with the addition of Great Britain; and will therefore see it their interest to prevent a coalition; but should they refuse, we shall be but where we are; whereas without trying we shall never know whether they will aid us or not:

That the present campaign may be unsuccessful, and therefore we had better propose an alliance while our affairs wear a hopeful aspect:

That to wait the event of this compaign will certainly work delay, because during this summer France may assist us effectually by cutting off those supplies of provisions from England and Ireland on which the enemy's armies here are to depend; or by setting in motion the great power they have collected in the West Indies, and calling our enemy to the defence of the possessions they have there:

That it would be idle to lose time in settling the terms of alliance, till we had first determined we would enter into alliance:

That it is necessary to lose no time in opening a trade for our people, who will want clothes, and will want money too for the paiment of taxes:

And that the only misfortune is that we did not enter into alliance with France six months sooner, as, besides opening their ports for the vent of our last year's produce, they might have marched an army into Germany and prevented the petty princes there from selling their unhappy subjects to subdue us.

It appearing in the course of these debates that the colonies of N. York, N. Jersey Pennsylvania, Delaware and Maryland [and South Carolina] were not yet matured for falling from the parent stem, but that they were fast advancing to that state, it was thought most prudent to wait a while for them, and to postpone the final decision to July 1. but that this might occasion as little delay as possible, a committee was appointed to prepare a declaration of independance. the commee were J. Adams, Dr Franklin, Roger Sherman, Robert R. Livingston and myself. committees were also appointed at the same time to prepare a plan of confederation for the colonies, and to state the terms proper to be proposed for foreign alliance. the com-

mittee for drawing the declaration of independance desired me to
do it. . . .

The rush toward independence could not be halted. The new,
radical-dominated Provincial Conference in Pennsylvania empowered that colony's delegates "to concur in a vote of Congress
declaring the United Colonies free and independent States." New
Jersey, Delaware, and Maryland followed, giving their delegates,
expressly or by implication, authority to vote for independence;
only New York failed to rescind its instructions against independence. The question was brought up again on July 1. Jefferson
recorded in his notes what transpired:

> Printed: Ford, *Journals of the Continental Congress,* VI,
> p. 1092.

. . . On Monday the 1ˢᵗ of July the house resolved itself into a
committee of the whole and resumed the consideration of the original
motion made by the delegates of Virginia, which being again debated
through the day, was carried in the affirmative by the votes of N.
Hampshire, Connecticut, Massachusetts, Rhode island, N. Jersey,
Maryland, Virginia, N. Carolina, and Georgia. S. Carolina and Pennsylvania voted against it. Delaware having but two members present
they were divided: the delegates for N. York declared they were for
it themselves, and were assured their constituents were for it, but that
their instructions, having been drawn near a twelvemonth before,
when reconciliation was still the general object, they were enjoined
by them to do nothing which should impede that object. they therefore thought themselves not justifiable in voting on either side, and
asked leave to withdraw from the question, which was given them.
the commee rose and reported their resolution to the house. Mr.
Rutlege of S. Carolina then requested the determination might be put
off to the next day, as he believed his collegues, tho they disapproved
of the resolution, would then join in it for the sake of unanimity. the
ultimate question whether the house would agree to the resolution of
the commee, was accordingly postponed to the next day, when it was
again moved and S. Carolina concurred in voting for it. in the mean
time a third member had come post from the Delaware counties and

turned the vote of that colony in favour of the resolution. members of a different sentiment attending that morning from Pennsylvania also, their vote was changed, so that the whole 12 colonies, who were authorized to vote at all, gave their voices for it; and within a few days the convention of N. York approved of it, and thus supplied the void occasioned by the withdrawing of their delegates from the vote.

The twelve delegations, with the delegates from New York abstaining, formally voted on July 2, 1776:

> Printed: Ford, *Journals of the Continental Congress*, V, p. 507.

Resolved, That these United Colonies are, and, of right, ought to be, Free and Independent States; that they are absolved from all allegiance to the British crown, and that all political connexion between them, and the state of Great Britain, is, and ought to be, totally dissolved.

The die was cast, John Adams rejoiced to his wife the next day:

> Printed: Adams, *The Works of John Adams*, IX, pp. 417-420.

. . . Yesterday, the greatest question was decided, which ever was debated in America, and a greater, perhaps, never was nor will be decided among men. A resolution was passed without one dissenting colony, "that these United Colonies are, and of right ought to be, free and independent States, and as such they have, and of right ought to have, full power to make war, conclude peace, establish commerce, and to do all other acts and things which other States may rightfully do." You will see in a few days a Declaration setting forth the causes which have impelled us to this mighty revolution, and the reasons which will justify it in the sight of God and man. A plan of confederation will be taken up in a few days.

When I look back to the year 1761, and recollect the argument concerning writs of assistance in the superior court, which I have

ROAD TO INDEPENDENCE

hitherto considered as the commencement of this controversy between Great Britain and America, and run through the whole period,
from that time to this, and recollect the series of political events, the
chain of causes and effects, I am surprised at the suddenness as well
as greatness of this revolution. Britain has been filled with folly, and
America with wisdom. At least, this is my judgment. Time must
determine. It is the will of Heaven that the two countries should be
sundered forever. It may be the will of Heaven that America shall
suffer calamities still more wasting, and distresses yet more dreadful.
If this is to be the case, it will have this good effect at least. It will
inspire us with many virtues, which we have not, and correct many
errors, follies and vices which threaten to disturb, dishonor, and
destroy us. The furnace of affliction produces refinement, in States as
well as individuals. And the new governments we are assuming in
every part will require a purification from our vices, and an augmentation of our virtues, or they will be no blessings. The people will
have unbounded power, and the people are extremely addicted to
corruption and venality, as well as the great. But I must submit all
my hopes and fears to an overruling Providence, in which, unfashionable as the faith may be, I firmly believe.

Had a Declaration of Independency been made seven months ago,
it would have been attended with many great and glorious effects.
We might, before this hour, have formed alliances with foreign
States. We should have mastered Quebec, and been in possession of
Canada. . . .

But, on the other hand, the delay of this declaration to this time
has many great advantages attending it. The hopes of reconciliation,
which were fondly entertained by multitudes of honest and well-
meaning, though weak and mistaken people, have been gradually and,
at last, totally extinguished. Time has been given for the whole
people maturely to consider the great question of independence, and
to ripen their judgment, dissipate their fears, and allure their hopes,
by discussing it in newspapers and pamphlets, by debating it in assemblies, conventions, committees of safety and inspection, in town and
county meetings, as well as in private conversations, so that the
whole people, in every colony of the thirteen, have now adopted it as
their own act. This will cement the union, and avoid those heats, and
perhaps convulsions, which might have been occasioned by such a
declaration six months ago.

But the day is past. The second day of July, 1776, will be the most memorable epocha in the history of America. I am apt to believe that it will be celebrated by succeeding generations as the great anniversary festival. It ought to be commemorated, as the day of deliverance, by solemn acts of devotion to God Almighty. It ought to be solemnized with pomp and parade, with shows, games, sports, guns, bells, bonfires, and illuminations, from one end of this continent to the other, from this time forward, forevermore.

You will think me transported with enthusiasm, but I am not. I am well aware of the toil, and blood, and treasure, that it will cost us to maintain this declaration, and support and defend these States. Yet, through all the gloom, I can see the rays of ravishing light and glory. I can see that the end is more than worth all the means, and that posterity will triumph in that day's transaction, even although we should rue it, which I trust in God we shall not.

Having thus declared for independence, the Congress proceeded to justify its action to the world. The committee appointed to draft the declaration had asked Thomas Jefferson to prepare a draft. Again resolving itself into a committee of the whole, Congress debated his draft; agreed upon a number of changes of phraseology; and made two significant deletions—one a passage severely condemning the people of Britain; the other Jefferson's attack on the slave trade. On the evening of July 4, the debate ended and the committee of the whole reported the amended declaration to the house. As two days before, twelve delegations voted aye, with New York abstaining. Finding no longer safety for their life, liberty, and property under the British constitution, the colonists appealed to the law of nature and nature's God to justify their rebellion against the mother country:

Printed: Ford, *Journals of the Continental Congress,* V, pp. 510-515.

The unanimous Declaration of the thirteen United States of America.

When, in the Course of human events, it becomes necessary for one people to dissolve the political bands which have connected them with another, and to assume, among the Powers of the earth, the separate and equal station to which the Laws of Nature and of Nature's God entitle them, a decent respect to the opinions of mankind requires that they should declare the causes which impel them to the separation.

We hold these truths to be self-evident, that all men are created equal, that they are endowed by their Creator with certain unalienable Rights, that among these, are Life, Liberty, and the pursuit of Happiness. That, to secure these rights, Governments are instituted among Men, deriving their just Powers from the consent of the governed. That, whenever any form of Government becomes destructive of these ends, it is the Right of the People to alter or to abolish it, and to institute new Government, laying its foundation on such Principles, and organizing its Powers in such form, as to them shall seem most likely to effect their Safety and Happiness. Prudence, indeed, will dictate that Governments long established should not be changed for light and transient causes; and, accordingly, all experience hath shewn, that mankind are more disposed to suffer, while evils are sufferable, than to right themselves by abolishing the forms to which they are accustomed. But, when a long train of abuses and usurpations, pursuing invariably the same Object, evinces a design to reduce them under absolute Despotism, it is their right, it is their duty, to throw off such Government, and to provide new Guards for their future Security. Such has been the patient sufferance of these Colonies; and such is now the necessity which constrains them to alter their former Systems of Government. The history of the present King of Great Britain is a history of repeated injuries and usurpations, all having in direct object the establishment of an absolute Tyranny over these States. To prove this, let Facts be submitted to a candid world.

He has refused his Assent to Laws the most wholesome and necessary for the public good.

He has forbidden his Governors to pass Laws of immediate and pressing importance, unless suspended in their operation till his Assent should be obtained; and when so suspended, he has utterly neglected to attend to them.

He has refused to pass other Laws for the accommodation of large districts of People, unless those People would relinquish the right of Representation in the legislature; a right inestimable to them and formidable to tyrants only.

He has called together legislative bodies at places unusual, uncomfortable, and distant from the depository of their Public Records, for the sole Purpose of fatiguing them into compliance with his measures.

He has dissolved Representative Houses repeatedly, for opposing, with manly firmness, his invasions on the rights of the People.

He has refused for a long time, after such dissolutions, to cause others to be elected; whereby the Legislative Powers, incapable of Annihilation, have returned to the People at large for their exercise; the State remaining in the mean time exposed to all the dangers of invasion from without, and convulsions within.

He has endeavoured to prevent the Population of these States; for that purpose obstructing the Laws for Naturalization of Foreigners; refusing to pass others to encourage their migrations hither, and raising the conditions of new Appropriations of Lands.

He has obstructed the Administration of Justice, by refusing his Assent to Laws for establishing Judiciary Powers.

He has made Judges dependent on his Will alone, for the tenure of their offices, and the amount and payment of their salaries.

He has erected a multitude of New Offices, and sent hither swarms of Officers to harrass our People, and eat out their substance.

He has kept among us, in times of Peace, Standing Armies, without the Consent of our legislatures.

He has affected to render the Military independent of and superior to the Civil Power.

He has combined with others to subject us to a jurisdiction foreign to our constitution, and unacknowledged by our laws; giving his Assent to their Acts of pretended Legislation:

For quartering large bodies of armed troops among us:

For protecting them, by a mock Trial, from Punishment for any Murders which they should commit on the Inhabitants of these States:

For cutting off our Trade with all parts of the world:

For imposing Taxes on us without our Consent:

For depriving us, in many cases, of the benefits of Trial by Jury:

For transporting us beyond Seas to be tried for pretended offences:

For abolishing the free System of English Laws in a neighbouring province, establishing therein an Arbitrary government, and enlarging its Boundaries, so as to render it at once an example and fit instrument for introducing the same absolute rule into these Colonies:

For taking away our Charters, abolishing our most valuable Laws, and altering fundamentally the Forms of our Governments:

For suspending our own Legislatures, and declaring themselves invested with Power to legislate for us in all cases whatsoever.

He has abdicated Government here, by declaring us out of his protection, and waging War against us.

He has plundered our seas, ravaged our Coasts, burnt our towns, and destroyed the Lives of our People.

He is at this time transporting large Armies of foreign Mercenaries to compleat the works of death, desolation and tyranny, already begun with circumstances of Cruelty and perfidy scarcely paralleled in the most barbarous ages, and totally unworthy the Head of a civilized nation.

He has constrained our fellow Citizens, taken Captive on the high Seas, to bear Arms against their Country, to become the executioners of their friends and Brethren, or to fall themselves by their Hands.

He has excited domestic insurrections amongst us, and has endeavoured to bring on the inhabitants of our frontiers, the merciless Indian Savages, whose known rule of warfare, is an undistinguished destruction of all ages, sexes and conditions.

In every stage of these Oppressions, We have Petitioned for Redress, in the most humble terms: Our repeated Petitions, have been answered only by repeated injury. A Prince, whose character is thus marked by every act which may define a Tyrant, is unfit to be the ruler of a free People.

Nor have We been wanting in attentions to our Brittish brethren. We have warned them from time to time of attempts by their legislature to extend an unwarrantable jurisdiction over us. We have reminded them of the circumstances of our emigration and settlement here. We have appealed to their native justice and magnanimity, and we have conjured them by the ties of our common kindred, to disavow these usurpations, which, would inevitably interrupt our connexions and correspondence. They too have been deaf to the voice of justice and of consanguinity. We must, therefore, acquiesce in the necessity, which denounces our Separation, and hold them, as we hold the rest of mankind, Enemies in War, in Peace Friends. *We, therefore,* the Representatives of the *united States of America,* in GENERAL CONGRESS assembled, appealing to the Supreme Judge of the World for the rectitude of our intentions, DO, in the Name, and by Authority of the good People of these Colonies, solemnly PUBLISH and DECLARE, That these United Colonies are, and of Right, ought to be *Free and Independent States;* that they are Absolved from all Allegiance to the British Crown, and that all political connexion between them and the State of Great Britain, is and ought to be totally dissolved; and that, as FREE and INDEPENDENT STATES, they have full Power to levy War, conclude Peace, contract Alliances, establish Commerce, and to do all other Acts and Things which INDEPENDENT STATES may of right do. AND for the support of this Declaration, with a firm reliance on the protection of divine Providence, we mutually pledge to each other our Lives, our Fortunes, and our sacred Honour.

||The foregoing declaration was, by order of Congress, engrossed, and signed by the following members:||

JOHN HANCOCK.

JOSIAH BARTLETT, W^M WHIPPLE, SAM^L ADAMS, JOHN ADAMS, ROB^T TREAT PAINE, ELBRIDGE GERRY, STEPH. HOPKINS, WILLIAM ELLERY, ROGER SHERMAN, SAM^EL HUNTINGTON, W^M WILLIAMS, OLIVER WOLCOTT, MATTHEW THORNTON, W^M FLOYD, PHIL LIVINGSTON, FRAN^S LEWIS, LEWIS MORRIS, RICH^D STOCKTON, GEO. TAYLOR, JAMES WILSON, GEO. ROSS, CÆSAR RODNEY, GEO READ, THOS M:KEAN, SAMUEL CHASE, W^M PACA, THO^S STONE, CHARLES CARROLL of Carrollton, GEORGE WYTHE, RICHARD HENRY LEE, TH. JEFFERSON, BENJ^A HARRISON, THO^S NELSON, JR., FRANCIS LIGHTFOOT LEE, CARTER BRAXTON, W^M HOOPER, JNO WITHERSPOON, FRA^S HOPKINSON, JOHN HART, ABRA CLARK, ROB^T MORRIS, BENJAMIN RUSH, BENJ^A FRANKLIN, JOHN MORTON, GEO CLYMER, JA^S SMITH, JOSEPH HEWES, JOHN PENN, EDWARD RUTLEDGE, THO^S HEYWARD, JUN^r, THOMAS LYNCH, Junr, ARTHUR MIDDLETON, BUTTON GWINNETT, LYMAN HALL, GEO WALTON.

SELECT BIBLIOGRAPHY

Adams, Randolph G., *Political Ideas of the American Revolution* (Durham, N.C., 1922).
Abernethy, Thomas P., *Western Lands and the American Revolution* (New York, 1937).
Alden, John R., *The American Revolution, 1775–1783* (New York, 1954).
Alden, John R., *General Gage in America* (Baton Rouge, La., 1948).
Alden, John R., *The South in the American Revolution* (Baton Rouge, La., 1957).
Alvord, Clarence W., *The Mississippi Valley in British Politics* (2 vols., Cleveland, 1917).
Andrews, Charles M., *The Colonial Background of the American Revolution: Four Essays in American Colonial History* (New Haven, 1931).
Becker, Carl L., *The Declaration of Independence: A Study in the History of Political Ideas* (New York, 1922).
Becker, Carl L., *The History of Political Parties in the Province of. New York, 1760–1776* (Madison, Wis., 1960).
Boyd, Julian, *Anglo-American Union: Joseph Galloway's Plans to Preserve the British Empire, 1774–1778* (Philadelphia, 1941).
Brooke, John, *The Chatham Administration, 1766–1768* (London, 1956).
Brooke, John, "Party in the Eighteenth Century," in Alex Natan, ed., *Silver Renaissance: Essays in Eighteenth Century English History* (London, 1961).

Brown, Robert E., *Middle-Class Democracy and the Revolution in Massachusetts, 1691–1780* (Ithaca, N.Y., 1955).

Burnett, Edmund C., *The Continental Congress* (New York, 1941).

Channing, Edward, *A History of the United States* (6 vols., New York, 1905–1925), vol. III.

Clark, Dora Mae, *The Rise of the British Treasury: Colonial Administration in the Eighteenth Century* (New Haven, 1960).

Commager, Henry Steele, & Morris, Richard B., *The Spirit of 'Seventy-Six* (2 vols., Indianapolis and New York, 1958).

.. Davidson, Philip, *Propaganda and the American Revolution, 1763–1783* (Chapel Hill, N.C., 1941).

Dickerson, Oliver M., *The Navigation Acts and the American Revolution* (Philadelphia, 1951).

Douglass, Elisha P., *Rebels and Democrats: The Struggle for Equal Political Rights and Majority Rule during the American Revolution* (Chapel Hill, N.C., 1955).

Gipson, Lawrence H., "The American Revolution as an Aftermath of the Great War for Empire, 1754–1765," *Political Science Quarterly*, LXV, No. 1 (March, 1950), 86–104.

Gipson, Lawrence H., *The British Empire before the American Revolution* (10 vols. to date, Caldwell, Idaho, and New York, 1936–   ).

Gipson, Lawrence H., *The Coming of the Revolution, 1763–1775* (New York, 1954).

Greene, Jack P., "The Role of the Lower Houses of Assembly in Eighteenth-Century Politics," *Journal of Southern History*, XXVII, No. 4 (November, 1961), 451–474.

Jensen, Merrill, ed., *American Colonial Documents to 1776* [*English Historical Documents*, IX] (New York, 1955).

Jensen, Merrill, *The Articles of Confederation: An Interpretation of the Social-Constitutional History of the American Revolution, 1774–1781* (paperback ed., Madison, Wis., 1959).

Knollenberg, Bernhard, *Origin of the American Revolution: 1759–1776* (New York, 1960).

Labaree, Leonard W., *Conservatism in Early America* (New York, 1948).

Labaree, Leonard W., *Royal Government in America: A Study of the British Colonial System before 1783* (New Haven, 1930).

Land, Aubrey, *The Dulanys of Maryland* (Baltimore, 1955).

Lovejoy, David S., "Rights Imply Equality: The Case Against Admiralty Jurisdiction in America, 1764–1776," *William and Mary Quarterly* 3rd Ser., XVI, No. 4 (October, 1959), 459–484.

Meade, Robert D., *Patrick Henry: Patriot in the Making* (Philadelphia, 1957).

Miller, John C., *Origins of the American Revolution* (Boston, 1943).

Miller, John C., *Sam Adams: Pioneer in Propaganda* (Boston, 1936).

Miller, John C., *Triumph of Freedom, 1775–1783* (Boston, 1948).

Morgan, Edmund S., *The Birth of the Republic, 1763–89* (Chicago, 1956).

Morgan, Edmund S., *Prologue to Revolution: Sources and Documents on the Stamp Act Crisis, 1764–1766* (Chapel Hill, N.C., 1959).

Morgan, Edmund S. and Helen M., *The Stamp Act Crisis: Prologue to Revolution* (Chapel Hill, N.C., 1953).

Morison, Samuel Eliot, ed., *Sources and Documents Illustrating the American Revolution 1764–1788 and the Formation of the Federal Constitution* (Oxford, 1929).

Morris, Richard B., ed., *The Era of the American Revolution* (New York, 1939).

Namier, Sir Lewis, *Crossroads of Power: Essays on England in the 18th Century* (London, 1962).

Namier, Sir Lewis, *England in the Age of the American Revolution* (2nd ed., London, 1961).

Namier, Sir Lewis, *The Structure of Politics at the Accession of George III* (2nd ed., London, 1957).

Nettels, Curtis P., "British Mercantilism and the Economic Development of the Thirteen Colonies," *Journal of Economic History*, XII (Spring, 1952), 105–114.

Nettels, Curtis P., *George Washington and American Independence* (Boston, 1951).

Pares, Richard, *King George III and the Politicians* (Oxford, 1953).

Ritcheson, Charles R., *British Politics and the American Revolution* (Norman, Okla., 1954).

Robson, Eric, *The American Revolution, In Its Political and Military Aspects, 1763–1783* (London, 1955).

Scheer, George F. and Rankin, Hugh F., *Rebels and Redcoats* (Cleveland and New York, 1957).

Schlesinger, Arthur M., *The Colonial Merchants and the American Revolution* (New York, 1918).

Schlesinger, Arthur M., *Prelude to Independence: The Newspaper War on Britain, 1764–1776* (New York, 1958).

Smith, Page, *James Wilson, Founding Father, 1742–1798* (Chapel Hill, N.C., 1956).

Sosin, Jack H., *Whitehall and the Wilderness: The Middle West in British Colonial Policy, 1760–1775* (Lincoln, Nebr., 1961).

Tate, Thad. W., "The Coming of the Revolution in Virginia: Britain's Challenge to Virginia's Ruling Class, 1763–1776," *William and Mary Quarterly*, 3rd Ser., XIX, No. 3 (July, 1962), 323–343.

Tyler, Moses Coit, *Patrick Henry* (Boston and New York, 1887).

Ubbelohde, Carl, *The Vice-Admiralty Courts and the American Revolution* (Chapel Hill, N.C., 1960).

Van Doren, Carl, *Benjamin Franklin* (New York, 1938).

Van Tyne, Claude H., *The Causes of the American Revolution* (Boston, 1922).

Watson, J. Steven, *The Reign of George III, 1760–1815* (Oxford, 1960).

Wright, Esmond, *Fabric of Freedom, 1763–1800* (New York, 1961).